FREE Study Skills DVD Offer

Dear Customer,

Thank you for your purchase from Mometrix! We consider it an honor and a privilege that you have purchased our product and we want to ensure your satisfaction.

As a way of showing our appreciation and to help us better serve you, we have developed a Study Skills DVD that we would like to give you for FREE. This DVD covers our *best practices* for getting ready for your exam, from how to use our study materials to how to best prepare for the day of the test.

All that we ask is that you email us with feedback that would describe your experience so far with our product. Good, bad, or indifferent, we want to know what you think!

To get your FREE Study Skills DVD, email freedvd@mometrix.com with *FREE STUDY SKILLS DVD* in the subject line and the following information in the body of the email:

- The name of the product you purchased.
- Your product rating on a scale of 1-5, with 5 being the highest rating.
- Your feedback. It can be long, short, or anything in between. We just want to know your impressions and experience so far with our product. (Good feedback might include how our study material met your needs and ways we might be able to make it even better. You could highlight features that you found helpful or features that you think we should add.)
- Your full name and shipping address where you would like us to send your free DVD.

If you have any questions or concerns, please don't hesitate to contact me directly.

Thanks again!

Sincerely,

Jay Willis
Vice President
jay.willis@mometrix.com
1-800-673-8175

College Math Placement

Test Prep Secrets

College Math Placement Test Study Guide

3 Practice Exams

Review Video Tutorials

2nd Edition
also covers
the ACCUPLACER
and TSI

Written and edited by Mometrix Test Prep

Printed in the United States of America

This paper meets the requirements of ANSI/NISO Z39.48-1992 (Permanence of Paper).

Mometrix offers volume discount pricing to institutions. For more information or a price quote, please contact our sales department at sales@mometrix.com or 888-248-1219.

Mometrix Media LLC is not affiliated with or endorsed by any official testing organization. All organizational and test names are trademarks of their respective owners.

Paperback
ISBN 13: 978-1-5167-1314-1
ISBN 10: 1-5167-1314-1

DEAR FUTURE EXAM SUCCESS STORY

First of all, **THANK YOU** for purchasing Mometrix study materials!

Second, congratulations! You are one of the few determined test-takers who are committed to doing whatever it takes to excel on your exam. **You have come to the right place.** We developed these study materials with one goal in mind: to deliver you the information you need in a format that's concise and easy to use.

In addition to optimizing your guide for the content of the test, we've outlined our recommended steps for breaking down the preparation process into small, attainable goals so you can make sure you stay on track.

We've also analyzed the entire test-taking process, identifying the most common pitfalls and showing how you can overcome them and be ready for any curveball the test throws you.

Standardized testing is one of the biggest obstacles on your road to success, which only increases the importance of doing well in the high-pressure, high-stakes environment of test day. Your results on this test could have a significant impact on your future, and this guide provides the information and practical advice to help you achieve your full potential on test day.

Your success is our success

We would love to hear from you! If you would like to share the story of your exam success or if you have any questions or comments in regard to our products, please contact us at **800-673-8175** or **support@mometrix.com**.

Thanks again for your business and we wish you continued success!

Sincerely,
The Mometrix Test Preparation Team

TABLE OF CONTENTS

Introduction

Thank you for purchasing this resource! You have made the choice to prepare yourself for a test that could have a huge impact on your future, and this guide is designed to help you be fully ready for test day. Obviously, it's important to have a solid understanding of the test material, but you also need to be prepared for the unique environment and stressors of the test, so that you can perform to the best of your abilities.

For this purpose, the first section that appears in this guide is the **Secret Keys**. We've devoted countless hours to meticulously researching what works and what doesn't, and we've boiled down our findings to the five most impactful steps you can take to improve your performance on the test. We start at the beginning with study planning and move through the preparation process, all the way to the testing strategies that will help you get the most out of what you know when you're finally sitting in front of the test.

We recommend that you start preparing for your test as far in advance as possible. However, if you've bought this guide as a last-minute study resource and only have a few days before your test, we recommend that you skip over the first two Secret Keys since they address a long-term study plan.

If you struggle with **test anxiety**, we strongly encourage you to check out our recommendations for how you can overcome it. Test anxiety is a formidable foe, but it can be beaten, and we want to make sure you have the tools you need to defeat it.

1

Secret Key #1 – Plan Big, Study Small

There's a lot riding on your performance. If you want to ace this test, you're going to need to keep your skills sharp and the material fresh in your mind. You need a plan that lets you review everything you need to know while still fitting in your schedule. We'll break this strategy down into three categories.

Information Organization

Start with the information you already have: the official test outline. From this, you can make a complete list of all the concepts you need to cover before the test. Organize these concepts into groups that can be studied together, and create a list of any related vocabulary you need to learn so you can brush up on any difficult terms. You'll want to keep this vocabulary list handy once you actually start studying since you may need to add to it along the way.

Time Management

Once you have your set of study concepts, decide how to spread them out over the time you have left before the test. Break your study plan into small, clear goals so you have a manageable task for each day and know exactly what you're doing. Then just focus on one small step at a time. When you manage your time this way, you don't need to spend hours at a time studying. Studying a small block of content for a short period each day helps you retain information better and avoid stressing over how much you have left to do. You can relax knowing that you have a plan to cover everything in time. In order for this strategy to be effective though, you have to start studying early and stick to your schedule. Avoid the exhaustion and futility that comes from last-minute cramming!

Study Environment

The environment you study in has a big impact on your learning. Studying in a coffee shop, while probably more enjoyable, is not likely to be as fruitful as studying in a quiet room. It's important to keep distractions to a minimum. You're only planning to study for a short block of time, so make the most of it. Don't pause to check your phone or get up to find a snack. It's also important to **avoid multitasking**. Research has consistently shown that multitasking will make your studying dramatically less effective. Your study area should also be comfortable and well-lit so you don't have the distraction of straining your eyes or sitting on an uncomfortable chair.

The time of day you study is also important. You want to be rested and alert. Don't wait until just before bedtime. Study when you'll be most likely to comprehend and remember. Even better, if you know what time of day your test will be, set that time aside for study. That way your brain will be used to working on that subject at that specific time and you'll have a better chance of recalling information.

Finally, it can be helpful to team up with others who are studying for the same test. Your actual studying should be done in as isolated an environment as possible, but the work of organizing the information and setting up the study plan can be divided up. In between study sessions, you can discuss with your teammates the concepts that you're all studying and quiz each other on the details. Just be sure that your teammates are as serious about the test as you are. If you find that your study time is being replaced with social time, you might need to find a new team.

Secret Key #2 – Make Your Studying Count

You're devoting a lot of time and effort to preparing for this test, so you want to be absolutely certain it will pay off. This means doing more than just reading the content and hoping you can remember it on test day. It's important to make every minute of study count. There are two main areas you can focus on to make your studying count:

Retention

It doesn't matter how much time you study if you can't remember the material. You need to make sure you are retaining the concepts. To check your retention of the information you're learning, try recalling it at later times with minimal prompting. Try carrying around flashcards and glance at one or two from time to time or ask a friend who's also studying for the test to quiz you.

To enhance your retention, look for ways to put the information into practice so that you can apply it rather than simply recalling it. If you're using the information in practical ways, it will be much easier to remember. Similarly, it helps to solidify a concept in your mind if you're not only reading it to yourself but also explaining it to someone else. Ask a friend to let you teach them about a concept you're a little shaky on (or speak aloud to an imaginary audience if necessary). As you try to summarize, define, give examples, and answer your friend's questions, you'll understand the concepts better and they will stay with you longer. Finally, step back for a big picture view and ask yourself how each piece of information fits with the whole subject. When you link the different concepts together and see them working together as a whole, it's easier to remember the individual components.

Finally, practice showing your work on any multi-step problems, even if you're just studying. Writing out each step you take to solve a problem will help solidify the process in your mind, and you'll be more likely to remember it during the test.

Modality

Modality simply refers to the means or method by which you study. Choosing a study modality that fits your own individual learning style is crucial. No two people learn best in exactly the same way, so it's important to know your strengths and use them to your advantage.

For example, if you learn best by visualization, focus on visualizing a concept in your mind and draw an image or a diagram. Try color-coding your notes, illustrating them, or creating symbols that will trigger your mind to recall a learned concept. If you learn best by hearing or discussing information, find a study partner who learns the same way or read aloud to yourself. Think about how to put the information in your own words. Imagine that you are giving a lecture on the topic and record yourself so you can listen to it later.

For any learning style, flashcards can be helpful. Organize the information so you can take advantage of spare moments to review. Underline key words or phrases. Use different colors for different categories. Mnemonic devices (such as creating a short list in which every item starts with the same letter) can also help with retention. Find what works best for you and use it to store the information in your mind most effectively and easily.

Secret Key #3 – Practice the Right Way

Your success on test day depends not only on how many hours you put into preparing, but also on whether you prepared the right way. It's good to check along the way to see if your studying is paying off. One of the most effective ways to do this is by taking practice tests to evaluate your progress. Practice tests are useful because they show exactly where you need to improve. Every time you take a practice test, pay special attention to these three groups of questions:

- The questions you got wrong
- The questions you had to guess on, even if you guessed right
- The questions you found difficult or slow to work through

This will show you exactly what your weak areas are, and where you need to devote more study time. Ask yourself why each of these questions gave you trouble. Was it because you didn't understand the material? Was it because you didn't remember the vocabulary? Do you need more repetitions on this type of question to build speed and confidence? Dig into those questions and figure out how you can strengthen your weak areas as you go back to review the material.

Additionally, many practice tests have a section explaining the answer choices. It can be tempting to read the explanation and think that you now have a good understanding of the concept. However, an explanation likely only covers part of the question's broader context. Even if the explanation makes sense, **go back and investigate** every concept related to the question until you're positive you have a thorough understanding.

As you go along, keep in mind that the practice test is just that: practice. Memorizing these questions and answers will not be very helpful on the actual test because it is unlikely to have any of the same exact questions. If you only know the right answers to the sample questions, you won't be prepared for the real thing. **Study the concepts** until you understand them fully, and then you'll be able to answer any question that shows up on the test.

It's important to wait on the practice tests until you're ready. If you take a test on your first day of study, you may be overwhelmed by the amount of material covered and how much you need to learn. Work up to it gradually.

On test day, you'll need to be prepared for answering questions, managing your time, and using the test-taking strategies you've learned. It's a lot to balance, like a mental marathon that will have a big impact on your future. Like training for a marathon, you'll need to start slowly and work your way up. When test day arrives, you'll be ready.

Start with the strategies you've read in the first two Secret Keys—plan your course and study in the way that works best for you. If you have time, consider using multiple study resources to get different approaches to the same concepts. It can be helpful to see difficult concepts from more than one angle. Then find a good source for practice tests. Many times, the test website will suggest potential study resources or provide sample tests.

Practice Test Strategy

If you're able to find at least three practice tests, we recommend this strategy:

UNTIMED AND OPEN-BOOK PRACTICE

Take the first test with no time constraints and with your notes and study guide handy. Take your time and focus on applying the strategies you've learned.

TIMED AND OPEN-BOOK PRACTICE

Take the second practice test open-book as well, but set a timer and practice pacing yourself to finish in time.

TIMED AND CLOSED-BOOK PRACTICE

Take any other practice tests as if it were test day. Set a timer and put away your study materials. Sit at a table or desk in a quiet room, imagine yourself at the testing center, and answer questions as quickly and accurately as possible.

Keep repeating timed and closed-book tests on a regular basis until you run out of practice tests or it's time for the actual test. Your mind will be ready for the schedule and stress of test day, and you'll be able to focus on recalling the material you've learned.

Secret Key #4 – Pace Yourself

Once you're fully prepared for the material on the test, your biggest challenge on test day will be managing your time. Just knowing that the clock is ticking can make you panic even if you have plenty of time left. Work on pacing yourself so you can build confidence against the time constraints of the exam. Pacing is a difficult skill to master, especially in a high-pressure environment, so **practice is vital**.

Set time expectations for your pace based on how much time is available. For example, if a section has 60 questions and the time limit is 30 minutes, you know you have to average 30 seconds or less per question in order to answer them all. Although 30 seconds is the hard limit, set 25 seconds per question as your goal, so you reserve extra time to spend on harder questions. When you budget extra time for the harder questions, you no longer have any reason to stress when those questions take longer to answer.

Don't let this time expectation distract you from working through the test at a calm, steady pace, but keep it in mind so you don't spend too much time on any one question. Recognize that taking extra time on one question you don't understand may keep you from answering two that you do understand later in the test. If your time limit for a question is up and you're still not sure of the answer, mark it and move on, and come back to it later if the time and the test format allow. If the testing format doesn't allow you to return to earlier questions, just make an educated guess; then put it out of your mind and move on.

On the easier questions, be careful not to rush. It may seem wise to hurry through them so you have more time for the challenging ones, but it's not worth missing one if you know the concept and just didn't take the time to read the question fully. Work efficiently but make sure you understand the question and have looked at all of the answer choices, since more than one may seem right at first.

Even if you're paying attention to the time, you may find yourself a little behind at some point. You should speed up to get back on track, but do so wisely. Don't panic; just take a few seconds less on each question until you're caught up. Don't guess without thinking, but do look through the answer choices and eliminate any you know are wrong. If you can get down to two choices, it is often worthwhile to guess from those. Once you've chosen an answer, move on and don't dwell on any that you skipped or had to hurry through. If a question was taking too long, chances are it was one of the harder ones, so you weren't as likely to get it right anyway.

On the other hand, if you find yourself getting ahead of schedule, it may be beneficial to slow down a little. The more quickly you work, the more likely you are to make a careless mistake that will affect your score. You've budgeted time for each question, so don't be afraid to spend that time. Practice an efficient but careful pace to get the most out of the time you have.

Secret Key #5 – Have a Plan for Guessing

When you're taking the test, you may find yourself stuck on a question. Some of the answer choices seem better than others, but you don't see the one answer choice that is obviously correct. What do you do?

The scenario described above is very common, yet most test takers have not effectively prepared for it. Developing and practicing a plan for guessing may be one of the single most effective uses of your time as you get ready for the exam.

In developing your plan for guessing, there are three questions to address:

- When should you start the guessing process?
- How should you narrow down the choices?
- Which answer should you choose?

When to Start the Guessing Process

Unless your plan for guessing is to select C every time (which, despite its merits, is not what we recommend), you need to leave yourself enough time to apply your answer elimination strategies. Since you have a limited amount of time for each question, that means that if you're going to give yourself the best shot at guessing correctly, you have to decide quickly whether or not you will guess.

Of course, the best-case scenario is that you don't have to guess at all, so first, see if you can answer the question based on your knowledge of the subject and basic reasoning skills. Focus on the key words in the question and try to jog your memory of related topics. Give yourself a chance to bring the knowledge to mind, but once you realize that you don't have (or you can't access) the knowledge you need to answer the question, it's time to start the guessing process.

It's almost always better to start the guessing process too early than too late. It only takes a few seconds to remember something and answer the question from knowledge. Carefully eliminating wrong answer choices takes longer. Plus, going through the process of eliminating answer choices can actually help jog your memory.

Summary: Start the guessing process as soon as you decide that you can't answer the question based on your knowledge.

7

How to Narrow Down the Choices

The next chapter in this book (**Test-Taking Strategies**) includes a wide range of strategies for how to approach questions and how to look for answer choices to eliminate. You will definitely want to read those carefully, practice them, and figure out which ones work best for you. Here though, we're going to address a mindset rather than a particular strategy.

Your chances of guessing an answer correctly depend on how many options you are choosing from.

How many choices you have	How likely you are to guess correctly
5	20%
4	25%
3	33%
2	50%
1	100%

You can see from this chart just how valuable it is to be able to eliminate incorrect answers and make an educated guess, but there are two things that many test takers do that cause them to miss out on the benefits of guessing:

- Accidentally eliminating the correct answer
- Selecting an answer based on an impression

We'll look at the first one here, and the second one in the next section.

To avoid accidentally eliminating the correct answer, we recommend a thought exercise called **the $5 challenge**. In this challenge, you only eliminate an answer choice from contention if you are willing to bet $5 on it being wrong. Why $5? Five dollars is a small but not insignificant amount of money. It's an amount you could afford to lose but wouldn't want to throw away. And while losing $5 once might not hurt too much, doing it twenty times will set you back $100. In the same way, each small decision you make—eliminating a choice here, guessing on a question there—won't by itself impact your score very much, but when you put them all together, they can make a big difference. By holding each answer choice elimination decision to a higher standard, you can reduce the risk of accidentally eliminating the correct answer.

The $5 challenge can also be applied in a positive sense: If you are willing to bet $5 that an answer choice *is* correct, go ahead and mark it as correct.

Summary: Only eliminate an answer choice if you are willing to bet $5 that it is wrong.

Which Answer to Choose

You're taking the test. You've run into a hard question and decided you'll have to guess. You've eliminated all the answer choices you're willing to bet $5 on. Now you have to pick an answer. Why do we even need to talk about this? Why can't you just pick whichever one you feel like when the time comes?

The answer to these questions is that if you don't come into the test with a plan, you'll rely on your impression to select an answer choice, and if you do that, you risk falling into a trap. The test writers know that everyone who takes their test will be guessing on some of the questions, so they intentionally write wrong answer choices to seem plausible. You still have to pick an answer though, and if the wrong answer choices are designed to look right, how can you ever be sure that you're not falling for their trap? The best solution we've found to this dilemma is to take the decision out of your hands entirely. Here is the process we recommend:

Once you've eliminated any choices that you are confident (willing to bet $5) are wrong, select the first remaining choice as your answer.

Whether you choose to select the first remaining choice, the second, or the last, the important thing is that you use some preselected standard. Using this approach guarantees that you will not be enticed into selecting an answer choice that looks right, because you are not basing your decision on how the answer choices look.

This is not meant to make you question your knowledge. Instead, it is to help you recognize the difference between your knowledge and your impressions. There's a huge difference between thinking an answer is right because of what you know, and thinking an answer is right because it looks or sounds like it should be right.

Summary: To ensure that your selection is appropriately random, make a predetermined selection from among all answer choices you have not eliminated.

Test-Taking Strategies

This section contains a list of test-taking strategies that you may find helpful as you work through the test. By taking what you know and applying logical thought, you can maximize your chances of answering any question correctly!

It is very important to realize that every question is different and every person is different: no single strategy will work on every question, and no single strategy will work for every person. That's why we've included all of them here, so you can try them out and determine which ones work best for different types of questions and which ones work best for you.

Question Strategies

READ CAREFULLY

Read the question and answer choices carefully. Don't miss the question because you misread the terms. You have plenty of time to read each question thoroughly and make sure you understand what is being asked. Yet a happy medium must be attained, so don't waste too much time. You must read carefully, but efficiently.

CONTEXTUAL CLUES

Look for contextual clues. If the question includes a word you are not familiar with, look at the immediate context for some indication of what the word might mean. Contextual clues can often give you all the information you need to decipher the meaning of an unfamiliar word. Even if you can't determine the meaning, you may be able to narrow down the possibilities enough to make a solid guess at the answer to the question.

PREFIXES

If you're having trouble with a word in the question or answer choices, try dissecting it. Take advantage of every clue that the word might include. Prefixes and suffixes can be a huge help. Usually they allow you to determine a basic meaning. Pre- means before, post- means after, pro - is positive, de- is negative. From prefixes and suffixes, you can get an idea of the general meaning of the word and try to put it into context.

HEDGE WORDS

Watch out for critical hedge words, such as *likely, may, can, sometimes, often, almost, mostly, usually, generally, rarely,* and *sometimes.* Question writers insert these hedge phrases to cover every possibility. Often an answer choice will be wrong simply because it leaves no room for exception. Be on guard for answer choices that have definitive words such as *exactly* and *always.*

SWITCHBACK WORDS

Stay alert for *switchbacks.* These are the words and phrases frequently used to alert you to shifts in thought. The most common switchback words are *but, although,* and *however.* Others include *nevertheless, on the other hand, even though, while, in spite of, despite, regardless of.* Switchback words are important to catch because they can change the direction of the question or an answer choice.

FACE VALUE

When in doubt, use common sense. Accept the situation in the problem at face value. Don't read too much into it. These problems will not require you to make wild assumptions. If you have to go beyond creativity and warp time or space in order to have an answer choice fit the question, then you should move on and consider the other answer choices. These are normal problems rooted in reality. The applicable relationship or explanation may not be readily apparent, but it is there for you to figure out. Use your common sense to interpret anything that isn't clear.

Answer Choice Strategies

ANSWER SELECTION

The most thorough way to pick an answer choice is to identify and eliminate wrong answers until only one is left, then confirm it is the correct answer. Sometimes an answer choice may immediately seem right, but be careful. The test writers will usually put more than one reasonable answer choice on each question, so take a second to read all of them and make sure that the other choices are not equally obvious. As long as you have time left, it is better to read every answer choice than to pick the first one that looks right without checking the others.

ANSWER CHOICE FAMILIES

An answer choice family consists of two (in rare cases, three) answer choices that are very similar in construction and cannot all be true at the same time. If you see two answer choices that are direct opposites or parallels, one of them is usually the correct answer. For instance, if one answer choice says that quantity x increases and another either says that quantity x decreases (opposite) or says that quantity y increases (parallel), then those answer choices would fall into the same family. An answer choice that doesn't match the construction of the answer choice family is more likely to be incorrect. Most questions will not have answer choice families, but when they do appear, you should be prepared to recognize them.

ELIMINATE ANSWERS

Eliminate answer choices as soon as you realize they are wrong, but make sure you consider all possibilities. If you are eliminating answer choices and realize that the last one you are left with is also wrong, don't panic. Start over and consider each choice again. There may be something you missed the first time that you will realize on the second pass.

AVOID FACT TRAPS

Don't be distracted by an answer choice that is factually true but doesn't answer the question. You are looking for the choice that answers the question. Stay focused on what the question is asking for so you don't accidentally pick an answer that is true but incorrect. Always go back to the question and make sure the answer choice you've selected actually answers the question and is not merely a true statement.

EXTREME STATEMENTS

In general, you should avoid answers that put forth extreme actions as standard practice or proclaim controversial ideas as established fact. An answer choice that states the "process should be used in certain situations, if..." is much more likely to be correct than one that states the "process should be discontinued completely." The first is a calm rational statement and doesn't even make a definitive, uncompromising stance, using a hedge word *if* to provide wiggle room, whereas the second choice is a radical idea and far more extreme.

BENCHMARK

As you read through the answer choices and you come across one that seems to answer the question well, mentally select that answer choice. This is not your final answer, but it's the one that will help you evaluate the other answer choices. The one that you selected is your benchmark or standard for judging each of the other answer choices. Every other answer choice must be compared to your benchmark. That choice is correct until proven otherwise by another answer choice beating it. If you find a better answer, then that one becomes your new benchmark. Once you've decided that no other choice answers the question as well as your benchmark, you have your final answer.

PREDICT THE ANSWER

Before you even start looking at the answer choices, it is often best to try to predict the answer. When you come up with the answer on your own, it is easier to avoid distractions and traps because you will know exactly what to look for. The right answer choice is unlikely to be word-for-word what you came up with, but it should be a close match. Even if you are confident that you have the right answer, you should still take the time to read each option before moving on.

General Strategies

TOUGH QUESTIONS

If you are stumped on a problem or it appears too hard or too difficult, don't waste time. Move on! Remember though, if you can quickly check for obviously incorrect answer choices, your chances of guessing correctly are greatly improved. Before you completely give up, at least try to knock out a couple of possible answers. Eliminate what you can and then guess at the remaining answer choices before moving on.

CHECK YOUR WORK

Since you will probably not know every term listed and the answer to every question, it is important that you get credit for the ones that you do know. Don't miss any questions through careless mistakes. If at all possible, try to take a second to look back over your answer selection and make sure you've selected the correct answer choice and haven't made a costly careless mistake (such as marking an answer choice that you didn't mean to mark). This quick double check should more than pay for itself in caught mistakes for the time it costs.

PACE YOURSELF

It's easy to be overwhelmed when you're looking at a page full of questions; your mind is confused and full of random thoughts, and the clock is ticking down faster than you would like. Calm down and maintain the pace that you have set for yourself. Especially as you get down to the last few minutes of the test, don't let the small numbers on the clock make you panic. As long as you are on track by monitoring your pace, you are guaranteed to have time for each question.

DON'T RUSH

It is very easy to make errors when you are in a hurry. Maintaining a fast pace in answering questions is pointless if it makes you miss questions that you would have gotten right otherwise. Test writers like to include distracting information and wrong answers that seem right. Taking a little extra time to avoid careless mistakes can make all the difference in your test score. Find a pace that allows you to be confident in the answers that you select.

KEEP MOVING

Panicking will not help you pass the test, so do your best to stay calm and keep moving. Taking deep breaths and going through the answer elimination steps you practiced can help to break through a stress barrier and keep your pace.

Final Notes

The combination of a solid foundation of content knowledge and the confidence that comes from practicing your plan for applying that knowledge is the key to maximizing your performance on test day. As your foundation of content knowledge is built up and strengthened, you'll find that the strategies included in this chapter become more and more effective in helping you quickly sift through the distractions and traps of the test to isolate the correct answer.

Now it's time to move on to the test content chapters of this book, but be sure to keep your goal in mind. As you read, think about how you will be able to apply this information on the test. If you've already seen sample questions for the test and you have an idea of the question format and style, try to come up with questions of your own that you can answer based on what you're reading. This will give you valuable practice applying your knowledge in the same ways you can expect to on test day.

Good luck and good studying!

Numbers and Operations

CLASSIFICATIONS OF NUMBERS

Numbers are the basic building blocks of mathematics. Specific features of numbers are identified by the following terms:

Integer – any positive or negative whole number, including zero. Integers do not include fractions $\left(\frac{1}{3}\right)$, decimals (0.56), or mixed numbers $\left(7\frac{3}{4}\right)$.

Prime number – any whole number greater than 1 that has only two factors, itself and 1; that is, a number that can be divided evenly only by 1 and itself.

Composite number – any whole number greater than 1 that has more than two different factors; in other words, any whole number that is not a prime number. For example: The composite number 8 has the factors of 1, 2, 4, and 8.

Even number – any integer that can be divided by 2 without leaving a remainder. For example: 2, 4, 6, 8, and so on.

Odd number – any integer that cannot be divided evenly by 2. For example: 3, 5, 7, 9, and so on.

Decimal number – any number that uses a decimal point to show the part of the number that is less than one. Example: 1.234.

Decimal point – a symbol used to separate the ones place from the tenths place in decimals or dollars from cents in currency.

Decimal place – the position of a number to the right of the decimal point. In the decimal 0.123, the 1 is in the first place to the right of the decimal point, indicating tenths; the 2 is in the second place, indicating hundredths; and the 3 is in the third place, indicating thousandths.

The **decimal**, or base 10, system is a number system that uses ten different digits (0, 1, 2, 3, 4, 5, 6, 7, 8, 9). An example of a number system that uses something other than ten digits is the **binary**, or base 2, number system, used by computers, which uses only the numbers 0 and 1. It is thought that the decimal system originated because people had only their 10 fingers for counting.

Rational numbers include all integers, decimals, and fractions. Any terminating or repeating decimal number is a rational number.

Irrational numbers cannot be written as fractions or decimals because the number of decimal places is infinite and there is no recurring pattern of digits within the number. For example, pi (π) begins with 3.141592 and continues without terminating or repeating, so pi is an irrational number.

Real numbers are the set of all rational and irrational numbers.

THE NUMBER LINE

A number line is a graph to see the distance between numbers. Basically, this graph shows the relationship between numbers. So, a number line may have a point for zero and may show negative numbers on the left side of the line. Also, any positive numbers are placed on the right side of the line. For example, consider the points labeled on the following number line:

We can use the dashed lines on the number line to identify each point. Each dashed line between two whole numbers is $\frac{1}{4}$. The line halfway between two numbers is $\frac{1}{2}$.

NUMBERS IN WORD FORM AND PLACE VALUE

When writing numbers out in word form or translating word form to numbers, it is essential to understand how a place value system works. In the decimal or base-10 system, each digit of a number represents how many of the corresponding place value – a specific factor of 10 – are contained in the number being represented. To make reading numbers easier, every three digits to the left of the decimal place is preceded by a comma. The following table demonstrates some of the place values:

Power of 10	10^3	10^2	10^1	10^0	10^{-1}	10^{-2}	10^{-3}
Value	1,000	100	10	1	0.1	0.01	0.001
Place	thousands	hundreds	tens	ones	tenths	hundredths	thousandths

For example, consider the number 4,546.09, which can be separated into each place value like this:

4: thousands
5: hundreds
4: tens
6: ones
0: tenths
9: hundredths

This number in word form would be *four thousand five hundred forty-six and nine hundredths.*

ABSOLUTE VALUE

A precursor to working with negative numbers is understanding what **absolute values** are. A number's absolute value is simply the distance away from zero a number is on the number line. The absolute value of a number is always positive and is written $|x|$. For example, the absolute value of 3, written as $|3|$, is 3 because the distance between 0 and 3 on a number line is three units. Likewise, the absolute value of –3, written as $|-3|$, is 3 because the distance between 0 and –3 on a number line is three units. So, $|3| = |-3|$.

OPERATIONS

Mathematical expressions consist of a combination of values and operations. An **operation** is simply a mathematical process that takes some value(s) as input(s) and produces an output. Elementary operations are often written in the following form: *value operation value*. For instance, in the expression 1 + 2 the values are 1 and 2 and the operation is addition. Performing the operation gives the output of 3. In this way we can say that 1 + 2 and 3 are equal, or 1 + 2 = 3.

ADDITION

Addition increases the value of one quantity by the value of another quantity (both called **addends**). For example, 2 + 4 = 6; 8 + 9 = 17. The result is called the **sum**. With addition, the order does not matter, 4 + 2 = 2 + 4.

When adding signed numbers, if the signs are the same simply add the absolute values of the addends and apply the original sign to the sum. For example, $(+4) + (+8) = +12$ and $(-4) + (-8) = -12$. When the original signs are different, take the absolute values of the addends and subtract the smaller value from the larger value, then apply the original sign of the larger value to the difference. For instance, $(+4) + (-8) = -4$ and $(-4) + (+8) = +4$.

SUBTRACTION

Subtraction is the opposite operation to addition; it decreases the value of one quantity (the **minuend**) by the value of another quantity (the **subtrahend**). For example, $6 - 4 = 2$; $17 - 8 = 9$. The result is called the **difference**. Note that with subtraction, the order does matter, $6 - 4 \neq 4 - 6$.

For subtracting signed numbers, change the sign of the subtrahend and then follow the same rules used for addition. For example, $(+4) - (+8) = (+4) + (-8) = -4$.

> **Review Video: Addition and Subtraction**
> Visit mometrix.com/academy and enter code: 521157

MULTIPLICATION

Multiplication can be thought of as repeated addition. One number (the **multiplier**) indicates how many times to add the other number (the **multiplicand**) to itself. For example, 3×2 (three times two) $= 2 + 2 + 2 = 6$. With multiplication, the order does not matter: $2 \times 3 = 3 \times 2$ or $3 + 3 = 2 + 2 + 2$, either way the result (the **product**) is the same.

If the signs are the same the product is positive when multiplying signed numbers. For example, $(+4) \times (+8) = +32$ and $(-4) \times (-8) = +32$. If the signs are opposite, the product is negative. For example, $(+4) \times (-8) = -32$ and $(-4) \times (+8) = -32$. When more than two factors are multiplied together, the sign of the product is determined by how many negative factors are present. If there are an odd number of negative factors then the product is negative, whereas an even number of negative factors indicates a positive product. For instance, $(+4) \times (-8) \times (-2) = +64$ and $(-4) \times (-8) \times (-2) = -64$.

DIVISION

Division is the opposite operation to multiplication; one number (the **divisor**) tells us how many parts to divide the other number (the **dividend**) into. The result of division is called the **quotient**. For example, $20 \div 4 = 5$; if 20 is split into 4 equal parts, each part is 5. With division, the order of the numbers does matter, $20 \div 4 \neq 4 \div 20$.

The rules for dividing signed numbers are similar to multiplying signed numbers. If the dividend and divisor have the same sign, the quotient is positive. If the dividend and divisor have opposite signs, the quotient is negative. For example, $(-4) \div (+8) = -0.5$.

> **Review Video: Multiplication and Division**
> Visit mometrix.com/academy and enter code: 643326

PARENTHESES

Parentheses are used to designate which operations should be done first when there are multiple operations. Example: $4 - (2 + 1) = 1$; the parentheses tell us that we must add 2 and 1, and then subtract the sum from 4, rather than subtracting 2 from 4 and then adding 1 (this would give us an answer of 3).

> **Review Video: Mathematical Parentheses**
> Visit mometrix.com/academy and enter code: 978600

EXPONENTS

An **exponent** is a superscript number placed next to another number at the top right. It indicates how many times the base number is to be multiplied by itself. Exponents provide a shorthand way

to write what would be a longer mathematical expression, for example: $2^4 = 2 \times 2 \times 2 \times 2$. A number with an exponent of 2 is said to be "squared," while a number with an exponent of 3 is said to be "cubed." The value of a number raised to an exponent is called its power. So, 8^4 is read as "8 to the 4th power," or "8 raised to the power of 4."

The properties of exponents are as follows:

Property	Description
$a^1 = a$	Any number to the power of 1 is equal to itself
$1^n = 1$	The number 1 raised to any power is equal to 1
$a^0 = 1$	Any number raised to the power of 0 is equal to 1
$a^n \times a^m = a^{n+m}$	Add exponents to multiply powers of the same base number
$a^n \div a^m = a^{n-m}$	Subtract exponents to divide powers of the same base number
$(a^n)^m = a^{n \times m}$	When a power is raised to a power, the exponents are multiplied
$(a \times b)^n = a^n \times b^n$ $(a \div b)^n = a^n \div b^n$	Multiplication and division operations inside parentheses can be raised to a power. This is the same as each term being raised to that power.
$a^{-n} = \dfrac{1}{a^n}$	A negative exponent is the same as the reciprocal of a positive exponent

Note that exponents do not have to be integers. Fractional or decimal exponents follow all the rules above as well. Example: $5^{\frac{1}{4}} \times 5^{\frac{3}{4}} = 5^{\frac{1}{4}+\frac{3}{4}} = 5^1 = 5$.

Review Video: Exponents
Visit mometrix.com/academy and enter code: 600998

Review Video: Laws of Exponents
Visit mometrix.com/academy and enter code: 532558

ROOTS

A **root**, such as a square root, is another way of writing a fractional exponent. Instead of using a superscript, roots use the radical symbol ($\sqrt{}$) to indicate the operation. A radical will have a number underneath the bar, and may sometimes have a number in the upper left: $\sqrt[n]{a}$, read as "the nth root of a." The relationship between radical notation and exponent notation can be described by this equation: $\sqrt[n]{a} = a^{\frac{1}{n}}$. The two special cases of $n = 2$ and $n = 3$ are called square roots and cube roots. If there is no number to the upper left, it is understood to be a square root ($n = 2$). Nearly all of the roots you encounter will be square roots. A square root is the same as a number raised to the one-half power. When we say that a is the square root of b ($a = \sqrt{b}$), we mean that a multiplied by itself equals b: ($a \times a = b$).

A **perfect square** is a number that has an integer for its square root. There are 10 perfect squares from 1 to 100: 1, 4, 9, 16, 25, 36, 49, 64, 81, 100 (the squares of integers 1 through 10).

Review Video: Roots
Visit mometrix.com/academy and enter code: 795655

Review Video: Square Root and Perfect Square
Visit mometrix.com/academy and enter code: 648063

ORDER OF OPERATIONS

Order of operations is a set of rules that dictates the order in which we must perform each operation in an expression so that we will evaluate it accurately. If we have an expression that includes multiple different operations, order of operations tells us which operations to do first. The most common mnemonic for order of operations is **PEMDAS**, or "Please Excuse My Dear Aunt Sally." PEMDAS stands for parentheses, exponents, multiplication, division, addition, and subtraction. It is important to understand that multiplication and division have equal precedence, as do addition and subtraction, so those pairs of operations are simply worked from left to right in order.

For example, evaluating the expression $5 + 20 \div 4 \times (2 + 3) - 6$ using the correct order of operations would be done like this:

- **P:** Perform the operations inside the parentheses: $(2 + 3) = 5$
- **E:** Simplify the exponents.
 - The equation now looks like this: $5 + 20 \div 4 \times 5 - 6$
- **MD:** Perform multiplication and division from left to right: $20 \div 4 = 5$; then $5 \times 5 = 25$
 - The equation now looks like this: $5 + 25 - 6$
- **AS:** Perform addition and subtraction from left to right: $5 + 25 = 30$; then $30 - 6 = 24$

> **Review Video: Order of Operations**
> Visit mometrix.com/academy and enter code: 259675

SUBTRACTION WITH REGROUPING

A great way to make use of some of the features built into the decimal system would be regrouping when attempting longform subtraction operations. When subtracting within a place value, sometimes the minuend is smaller than the subtrahend, **regrouping** enables you to 'borrow' a unit from a place value to the left in order to get a positive difference. For example, consider subtracting 189 from 525 with regrouping.

First, set up the subtraction problem in vertical form:

```
   525
 - 189
```

Notice that the numbers in the ones and tens columns of 525 are smaller than the numbers in the ones and tens columns of 189. This means you will need to use regrouping to perform subtraction:

```
   5  2  5
 - 1  8  9
```

To subtract 9 from 5 in the ones column you will need to borrow from the 2 in the tens columns:

```
   5  1  15
 - 1  8   9
          6
```

Next, to subtract 8 from 1 in the tens column you will need to borrow from the 5 in the hundreds column:

```
    4    11   15
 –  1     8    9
         3    6
```

Last, subtract the 1 from the 4 in the hundreds column:

```
    4    11   15
 –  1     8    9
    3    3    6
```

FACTORS AND GREATEST COMMON FACTOR

Factors are numbers that are multiplied together to obtain a **product**. For example, in the equation $2 \times 3 = 6$, the numbers 2 and 3 are factors. A **prime number** has only two factors (1 and itself), but other numbers can have many factors.

A **common factor** is a number that divides exactly into two or more other numbers. For example, the factors of 12 are 1, 2, 3, 4, 6, and 12, while the factors of 15 are 1, 3, 5, and 15. The common factors of 12 and 15 are 1 and 3.

A **prime factor** is also a prime number. Therefore, the prime factors of 12 are 2 and 3. For 15, the prime factors are 3 and 5.

The **greatest common factor** (GCF) is the largest number that is a factor of two or more numbers. For example, the factors of 15 are 1, 3, 5, and 15; the factors of 35 are 1, 5, 7, and 35. Therefore, the greatest common factor of 15 and 35 is 5.

> **Review Video: Factors**
> Visit mometrix.com/academy and enter code: 920086
>
> **Review Video: Greatest Common Factor (GCF)**
> Visit mometrix.com/academy and enter code: 838699

MULTIPLES AND LEAST COMMON MULTIPLE

Often listed out in multiplication tables, **multiples** are integer increments of a given factor. In other words, dividing a multiple by the factor number will result in an integer. For example, the multiples of 7 include: $1 \times 7 = 7$, $2 \times 7 = 14$, $3 \times 7 = 21$, $4 \times 7 = 28$, $5 \times 7 = 35$. Dividing 7, 14, 21, 28, or 35 by 7 will result in the integers 1, 2, 3, 4, and 5, respectively.

The **least common multiple** (**LCM**) is the smallest number that is a multiple of two or more numbers. For example, the multiples of 3 include 3, 6, 9, 12, 15, etc.; the multiples of 5 include 5, 10, 15, 20, etc. Therefore, the least common multiple of 3 and 5 is 15.

> **Review Video: Multiples**
> Visit mometrix.com/academy and enter code: 626738
>
> **Review Video: Multiples and Least Common Multiple (LCM)**
> Visit mometrix.com/academy and enter code: 520269

Practice

P1. Write the place value of each digit in 14,059.826

P2. Write out each of the following in words:

(a) 29
(b) 478
(c) 98,542
(d) 0.06
(e) 13.113

P3. Write each of the following in numbers:

(a) nine thousand four hundred thirty-five
(b) three hundred two thousand eight hundred seventy-six
(c) nine hundred one thousandths
(d) nineteen thousandths
(e) seven thousand one hundred forty-two and eighty-five hundredths

P4. Demonstrate how to subtract 477 from 620 using regrouping.

P5. Simplify the following expressions with exponents:

(a) 37^0
(b) 1^{30}
(c) $2^3 \times 2^4 \times 2^x$
(d) $(3^x)^3$
(e) $(12 \div 3)^2$

Mometrix

Practice Solutions

P1. The place value for each digit would be as follows:

Digit	Place Value
1	ten-thousands
4	thousands
0	hundreds
5	tens
9	ones
8	tenths
2	hundredths
6	thousandths

P2. Each written out in words would be:

(a) twenty-nine
(b) four hundred seventy-eight
(c) ninety-eight thousand five hundred forty-two
(d) six hundredths
(e) thirteen and one hundred thirteen thousandths

P3. Each in numeric form would be:

(a) 9,435
(b) 302,876
(c) 0.901
(d) 0.019
(e) 7,142.85

P4. First, set up the subtraction problem in vertical form:

```
    6   2   0
−   4   7   7
```

To subtract 7 from 0 in the ones column you will need to borrow from the 2 in the tens column:

```
    6   1   10
−   4   7   7
                3
```

Next, to subtract 7 from the 1 that's still in the tens column you will need to borrow from the 6 in the hundreds column:

```
    5   11   10
−   4   7    7
            4    3
```

23

Lastly, subtract 4 from the 5 remaining in the hundreds column:

$$
\begin{array}{r}
5\ \ 11\ \ 10 \\
-\ \ 4\ \ \ \ 7\ \ \ \ 7 \\
\hline
1\ \ \ \ 4\ \ \ \ 3
\end{array}
$$

P5. Using the properties of exponents and the proper order of operations:

(a) Any number raised to the power of 0 is equal to 1: $37^0 = 1$
(b) The number 1 raised to any power is equal to 1: $1^{30} = 1$
(c) Add exponents to multiply powers of the same base: $2^3 \times 2^4 \times 2^x = 2^{(3+4+x)} = 2^{(7+x)}$
(d) When a power is raised to a power, the exponents are multiplied: $(3^x)^3 = 3^{3x}$
(e) Perform the operation inside the parentheses first: $(12 \div 3)^2 = 4^2 = 16$

Rational Numbers

FRACTIONS

A **fraction** is a number that is expressed as one integer written above another integer, with a dividing line between them $\left(\frac{x}{y}\right)$. It represents the **quotient** of the two numbers "x divided by y." It can also be thought of as x out of y equal parts.

The top number of a fraction is called the **numerator**, and it represents the number of parts under consideration. The 1 in $\frac{1}{4}$ means that 1 part out of the whole is being considered in the calculation. The bottom number of a fraction is called the **denominator**, and it represents the total number of equal parts. The 4 in $\frac{1}{4}$ means that the whole consists of 4 equal parts. A fraction cannot have a denominator of zero; this is referred to as "*undefined.*"

Fractions can be manipulated, without changing the value of the fraction, by multiplying or dividing (but not adding or subtracting) both the numerator and denominator by the same number. If you divide both numbers by a common factor, you are **reducing** or simplifying the fraction. Two fractions that have the same value but are expressed differently are known as **equivalent fractions**. For example, $\frac{2}{10}, \frac{3}{15}, \frac{4}{20}$, and $\frac{5}{25}$ are all equivalent fractions. They can also all be reduced or simplified to $\frac{1}{5}$.

When two fractions are manipulated so that they have the same denominator, this is known as finding a **common denominator**. The number chosen to be that common denominator should be the least common multiple of the two original denominators. Example: $\frac{3}{4}$ and $\frac{5}{6}$; the least common multiple of 4 and 6 is 12. Manipulating to achieve the common denominator: $\frac{3}{4} = \frac{9}{12}; \frac{5}{6} = \frac{10}{12}$.

PROPER FRACTIONS AND MIXED NUMBERS

A fraction whose denominator is greater than its numerator is known as a **proper fraction**, while a fraction whose numerator is greater than its denominator is known as an **improper fraction**. Proper fractions have values *less than one* and improper fractions have values *greater than one*.

A **mixed number** is a number that contains both an integer and a fraction. Any improper fraction can be rewritten as a mixed number. Example: $\frac{8}{3} = \frac{6}{3} + \frac{2}{3} = 2 + \frac{2}{3} = 2\frac{2}{3}$. Similarly, any mixed number can be rewritten as an improper fraction. Example: $1\frac{3}{5} = 1 + \frac{3}{5} = \frac{5}{5} + \frac{3}{5} = \frac{8}{5}$.

> **Review Video: <u>Proper and Improper Fractions and Mixed Numbers</u>**
> Visit mometrix.com/academy and enter code: 211077
>
> **Review Video: <u>Fractions</u>**
> Visit mometrix.com/academy and enter code: 262335

OPERATIONS WITH FRACTIONS

ADDING AND SUBTRACTING FRACTIONS

If two fractions have a common denominator, they can be added or subtracted simply by adding or subtracting the two numerators and retaining the same denominator. If the two fractions do not already have the same denominator, one or both of them must be manipulated to achieve a common denominator before they can be added or subtracted. Example: $\frac{1}{2} + \frac{1}{4} = \frac{2}{4} + \frac{1}{4} = \frac{3}{4}$.

> **Review Video: Adding and Subtracting Fractions**
> Visit mometrix.com/academy and enter code: 378080

MULTIPLYING FRACTIONS

Two fractions can be multiplied by multiplying the two numerators to find the new numerator and the two denominators to find the new denominator. Example: $\frac{1}{3} \times \frac{2}{3} = \frac{1 \times 2}{3 \times 3} = \frac{2}{9}$.

> **Review Video: Multiplying Fractions**
> Visit mometrix.com/academy and enter code: 638849

DIVIDING FRACTIONS

Two fractions can be divided by flipping the numerator and denominator of the second fraction and then proceeding as though it were a multiplication. Example: $\frac{2}{3} \div \frac{3}{4} = \frac{2}{3} \times \frac{4}{3} = \frac{8}{9}$.

> **Review Video: Dividing Fractions**
> Visit mometrix.com/academy and enter code: 300874

DECIMALS

Decimals are one way to represent parts of a whole. Using the place value system, each digit to the right of a decimal point denotes the number of units of a corresponding *negative* power of ten. For example, consider the decimal 0.24. We can use a model to represent the decimal. Since a dime is worth one-tenth of a dollar and a penny is worth one-hundredth of a dollar, one possible model to represent this fraction is to have 2 dimes representing the 2 in the tenths place and 4 pennies representing the 4 in the hundredths place:

To write the decimal as a fraction, put the decimal in the numerator with 1 in the denominator. Multiply the numerator and denominator by tens until there are no more decimal places. Then simplify the fraction to lowest terms. For example, converting 0.24 to a fraction:

$$0.24 = \frac{0.24}{1} = \frac{0.24 \times 100}{1 \times 100} = \frac{24}{100} = \frac{6}{25}$$

> **Review Video: Decimals**
> Visit mometrix.com/academy and enter code: 837268

OPERATIONS WITH DECIMALS

ADDING AND SUBTRACTING DECIMALS

When adding and subtracting decimals, the decimal points must always be aligned. Adding decimals is just like adding regular whole numbers. Example: $4.5 + 2 = 6.5$.

If the problem-solver does not properly align the decimal points, an incorrect answer of 4.7 may result. An easy way to add decimals is to align all of the decimal points in a vertical column visually. This will allow one to see exactly where the decimal should be placed in the final answer. Begin adding from right to left. Add each column in turn, making sure to carry the number to the left if a column adds up to more than 9. The same rules apply to the subtraction of decimals.

> **Review Video: Adding and Subtracting Decimals**
> Visit mometrix.com/academy and enter code: 381101

MULTIPLYING DECIMALS

A simple multiplication problem has two components: a **multiplicand** and a **multiplier**. When multiplying decimals, work as though the numbers were whole rather than decimals. Once the final product is calculated, count the number of places to the right of the decimal in both the multiplicand and the multiplier. Then, count that number of places from the right of the product and place the decimal in that position.

For example, 12.3×2.56 has a total of three places to the right of the respective decimals. Multiply 123×256 to get 31488. Now, beginning on the right, count three places to the left and insert the decimal. The final product will be 31.488.

> **Review Video: Multiplying Decimals**
> Visit mometrix.com/academy and enter code: 731574

DIVIDING DECIMALS

Every division problem has a **divisor** and a **dividend**. The dividend is the number that is being divided. In the problem $14 \div 7$, 14 is the dividend and 7 is the divisor. In a division problem with decimals, the divisor must be converted into a whole number. Begin by moving the decimal in the divisor to the right until a whole number is created. Next, move the decimal in the dividend the same number of spaces to the right. For example, 4.9 into 24.5 would become 49 into 245. The decimal was moved one space to the right to create a whole number in the divisor, and then the same was done for the dividend. Once the whole numbers are created, the problem is carried out normally: $245 \div 49 = 5$.

> **Review Video: Dividing Decimals**
> Visit mometrix.com/academy and enter code: 560690

PERCENTAGES

Percentages can be thought of as fractions that are based on a whole of 100; that is, one whole is equal to 100%. The word **percent** means "per hundred." Percentage problems are often presented in three main ways:

- Find what percentage of some number another number is.
 - Example: What percentage of 40 is 8?
- Find what number is some percentage of a given number.
 - Example: What number is 20% of 40?
- Find what number another number is a given percentage of.
 - Example: What number is 8 20% of?

There are three components in each of these cases: a **whole** (W), a **part** (P), and a **percentage** (%). These are related by the equation: $P = W \times \%$. This can easily be rearranged into other forms that may suit different questions better: $\% = \frac{P}{W}$ and $W = \frac{P}{\%}$. Percentage problems are often also word problems. As such, a large part of solving them is figuring out which quantities are what. For example, consider the following word problem:

In a school cafeteria, 7 students choose pizza, 9 choose hamburgers, and 4 choose tacos. What percentage of student choose tacos?

To find the whole, you must first add all of the parts: $7 + 9 + 4 = 20$. The percentage can then be found by dividing the part by the whole ($\% = \frac{P}{W}$): $\frac{4}{20} = \frac{20}{100} = 20\%$.

> **Review Video: Percentages**
> Visit mometrix.com/academy and enter code: 141911
>
> **Review Video: Finding Percentage of Number Given Whole**
> Visit mometrix.com/academy and enter code: 932623

CONVERTING BETWEEN PERCENTAGES, FRACTIONS, AND DECIMALS

Converting decimals to percentages and percentages to decimals is as simple as moving the decimal point. To *convert from a decimal to a percentage*, move the decimal point **two places to the right**. To *convert from a percentage to a decimal*, move it **two places to the left**. It may be helpful to remember that the percentage number will always be larger than the equivalent decimal number. For example:

$$0.23 = 23\% \quad 5.34 = 534\% \quad 0.007 = 0.7\%$$
$$700\% = 7.00 \quad 86\% = 0.86 \quad 0.15\% = 0.0015$$

To convert a fraction to a decimal, simply divide the numerator by the denominator in the fraction. To convert a decimal to a fraction, put the decimal in the numerator with 1 in the denominator. Multiply the numerator and denominator by tens until there are no more decimal places. Then simplify the fraction to lowest terms. For example, converting 0.24 to a fraction:

$$0.24 = \frac{0.24}{1} = \frac{0.24 \times 100}{1 \times 100} = \frac{24}{100} = \frac{6}{25}$$

28

Fractions can be converted to a percentage by finding equivalent fractions with a denominator of 100. For example,

$$\frac{7}{10} = \frac{70}{100} = 70\% \quad \frac{1}{4} = \frac{25}{100} = 25\%$$

To convert a percentage to a fraction, divide the percentage number by 100 and reduce the fraction to its simplest possible terms. For example,

$$60\% = \frac{60}{100} = \frac{3}{5} \quad 96\% = \frac{96}{100} = \frac{24}{25}$$

Review Video: Converting Decimals to Fractions and Percentages
Visit mometrix.com/academy and enter code: 986765

Review Video: Converting Fractions to Percentages and Decimals
Visit mometrix.com/academy and enter code: 306233

Review Video: Converting Percentages to Decimals and Fractions
Visit mometrix.com/academy and enter code: 287297

RATIONAL NUMBERS

The term **rational** means that the number can be expressed as a ratio or fraction. That is, a number, r, is rational if and only if it can be represented by a fraction $\frac{a}{b}$ where a and b are integers and b does not equal 0. The set of rational numbers includes integers and decimals. If there is no finite way to represent a value with a fraction of integers, then the number is **irrational**. Common examples of irrational numbers include: $\sqrt{5}, \left(1 + \sqrt{2}\right),$ and π.

Review Video: Rational Numbers
Visit mometrix.com/academy and enter code: 280645

Practice

P1. What is 30% of 120?

P2. What is 150% of 20?

P3. What is 14.5% of 96?

P4. Simplify the following expressions:

(a) $\left(\frac{2}{5}\right)/\left(\frac{4}{7}\right)$

(b) $\frac{7}{8} - \frac{8}{16}$

(c) $\frac{1}{2} + \left(3\left(\frac{3}{4}\right) - 2\right) + 4$

(d) $0.22 + 0.5 - (5.5 + 3.3 \div 3)$

(e) $\frac{3}{2} + (4(0.5) - 0.75) + 2$

P5. Convert the following to a fraction and to a decimal: **(a)** 15%; **(b)** 24.36%

P6. Convert the following to a decimal and to a percentage. **(a)** 4/5; **(b)** $3\frac{2}{5}$

P7. A woman's age is thirteen more than half of 60. How old is the woman?

P8. A patient was given pain medicine at a dosage of 0.22 grams. The patient's dosage was then increased to 0.80 grams. By how much was the patient's dosage increased?

P9. At a hotel, $\frac{3}{4}$ of the 100 rooms are occupied today. Yesterday, $\frac{4}{5}$ of the 100 rooms were occupied. On which day were more of the rooms occupied and by how much more?

P10. At a school, 40% of the teachers teach English. If 20 teachers teach English, how many teachers work at the school?

P11. A patient was given blood pressure medicine at a dosage of 2 grams. The patient's dosage was then decreased to 0.45 grams. By how much was the patient's dosage decreased?

P12. Two weeks ago, $\frac{2}{3}$ of the 60 customers at a skate shop were male. Last week, $\frac{3}{6}$ of the 80 customers were male. During which week were there more male customers?

P13. Jane ate lunch at a local restaurant. She ordered a $4.99 appetizer, a $12.50 entrée, and a $1.25 soda. If she wants to tip her server 20%, how much money will she spend in all?

P14. According to a survey, about 82% of engineers were highly satisfied with their job. If 145 engineers were surveyed, how many reported that they were highly satisfied?

P15. A patient was given 40 mg of a certain medicine. Later, the patient's dosage was increased to 45 mg. What was the percent increase in his medication?

P16. Order the following rational numbers from least to greatest: 0.55, 17%, $\sqrt{25}$, $\frac{64}{4}$, $\frac{25}{50}$, 3.

P17. Order the following rational numbers from greatest to least: 0.3, 27%, $\sqrt{100}$, $\frac{72}{9}$, $\frac{1}{9}$, 4.5

Mometrix

Practice Solutions

P1. The word *of* indicates multiplication, so 30% of 120 is found by multiplying 120 by 30%. Change 30% to a decimal, then multiply: $120 \times 0.3 = 36$

P2. The word *of* indicates multiplication, so 150% of 20 is found by multiplying 20 by 150%. Change 150% to a decimal, then multiply: $20 \times 1.5 = 30$

P3. Change 14.5% to a decimal before multiplying. $0.145 \times 96 = 13.92$.

P4. Follow the order of operations and utilize properties of fractions to solve each:

(a) Rewrite the problem as a multiplication problem: $\frac{2}{5} \times \frac{7}{4} = \frac{2\times7}{5\times4} = \frac{14}{20}$. Make sure the fraction is reduced to lowest terms. Both 14 and 20 can be divided by 2.

$$\frac{14}{20} = \frac{14 \div 2}{20 \div 2} = \frac{7}{10}$$

(b) The denominators of $\frac{7}{8}$ and $\frac{8}{16}$ are 8 and 16, respectively. The lowest common denominator of 8 and 16 is 16 because 16 is the least common multiple of 8 and 16. Convert the first fraction to its equivalent with the newly found common denominator of 16: $\frac{7 \times 2}{8 \times 2} = \frac{14}{16}$. Now that the fractions have the same denominator, you can subtract them.

$$\frac{14}{16} - \frac{8}{16} = \frac{6}{16} = \frac{3}{8}$$

(c) When simplifying expressions, first perform operations within groups. Within the set of parentheses are multiplication and subtraction operations. Perform the multiplication first to get $\frac{1}{2} + \left(\frac{9}{4} - 2\right) + 4$. Then, subtract two to obtain $\frac{1}{2} + \frac{1}{4} + 4$. Finally, perform addition from left to right:

$$\frac{1}{2} + \frac{1}{4} + 4 = \frac{2}{4} + \frac{1}{4} + \frac{16}{4} = \frac{19}{4} = 4\frac{3}{4}$$

(d) First, evaluate the terms in the parentheses $(5.5 + 3.3 \div 3)$ using order of operations. $3.3 \div 3 = 1.1$, and $5.5 + 1.1 = 6.6$. Next, rewrite the problem: $0.22 + 0.5 - 6.6$. Finally, add and subtract from left to right: $0.22 + 0.5 = 0.72$; $0.72 - 6.6 = -5.88$. The answer is -5.88.

(e) First, simplify within the parentheses, then change the fraction to a decimal and perform addition from left to right:

$$\frac{3}{2} + (2 - 0.75) + 2 =$$
$$\frac{3}{2} + 1.25 + 2 =$$
$$1.5 + 1.25 + 2 = 4.75$$

P5. (a) 15% can be written as $\frac{15}{100}$. Both 15 and 100 can be divided by 5: $\frac{15 \div 5}{100 \div 5} = \frac{3}{20}$

When converting from a percentage to a decimal, drop the percent sign and move the decimal point two places to the left: $15\% = 0.15$

(b) 24.36% written as a fraction is $\frac{24.36}{100}$, or $\frac{2436}{10,000}$, which reduces to $\frac{609}{2500}$. 24.36% written as a decimal is 0.2436. Recall that dividing by 100 moves the decimal two places to the left.

P6. (a) Recall that in the decimal system the first decimal place is one tenth: $\frac{4 \times 2}{5 \times 2} = \frac{8}{10} = 0.8$

Percent means "per hundred." $\frac{4 \times 20}{5 \times 20} = \frac{80}{100} = 80\%$

(b) The mixed number $3\frac{2}{5}$ has a whole number and a fractional part. The fractional part $\frac{2}{5}$ can be written as a decimal by dividing 5 into 2, which gives 0.4. Adding the whole to the part gives 3.4.

To find the equivalent percentage, multiply the decimal by 100. $3.4(100) = 340\%$. Notice that this percentage is greater than 100%. This makes sense because the original mixed number $3\frac{2}{5}$ is greater than 1.

P7. "More than" indicates addition, and "of" indicates multiplication. The expression can be written as $\frac{1}{2}(60) + 13$. So, the woman's age is equal to $\frac{1}{2}(60) + 13 = 30 + 13 = 43$. The woman is 43 years old.

P8. The first step is to determine what operation (addition, subtraction, multiplication, or division) the problem requires. Notice the keywords and phrases "by how much" and "increased." "Increased" means that you go from a smaller amount to a larger amount. This change can be found by subtracting the smaller amount from the larger amount: 0.80 grams– 0.22 grams = 0.58 grams.

Remember to line up the decimal when subtracting:

$$
\begin{array}{r}
0.80 \\
-\ 0.22 \\
\hline
0.58
\end{array}
$$

P9. First, find the number of rooms occupied each day. To do so, multiply the fraction of rooms occupied by the number of rooms available:

$$\text{Number occupied} = \text{Fraction occupied} \times \text{Total number}$$
$$\text{Number of rooms occupied today} = \frac{3}{4} \times 100 = 75$$
$$\text{Number of rooms occupied} = \frac{4}{5} \times 100 = 80$$

The difference in the number of rooms occupied is: $80 - 75 = 5$ rooms

P10. To answer this problem, first think about the number of teachers that work at the school. Will it be more or less than the number of teachers who work in a specific department such as English? More teachers work at the school, so the number you find to answer this question will be greater than 20.

40% of the teachers are English teachers. "Of" indicates multiplication, and words like "is" and "are" indicate equivalence. Translating the problem into a mathematical sentence gives $40\% \times t = 20$, where t represents the total number of teachers. Solving for t gives $t = \frac{20}{40\%} = \frac{20}{0.40} = 50$. Fifty teachers work at the school.

P11. The decrease is represented by the difference between the two amounts:

$$2 \text{ grams} - 0.45 \text{ grams} = 1.55 \text{ grams}.$$

Remember to line up the decimal point before subtracting.

$$\begin{array}{r} 2.00 \\ -\ 0.45 \\ \hline 1.55 \end{array}$$

P12. First, you need to find the number of male customers that were in the skate shop each week. You are given this amount in terms of fractions. To find the actual number of male customers, multiply the fraction of male customers by the number of customers in the store.

$$\text{Actual number of male customers} = \text{fraction of male customers} \times \text{total customers}$$
$$\text{Number of male customers two weeks ago} = \frac{2}{3} \times 60 = \frac{120}{3} = 40$$
$$\text{Number of male customers last week} = \frac{3}{6} \times 80 = \frac{1}{2} \times 80 = \frac{80}{2} = 40$$

The number of male customers was the same both weeks.

P13. To find total amount, first find the sum of the items she ordered from the menu and then add 20% of this sum to the total.

$$\$4.99 + \$12.50 + \$1.25 = \$18.74$$

$$\$18.74 \times 20\% = (0.20)(\$18.74) = \$3.748 \approx \$3.75$$

$$\text{Total} = \$18.74 + \$3.75 = \$22.49$$

P14. 82% of 145 is $0.82 \times 145 = 118.9$. Because you can't have 0.9 of a person, we must round up to say that 119 engineers reported that they were highly satisfied with their jobs.

P15. To find the percent increase, first compare the original and increased amounts. The original amount was 40 mg, and the increased amount is 45 mg, so the dosage of medication was increased by 5 mg ($45 - 40 = 5$). Note, however, that the question asks not by how much the dosage increased but by what percentage it increased.

$$\text{Percent increase} = \frac{\text{new amount} - \text{original amount}}{\text{original amount}} \times 100\%$$
$$= \frac{45 \text{ mg} - 40 \text{ mg}}{40 \text{ mg}} \times 100\% = \frac{5}{40} \times 100\% = 0.125 \times 100\% = 12.5\%$$

P16. Recall that the term rational simply means that the number can be expressed as a ratio or fraction. Notice that each of the numbers in the problem can be written as a decimal or integer:

$$17\% = 0.1717$$
$$\sqrt{25} = 5$$
$$\frac{64}{4} = 16$$
$$\frac{25}{50} = \frac{1}{2} = 0.5$$

So, the answer is $17\%, \frac{25}{50}, 0.55, 3, \sqrt{25}, \frac{64}{4}$.

P17. Converting all the numbers to integers and decimals makes it easier to compare the values:

$$27\% = 0.27$$
$$\sqrt{100} = 10$$
$$\frac{72}{9} = 8$$
$$\frac{1}{9} \approx 0.11$$

So, the answer is $\sqrt{100}, \frac{72}{9}, 4.5, 0.3, 27\%, \frac{1}{9}$.

Review Video: <u>Ordering Rational Numbers</u>
Visit mometrix.com/academy and enter code: 419578

Proportions and Ratios

PROPORTIONS

A proportion is a relationship between two quantities that dictates how one changes when the other changes. A **direct proportion** describes a relationship in which a quantity increases by a set amount for every increase in the other quantity, or decreases by that same amount for every decrease in the other quantity. Example: Assuming a constant driving speed, the time required for a car trip increases as the distance of the trip increases. The distance to be traveled and the time required to travel are directly proportional.

Inverse proportion is a relationship in which an increase in one quantity is accompanied by a decrease in the other, or vice versa. Example: the time required for a car trip decreases as the speed increases, and increases as the speed decreases, so the time required is inversely proportional to the speed of the car.

Review Video: Proportions
Visit mometrix.com/academy and enter code: 505355

RATIOS

A **ratio** is a comparison of two quantities in a particular order. Example: If there are 14 computers in a lab, and the class has 20 students, there is a student to computer ratio of 20 to 14, commonly written as 20:14. Ratios are normally reduced to their smallest whole number representation, so 20:14 would be reduced to 10:7 by dividing both sides by 2.

Review Video: Ratios
Visit mometrix.com/academy and enter code: 996914

CONSTANT OF PROPORTIONALITY

When two quantities have a proportional relationship, there exists a **constant of proportionality** between the quantities; the product of this constant and one of the quantities is equal to the other quantity. For example, if one lemon costs $0.25, two lemons cost $0.50, and three lemons cost $0.75, there is a proportional relationship between the total cost of lemons and the number of lemons purchased. The constant of proportionality is the **unit price**, namely $0.25/lemon. Notice that the total price of lemons, t, can be found by multiplying the unit price of lemons, p, and the number of lemons, n: $t = pn$.

WORK/UNIT RATE

Unit rate expresses a quantity of one thing in terms of one unit of another. For example, if you travel 30 miles every two hours, a unit rate expresses this comparison in terms of one hour: in one hour you travel 15 miles, so your unit rate is 15 miles per hour. Other examples are how much one ounce of food costs (price per ounce) or figuring out how much one egg costs out of the dozen (price per 1 egg, instead of price per 12 eggs). The denominator of a unit rate is always 1. Unit rates are used to compare different situations to solve problems. For example, to make sure you get the best deal when deciding which kind of soda to buy, you can find the unit rate of each. If soda #1 costs $1.50 for a 1-liter bottle, and soda #2 costs $2.75 for a 2-liter bottle, it would be a better deal to buy soda #2, because its unit rate is only $1.375 per 1-liter, which is cheaper than soda #1. Unit rates can also help determine the length of time a given event will take. For example, if you can

paint 2 rooms in 4.5 hours, you can determine how long it will take you to paint 5 rooms by solving for the unit rate per room and then multiplying that by 5.

Review Video: <u>Rates and Unit Rates</u>
Visit mometrix.com/academy and enter code: 185363

SLOPE

On a graph with two points, (x_1, y_1) and (x_2, y_2), the **slope** is found with the formula $m = \frac{y_2 - y_1}{x_2 - x_1}$; where $x_1 \neq x_2$ and m stands for slope. If the value of the slope is **positive**, the line has an *upward direction* from left to right. If the value of the slope is **negative**, the line has a *downward direction* from left to right. Consider the following example:

A new book goes on sale in bookstores and online stores. In the first month, 5,000 copies of the book are sold. Over time, the book continues to grow in popularity. The data for the number of copies sold is in the table below.

# of Months on Sale	1	2	3	4	5
# of Copies Sold (In Thousands)	5	10	15	20	25

So, the number of copies that are sold and the time that the book is on sale is a proportional relationship. In this example, an equation can be used to show the data: $y = 5x$, where x is the number of months that the book is on sale. Also, y is the number of copies sold. So, the slope of the corresponding line is $\frac{\text{rise}}{\text{run}} = \frac{5}{1} = 5$.

Review Video: <u>Finding the Slope of a Line</u>
Visit mometrix.com/academy and enter code: 766664

FINDING AN UNKNOWN IN EQUIVALENT EXPRESSIONS

It is often necessary to apply information given about a rate or proportion to a new scenario. For example, if you know that Jedha can run a marathon (26 miles) in 3 hours, how long would it take her to run 10 miles at the same pace? Start by setting up equivalent expressions:

$$\frac{26 \text{ mi}}{3 \text{ hr}} = \frac{10 \text{ mi}}{x \text{ hr}}$$

Now, cross multiply and, solve for x:

$$26x = 30$$
$$x = \frac{30}{26} = \frac{15}{13}$$
$$x \cong 1.15 \text{ hrs } or \text{ 1 hr 9 min}$$

So, at this pace, Jedha could run 10 miles in about 1.15 hours or about 1 hour and 9 minutes.

Practice

P1. Solve the following for x.

(a) $\frac{45}{12} = \frac{15}{x}$

(b) $\frac{0.50}{2} = \frac{1.50}{x}$

(c) $\frac{40}{8} = \frac{x}{24}$

P2. At a school, for every 20 female students there are 15 male students. This same student ratio happens to exist at another school. If there are 100 female students at the second school, how many male students are there?

P3. In a hospital emergency room, there are 4 nurses for every 12 patients. What is the ratio of nurses to patients? If the nurse-to-patient ratio remains constant, how many nurses must be present to care for 24 patients?

P4. In a bank, the banker-to-customer ratio is 1:2. If seven bankers are on duty, how many customers are currently in the bank?

P5. Janice made $40 during the first 5 hours she spent babysitting. She will continue to earn money at this rate until she finishes babysitting in 3 more hours. Find how much money Janice earns per hour and the total she earned babysitting.

P6. The McDonalds are taking a family road trip, driving 300 miles to their cabin. It took them 2 hours to drive the first 120 miles. They will drive at the same speed all the way to their cabin. Find the speed at which the McDonalds are driving and how much longer it will take them to get to their cabin.

P7. It takes Andy 10 minutes to read 6 pages of his book. He has already read 150 pages in his book that is 210 pages long. Find how long it takes Andy to read 1 page and also find how long it will take him to finish his book if he continues to read at the same speed.

Practice Solutions

P1. First, cross multiply; then, solve for x:

(a) $45x = 12 \times 15$
$45x = 180$
$x = \frac{180}{45} = 4$

(b) $0.5x = 1.5 \times 2$
$0.5x = 3$
$x = \frac{3}{0.5} = 6$

(c) $8x = 40 \times 24$
$8x = 960$
$x = \frac{960}{8} = 120$

P2. One way to find the number of male students is to set up and solve a proportion.

$$\frac{\text{number of female students}}{\text{number of male students}} = \frac{20}{15} = \frac{100}{\text{number of male students}}$$

Represent the unknown number of male students as the variable x: $\frac{20}{15} = \frac{100}{x}$

Cross multiply and then solve for x:

$$20x = 15 \times 100$$
$$x = \frac{1500}{20}$$
$$x = 75$$

P3. The ratio of nurses to patients can be written as 4 to 12, 4:12, or $\frac{4}{12}$. Because four and twelve have a common factor of four, the ratio should be reduced to 1:3, which means that there is one nurse present for every three patients. If this ratio remains constant, there must be eight nurses present to care for 24 patients.

P4. Use proportional reasoning or set up a proportion to solve. Because there are twice as many customers as bankers, there must be fourteen customers when seven bankers are on duty. Setting up and solving a proportion gives the same result:

$$\frac{\text{number of bankers}}{\text{number of customers}} = \frac{1}{2} = \frac{7}{\text{number of customers}}$$

Represent the unknown number of patients as the variable x: $\frac{1}{2} = \frac{7}{x}$.

To solve for x, cross multiply: $1 \times x = 7 \times 2$, so $x = 14$.

P5. Janice earns \$8 per hour. This can be found by taking her initial amount earned, \$40, and dividing it by the number of hours worked, 5. Since $\frac{40}{5} = 8$, Janice makes \$8 in one hour. This can also be found by finding the unit rate, money earned per hour: $\frac{40}{5} = \frac{x}{1}$. Since cross multiplying yields $5x = 40$, and division by 5 shows that $x = 8$, Janice earns \$8 per hour.

Janice will earn \$64 babysitting in her 8 total hours (adding the first 5 hours to the remaining 3 gives the 8 hour total). Since Janice earns \$8 per hour and she worked 8 hours, $\frac{\$8}{\text{hr}} \times 8$ hrs $= \$64$. This can also be found by setting up a proportion comparing money earned to babysitting hours. Since she earns \$40 for 5 hours and since the rate is constant, she will earn a proportional amount in 8 hours: $\frac{40}{5} = \frac{x}{8}$. Cross multiplying will yield $5x = 320$, and division by 5 shows that $x = 64$.

P6. The McDonalds are driving 60 miles per hour. This can be found by setting up a proportion to find the unit rate, the number of miles they drive per one hour: $\frac{120}{2} = \frac{x}{1}$. Cross multiplying yields $2x = 120$ and division by 2 shows that $x = 60$.

Since the McDonalds will drive this same speed, it will take them another 3 hours to get to their cabin. This can be found by first finding how many miles the McDonalds have left to drive, which is $300 - 120 = 180$. The McDonalds are driving at 60 miles per hour, so a proportion can be set up to determine how many hours it will take them to drive 180 miles: $\frac{180}{x} = \frac{60}{1}$. Cross multiplying yields $60x = 180$, and division by 60 shows that $x = 3$. This can also be found by using the formula $D = r \times t$ (or distance = rate × time), where $180 = 60 \times t$, and division by 60 shows that $t = 3$.

P7. It takes Andy 10 minutes to read 6 pages, $\frac{10}{6} = 1\frac{2}{3}$ minutes, which is 1 minute and 40 seconds.

Next, determine how many pages Andy has left to read, $210 - 150 = 60$. Since it is now known that it takes him $1\frac{2}{3}$ minutes to read each page, then that rate must be multiplied by however many pages he has left to read (60) to find the time he'll need: $60 \times 1\frac{2}{3} = 100$, so it will take him 100 minutes, or 1 hour and 40 minutes, to read the rest of his book.

> **Review Video: <u>Proportions in the Real World</u>**
> Visit mometrix.com/academy and enter code: 221143

Expressions, Equations, and Inequalities

LINEAR EQUATIONS

Equations that can be written as $ax + b = 0$, where $a \neq 0$ are referred to as **one variable linear equations**. A solution to such an equation is called a **root**. In the case where we have the equation $5x + 10 = 0$, if we solve for x we get a solution of $x = -2$. In other words, the root of the equation is -2. This is found by first subtracting 10 from both sides, which gives $5x = -10$. Next, simply divide both sides by the coefficient of the variable, in this case 5, to get $x = -2$. This can be checked by plugging -2 back into the original equation $(5)(-2) + 10 = -10 + 10 = 0$.

The **solution set** is the set of all solutions of an equation. In our example, the solution set would simply be -2. If there were more solutions (there usually are in multivariable equations) then they would also be included in the solution set. When an equation has no true solutions, this is referred to as an **empty set**. Equations with identical solution sets are **equivalent equations**. An **identity** is a term whose value or determinant is equal to 1.

Linear equations can be written many ways. Below is a list of some forms linear equations can take:

- **Standard Form**: $Ax + By = C$; the slope is $\frac{-A}{B}$ and the y-intercept is $\frac{C}{B}$
- **Slope Intercept Form**: $y = mx + b$, where m is the slope and b is the y-intercept
- **Point-Slope Form**: $y - y_1 = m(x - x_1)$, where m is the slope and (x_1, y_1) is a point on the line
- **Two-Point Form**: $\frac{y - y_1}{x - x_1} = \frac{y_2 - y_1}{x_2 - x_1}$, where (x_1, y_1) and (x_2, y_2) are two points on the given line
- **Intercept Form**: $\frac{x}{x_1} + \frac{y}{y_1} = 1$, where $(x_1, 0)$ is the point at which a line intersects the x-axis, and $(0, y_1)$ is the point at which the same line intersects the y-axis

> **Review Video: Slope-Intercept and Point-Slope Forms**
> Visit mometrix.com/academy and enter code: 113216

SOLVING ONE-VARIABLE LINEAR EQUATIONS

Multiply all terms by the lowest common denominator to eliminate any fractions. Look for addition or subtraction to undo so you can isolate the variable on one side of the equal sign. Divide both sides by the coefficient of the variable. When you have a value for the variable, substitute this value into the original equation to make sure you have a true equation. Consider the following example:

Kim's savings are represented by the table below. Represent her savings, using an equation.

X (Months)	Y (Total Savings)
2	$1300
5	$2050
9	$3050
11	$3550
16	$4800

The table shows a function with a constant rate of change, or slope, of 250. Given the points on the table, the slopes can be calculated as $(2050 - 1300)/(5 - 2)$, $(3050 - 2050)/(9 - 5)$, $(3550 - 3050)/(11 - 9)$, and $(4800 - 3550)/(16 - 11)$, each of which equals 250. Thus, the table

40

shows a constant rate of change, indicating a linear function. The slope-intercept form of a linear equation is written as $y = mx + b$, where m represents the slope and b represents the y-intercept. Substituting the slope into this form gives $y = 250x + b$. Substituting corresponding x- and y-values from any point into this equation will give the y-intercept, or b. Using the point, (2, 1300), gives $1300 = 250(2) + b$, which simplifies as b = 800. Thus, her savings may be represented by the equation, $y = 250x + 800$.

RULES FOR MANIPULATING EQUATIONS

LIKE TERMS

Like terms are terms in an equation that have the same variable, regardless of whether or not they also have the same coefficient. This includes terms that *lack* a variable; all constants (i.e. numbers without variables) are considered like terms. If the equation involves terms with a variable raised to different powers, the like terms are those that have the variable raised to the same power.

For example, consider the equation $x^2 + 3x + 2 = 2x^2 + x - 7 + 2x$. In this equation, 2 and –7 are like terms; they are both constants. $3x$, x, and $2x$ are like terms: they all include the variable x raised to the first power. x^2 and $2x^2$ are like terms; they both include the variable x, raised to the second power. $2x$ and $2x^2$ are not like terms; although they both involve the variable x, the variable is not raised to the same power in both terms. The fact that they have the same coefficient, 2, is not relevant.

CARRYING OUT THE SAME OPERATION ON BOTH SIDES OF AN EQUATION

When solving an equation, the general procedure is to carry out a series of operations on both sides of an equation, choosing operations that will tend to simplify the equation when doing so. The reason why the same operation must be carried out on both sides of the equation is because that leaves the meaning of the equation unchanged, and yields a result that is equivalent to the original equation. This would not be the case if we carried out an operation on one side of an equation and not the other. Consider what an equation means: it is a statement that two values or expressions are equal. If we carry out the same operation on both sides of the equation—add 3 to both sides, for example—then the two sides of the equation are changed in the same way, and so remain equal. If we do that to only one side of the equation—add 3 to one side but not the other—then that wouldn't be true; if we change one side of the equation but not the other then the two sides are no longer equal.

ADVANTAGE OF COMBINING LIKE TERMS

Combining like terms refers to adding or subtracting like terms—terms with the same variable— and therefore reducing sets of like terms to a single term. The main advantage of doing this is that it simplifies the equation. Often combining like terms can be done as the first step in solving an equation, though it can also be done later, such as after distributing terms in a product.

For example, consider the equation $2(x + 3) + 3(2 + x + 3) = -4$. The 2 and the 3 in the second set of parentheses are like terms, and we can combine them, yielding $2(x + 3) + 3(x + 5) = -4$. Now we can carry out the multiplications implied by the parentheses, distributing outer 2 and 3 accordingly: $2x + 6 + 3x + 15 = -4$. The $2x$ and the $3x$ are like terms, and we can add them together: $5x + 6 + 15 = -4$. Now, the constants 6, 15, and –4 are also like terms, and we can combine them as well: subtracting 6 and 15 from both sides of the equation, we get $5x = -4 - 6 - 15$, or $5x = -25$, which simplifies further to $x = -5$.

CANCELING TERMS ON OPPOSITE SIDES OF AN EQUATION

Two terms on opposite sides of an equation can be canceled if and only if they *exactly* match each other. They must have the same variable raised to the same power and the same coefficient. For example, in the equation $3x + 2x^2 + 6 = 2x^2 - 6$, $2x^2$ appears on both sides of the equation, and can be canceled, leaving $3x + 6 = -6$. The 6 on each side of the equation can*not* be canceled, because it is added on one side of the equation and subtracted on the other. While they cannot be canceled, however, the 6 and –6 are like terms and can be combined, yielding $3x = -12$, which simplifies further to $x = -4$.

It's also important to note that the terms to be canceled must be independent terms and cannot be part of a larger term. For example, consider the equation $2(x + 6) = 3(x + 4) + 1$. We cannot cancel the xs, because even though they match each other they are part of the larger terms $2(x + 6)$ and $3(x + 4)$. We must first distribute the 2 and 3, yielding $2x + 12 = 3x + 12 + 1$. Now we see that the terms with the x's do not match, but the 12's do, and can be canceled, leaving $2x = 3x + 1$, which simplifies to $x = -1$.

PROCESS FOR MANIPULATING EQUATIONS

ISOLATING VARIABLES

To **isolate a variable** means to manipulate the equation so that the variable appears by itself on one side of the equation, and does not appear at all on the other side. Generally, an equation or inequality is considered to be solved once the variable is isolated and the other side of the equation or inequality is simplified as much as possible. In the case of a two-variable equation or inequality, only one variable need be isolated; it will not usually be possible to simultaneously isolate both variables.

For a linear equation—an equation in which the variable only appears raised to the first power—isolating a variable can be done by first moving all the terms with the variable to one side of the equation and all other terms to the other side. (*Moving* a term really means adding the inverse of the term to both sides; when a term is *moved* to the other side of the equation its sign is flipped.) Then combine like terms on each side. Finally, divide both sides by the coefficient of the variable, if applicable. The steps need not necessarily be done in this order, but this order will always work.

EQUATIONS WITH MORE THAN ONE SOLUTION

Some types of non-linear equation, such as equations involving squares of variables, may have more than one solution. For example, the equation $x^2 = 4$ has two solutions: 2 and –2. Equations with absolute values can also have multiple solutions: $|x| = 1$ has the solutions $x = 1$ and $x = -1$.

It is also possible for a linear equation to have more than one solution, but only if the equation is true regardless of the value of the variable. In this case, the equation is considered to have infinitely many solutions, because any possible value of the variable is a solution. We know a linear equation has infinitely many solutions if when we combine like terms the variables cancel, leaving a true statement. For example, consider the equation $2(3x + 5) = x + 5(x + 2)$. Distributing, we get $6x + 10 = x + 5x + 10$; combining like terms gives $6x + 10 = 6x + 10$, and the $6x$ terms cancel to leave $10 = 10$. This is clearly true, so the original equation is true for any value of x. We could also have canceled the 10s leaving $0 = 0$, but again this is clearly true—in general if both sides of the equation match exactly, it has infinitely many solutions.

EQUATIONS WITH NO SOLUTION

Some types of non-linear equation, such as equations involving squares of variables, may have no solution. For example, the equation $x^2 = -2$ has no solutions in the real numbers, because the square of any real number must be positive. Similarly, $|x| = -1$ has no solution, because the absolute value of a number is always positive.

It is also possible for an equation to have no solution even if does not involve any powers greater than one or absolute values or other special functions. For example, the equation $2(x + 3) + x = 3x$ has no solution. We can see that if we try to solve it: first we distribute, leaving $2x + 6 + x = 3x$. But now if we try to combine all the terms with the variable, we find that they cancel: we have $3x$ on the left and $3x$ on the right, canceling to leave us with $6 = 0$. This is clearly false. In general, whenever the variable terms in an equation cancel leaving different constants on both sides, it means that the equation has no solution. (If we are left with the *same* constant on both sides, the equation has infinitely many solutions instead.)

FEATURES OF EQUATIONS THAT REQUIRE SPECIAL TREATMENT

LINEAR EQUATIONS

A linear equation is an equation in which variables only appear by themselves: not multiplied together, not with exponents other than one, and not inside absolute value signs or any other functions. For example, the equation $x + 1 - 3x = 5 - x$ is a linear equation: while x appears multiple times, it never appears with an exponent other than one, or inside any function. The two-variable equation $2x - 3y = 5 + 2x$ is also a linear equation. In contrast, the equation $x^2 - 5 = 3x$ is *not* a linear equation, because it involves the term x^2. $\sqrt{x} = 5$ is not a linear equation, because it involves a square root. $(x - 1)^2 = 4$ is not a linear equation because even though there's no exponent on the x directly, it appears as part of an expression that is squared. The two-variable equation $x + xy - y = 5$ is not a linear equation because it includes the term xy, where two variables are multiplied together.

Linear equations can always be solved (or shown to have no solution) by combining like terms and performing simple operations on both sides of the equation. Some non-linear equations can also be solved by similar methods, but others may require more advanced methods of solution, if they can be solved analytically at all.

SOLVING EQUATIONS INVOLVING ROOTS

In an equation involving roots, the first step is to isolate the term with the root, if possible, and then raise both sides of the equation to the appropriate power to eliminate it. Consider an example equation, $2\sqrt{x + 1} - 1 = 3$. In this case, begin by adding 1 to both sides, yielding $2\sqrt{x + 1} = 4$, and then dividing both sides by 2, yielding $\sqrt{x + 1} = 2$. Now square both sides, yielding $x + 1 = 4$. Finally, subtracting 1 from both sides yields $x = 3$.

Squaring both sides of an equation may, however, yield a spurious solution—a solution to the squared equation that is *not* a solution of the original equation. It's therefore necessary to plug the solution back into the original equation to make sure it works. In this case, it does: $2\sqrt{3 + 1} - 1 = 2\sqrt{4} - 1 = 2(2) - 1 = 4 - 1 = 3$.

The same procedure applies for roots other than square roots. For example, given the equation $3 + \sqrt[3]{2x} = 5$, we can first subtract 3 from both sides, yielding $\sqrt[3]{2x} = 2$ and isolating the root. Raising both sides to the third power yields $2x = 2^3$, i.e. $2x = 8$. We can now divide both sides by 2 to get $x = 4$.

SOLVING EQUATIONS WITH EXPONENTS

To solve an equation involving an exponent, the first step is to isolate the variable with the exponent. We can then take the appropriate root of both sides to eliminate the exponent. For instance, for the equation $2x^3 + 17 = 5x^3 - 7$, we can subtract $5x^3$ from both sides to get $-3x^3 + 17 = -7$, and then subtract 17 from both sides to get $-3x^3 = -24$. Finally, we can divide both sides by –3 to get $x^3 = 8$. Finally, we can take the cube root of both sides to get $x = \sqrt[3]{8} = 2$.

One important but often overlooked point is that equations with an exponent greater than 1 may have more than one answer. The solution to $x^2 = 9$ isn't simply $x = 3$; it's $x = \pm 3$: that is, $x = 3$ or $x = -3$. For a slightly more complicated example, consider the equation $(x - 1)^2 - 1 = 3$. Adding one to both sides yields $(x - 1)^2 = 4$; taking the square root of both sides yields $x - 1 = 2$. We can then add 1 to both sides to get $x = 3$. However, there's a second solution: we also have the possibility that $x - 1 = -2$, in which case $x = -1$. Both $x = 3$ and $x = -1$ are valid solutions, as can be verified by substituting them both into the original equation.

SOLVING EQUATIONS WITH ABSOLUTE VALUES

When solving an equation with an absolute value, the first step is to isolate the absolute value term. We then consider the two possibilities: when the expression inside the absolute value is positive or when it is negative. In the former case, the expression in the absolute value equals the expression on the other side of the equation; in the latter, it equals the additive inverse of that expression—the expression times negative one. We consider each case separately, and finally check for spurious solutions.

For instance, consider solving $|2x - 1| + x = 5$ for x. We can first isolate the absolute value by moving the x to the other side: $|2x - 1| = -x + 5$. Now, we have two possibilities. First, that $2x - 1$ is positive, and hence $2x - 1 = -x + 5$. Rearranging and combining like terms yields $3x = 6$, and hence $x = 2$. The other possibility is that $2x - 1$ is negative, and hence $2x - 1 = -(-x + 5) = x - 5$. In this case, rearranging and combining like terms yields $x = -4$. Substituting $x = 2$ and $x = -4$ back into the original equation, we see that they are both valid solutions.

Note that the absolute value of a sum or difference applies to the sum or difference as a whole, not to the individual terms: in general, $|2x - 1|$ is not equal to $|2x + 1|$ or to $|2x| - 1$.

SPURIOUS SOLUTIONS

A **spurious solution** may arise when we square both sides of an equation as a step in solving it, or under certain other operations on the equation. It is a solution to the squared or otherwise modified equation that is *not* a solution of the original equation. To identify a spurious solution, it's useful when you solve an equation involving roots or absolute values to plug the solution back into the original equation to make sure it's valid.

CHOOSING WHICH VARIABLE TO ISOLATE IN TWO-VARIABLE EQUATIONS

Similar to methods for a one-variable equation, solving a two-variable equation involves isolating a variable: manipulating the equation so that a variable appears by itself on one side of the equation, and not at all on the other side. However, in a two-variable equation, you will usually only be able to isolate one of the variables; the other variable may appear on the other side along with constant terms, or with exponents or other functions.

Often one variable will be much more easily isolated than the other, and therefore that's the variable you should choose. If one variable appears with various exponents, and other only raised to the first power, the latter variable is the one to isolate: given the equation $a^2 + 2b = a^3 + b + 3$,

44

the b only appears to the first power, whereas a appears squared and cubed, so b is the variable that can be solved for: combining like terms and isolating the b on the left side of the equation, we get $b = a^3 - a^2 + 3$. If both variables are equally easy to isolate, then it's best to isolate the independent variable, if one is defined; if the two variables are x and y, the convention is that y is the independent variable.

WORKING WITH INEQUALITIES

Commonly in algebra and other upper-level fields of math you find yourself working with mathematical expressions that do not equal each other. The statement comparing such expressions with symbols such as < (less than) or > (greater than) is called an *inequality*. An example of an inequality is $7x > 5$. To solve for x, simply divide both sides by 7 and the solution is shown to be $x > \frac{5}{7}$. Graphs of the solution set of inequalities are represented on a number line. Open circles are used to show that an expression approaches a number but is never quite equal to that number.

Conditional inequalities are those with certain values for the variable that will make the condition true and other values for the variable where the condition will be false. **Absolute inequalities** can have any real number as the value for the variable to make the condition true, while there is no real number value for the variable that will make the condition false. Solving inequalities is done by following the same rules as for solving equations with the exception that when multiplying or dividing by a negative number the direction of the inequality sign must be flipped or reversed. **Double inequalities** are situations where two inequality statements apply to the same variable expression. An example of this is $-c < ax + b < c$.

DETERMINING SOLUTIONS TO INEQUALITIES

To determine whether a coordinate is a solution of an inequality, you can substitute the values of the coordinate into the inequality, simplify, and check whether the resulting statement holds true. For instance, to determine whether $(-2, 4)$ is a solution of the inequality $y \geq -2x + 3$, substitute the values into the inequality, $4 \geq -2(-2) + 3$. Simplify the right side of the inequality and the result is $4 \geq 7$, which is a false statement. Therefore, the coordinate is not a solution of the inequality. You can also use this method to determine which part of the graph of an inequality is shaded. The graph of $y \geq -2x + 3$ includes the solid line $y = -2x + 3$ and, since it excludes the point $(-2, 4)$ to the left of the line, it is shaded to the right of the line.

FLIPPING INEQUALITY SIGNS

When given an inequality, we can always turn the entire inequality around, swapping the two sides of the inequality and changing the inequality sign. For instance, $x + 2 > 2x - 3$ is equivalent to $2x - 3 < x + 2$. Aside from that, normally the inequality does not change if we carry out the same operation on both sides of the inequality. There is, however, one principal exception: if we *multiply* or *divide* both sides of the inequality by a *negative number*, the inequality is flipped. For example, if we take the inequality $-2x < 6$ and divide both sides by -2, the inequality flips and we are left with $x > -3$. This *only* applies to multiplication and division, and only with negative numbers. Multiplying or dividing both sides by a positive number, or adding or subtracting any number regardless of sign, does not flip the inequality.

COMPOUND INEQUALITIES

A **compound inequality** is an equality that consists of two inequalities combined with *and* or *or*. The two components of a proper compound inequality must be of opposite type: that is, one must be greater than (or greater than or equal to), the other less than (or less than or equal to). For instance, "$x + 1 < 2$ or $x + 1 > 3$" is a compound inequality, as is "$2x \geq 4$ and $2x \leq 6$." An *and* inequality can be written more compactly by having one inequality on each side of the common part: "$2x \geq 1$ and $2x \leq 6$," can also be written as $1 \leq 2x \leq 6$.

In order for the compound inequality to be meaningful, the two parts of an *and* inequality must overlap; otherwise no numbers satisfy the inequality. On the other hand, if the two parts of an *or* inequality overlap, then *all* numbers satisfy the inequality and as such is usually not meaningful.

Solving a compound inequality requires solving each part separately. For example, given the compound inequality "$x + 1 < 2$ or $x + 1 > 3$," the first inequality, $x + 1 < 2$, reduces to $x < 1$, and the second part, $x + 1 > 3$, reduces to $x > 2$, so the whole compound inequality can be written as "$x < 1$ or $x > 2$." Similarly, $1 \leq 2x \leq 6$ can be solved by dividing each term by 2, yielding $\frac{1}{2} \leq x \leq 3$.

SOLVING INEQUALITIES INVOLVING ABSOLUTE VALUES

To solve an inequality involving an absolute value, first isolate the term with the absolute value. Then proceed to treat the two cases separately as with an absolute value equation, but flipping the inequality in the case where the expression in the absolute value is negative (since that essentially involves multiplying both sides by -1.) The two cases are then combined into a compound inequality; if the absolute value is on the greater side of the inequality, then it is an *or* compound inequality, if on the lesser side, then it's an *and*.

Consider the inequality $2 + |x - 1| \geq 3$. We can isolate the absolute value term by subtracting 2 from both sides: $|x - 1| \geq 1$. Now, we're left with the two cases $x - 1 \geq 1$ or $x - 1 \leq -1$: note that in the latter, negative case, the inequality is flipped. $x - 1 \geq 1$ reduces to $x \geq 2$, and $x - 1 \leq -1$ reduces to $x \leq 0$. Since in the inequality $|x - 1| \geq 1$ the absolute value is on the greater side, the two cases combine into an *or* compound inequality, so the final, solved inequality is "$x \leq 0$ or $x \geq 2$."

SOLVING INEQUALITIES INVOLVING SQUARE ROOTS

Solving an inequality with a square root involves two parts. First, we solve the inequality as if it were an equation, isolating the square root and then squaring both sides of the equation. Second, we restrict the solution to the set of values of x for which the value inside the square root sign is non-negative.

For example, in the inequality, $\sqrt{x - 2} + 1 < 5$, we can isolate the square root by subtracting 1 from both sides, yielding $\sqrt{x - 2} < 4$. Squaring both sides of the inequality yields $x - 2 < 16$, so $x < 18$. Since we can't take the square root of a negative number, we also require the part inside the square root to be non-negative. In this case, that means $x - 2 \geq 0$. Adding 2 to both sides of the inequality yields $x \geq 2$. Our final answer is a compound inequality combining the two simple inequalities: $x \geq 2$ and $x < 18$, or $2 \leq x < 18$.

Note that we only get a compound inequality if the two simple inequalities are in opposite directions; otherwise we take the one that is more restrictive.

The same technique can be used for other even roots, such as fourth roots. It is *not*, however, used for cube roots or other odd roots—negative numbers *do* have cube roots, so the condition that the quantity inside the root sign cannot be negative does not apply.

SPECIAL CIRCUMSTANCES

Sometimes an inequality involving an absolute value or an even exponent is true for all values of x, and we don't need to do any further work to solve it. This is true if the inequality, once the absolute value or exponent term is isolated, says that term is greater than a negative number (or greater than or equal to zero). Since an absolute value or a number raised to an even exponent is *always* non-negative, this inequality is always true.

GRAPHICAL SOLUTIONS TO EQUATIONS AND INEQUALITIES

When equations are shown graphically, they are usually shown on a **Cartesian coordinate plane**. The Cartesian coordinate plane consists of two number lines placed perpendicular to each other, and intersecting at the zero point, also known as the origin. The horizontal number line is known as the x-axis, with positive values to the right of the origin, and negative values to the left of the origin. The vertical number line is known as the y-axis, with positive values above the origin, and negative values below the origin. Any point on the plane can be identified by an ordered pair in the form (x, y), called coordinates. The x-value of the coordinate is called the abscissa, and the y-value of the coordinate is called the ordinate. The two number lines divide the plane into **four quadrants**: I, II, III, and IV.

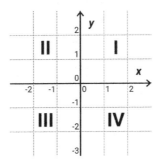

Note that in quadrant I $x > 0$ and $y > 0$, in quadrant II $x < 0$ and $y > 0$, in quadrant III $x < 0$ and $y < 0$, and in quadrant IV $x > 0$ and $y < 0$.

Recall that if the value of the slope of a line is positive, the line slopes upward from left to right. If the value of the slope is negative, the line slopes downward from left to right. If the y-coordinates are the same for two points on a line, the slope is 0 and the line is a **horizontal line**. If the x-coordinates are the same for two points on a line, there is no slope and the line is a **vertical line**. Two or more lines that have equivalent slopes are **parallel lines**. **Perpendicular lines** have slopes that are negative reciprocals of each other, such as $\frac{a}{b}$ and $\frac{-b}{a}$.

GRAPHING SIMPLE INEQUALITIES

To graph a simple inequality, we first mark on the number line the value that signifies the end point of the inequality. If the inequality is strict (involves a less than or greater than), we use a hollow circle; if it is not strict (less than or equal to or greater than or equal to), we use a solid circle. We then fill in the part of the number line that satisfies the inequality: to the left of the marked point for less than (or less than or equal to), to the right for greater than (or greater than or equal to).

For example, we would graph the inequality $x < 5$ by putting a hollow circle at 5 and filling in the part of the line to the left:

GRAPHING COMPOUND INEQUALITIES

To graph a compound inequality, we fill in both parts of the inequality for an *or* inequality, or the overlap between them for an *and* inequality. More specifically, we start by plotting the endpoints of each inequality on the number line. For an *or* inequality, we then fill in the appropriate side of the line for each inequality. Typically, the two component inequalities do not overlap, that means the shaded part is *outside* the two points. For an *and* inequality, we instead fill in the part of the line that meets both inequalities.

For the inequality "$x \leq -3$ or $x > 4$," we first put a solid circle at –3 and a hollow circle at 4. We then fill the parts of the line *outside* these circles:

GRAPHING INEQUALITIES INCLUDING ABSOLUTE VALUES

An inequality with an absolute value can be converted to a compound inequality. To graph the inequality, first convert it to a compound inequality, and then graph that normally. If the absolute value is on the greater side of the inequality, we end up with an *or* inequality; we plot the endpoints of the inequality on the number line and fill in the part of the line *outside* those points. If the absolute value is on the smaller side of the inequality, we end up with an *and* inequality; we plot the endpoints of the inequality on the number line and fill in the part of the line *between* those points.

For example, the inequality $|x + 1| \geq 4$ can be rewritten as $x \geq 3$ or $x \leq -5$. We place solid circles at the points 3 and -5 and fill in the part of the line *outside* them:

GRAPHING EQUATIONS IN TWO VARIABLES

One way of graphing an equation in two variables is to plot enough points to get an idea for its shape, and then draw the appropriate curve through those points. A point can be plotted by substituting in a value for one variable and solving for the other. If the equation is linear, we only need two points, and can then draw a straight line between them.

For example, consider the equation $y = 2x - 1$. This is a linear equation—both variables only appear raised to the first power—so we only need two points. When $x = 0$, $y = 2(0) - 1 = -1$.

48

When $x = 2$, $y = 2(2) - 1 = 3$. We can therefore choose the points $(0, -1)$ and $(2, 3)$, and draw a line between them:

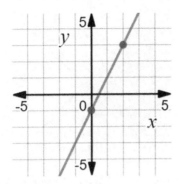

GRAPHING INEQUALITIES IN TWO VARIABLES

To graph an inequality in two variables, we first graph the border of the inequality. This means graphing the equation that we get if we replace the inequality sign with an equals sign. If the inequality is strict (> or <), we graph the border with a dashed or dotted line; if it is not strict (≥ or ≤), we use a solid line. We can then test any point not on the border to see if it satisfies the inequality. If it does, we shade in that side of the border; if not, we shade in the other side. As an example, consider $y > 2x + 2$. To graph this inequality, we first graph the border, $y = 2x + 2$. Since it is a strict inequality, we use a dashed line. Then, we choose a test point. This can be any point not on the border; in this case, we will choose the origin, $(0, 0)$. (This makes the calculation easy and is generally a good choice unless the border passes through the origin.) Putting this into the original inequality, we get $0 > 2(0) + 2$, i.e. $0 > 2$. This is *not* true, so we shade in the side of the border that does *not* include the point $(0, 0)$:

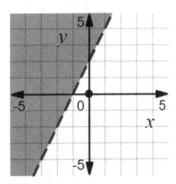

GRAPHING COMPOUND INEQUALITIES IN TWO VARIABLES

One way to graph a compound inequality in two variables is to first graph each of the component inequalities. For an *and* inequality, we then shade in only the parts where the two graphs overlap; for an *or* inequality, we shade in any region that pertains to either of the individual inequalities.

Consider the graph of "$y \geq x - 1$ *and* $y \leq -x$":

We first shade in the individual inequalities:

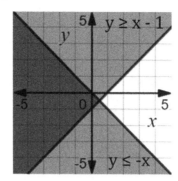

Now, since the compound inequality has an *and*, we only leave shaded the overlap—the part that pertains to *both* inequalities:

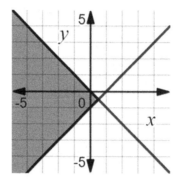

If instead the inequality had been "$y \geq x - 1$ *or* $y \leq -x$," our final graph would involve the *total* shaded area:

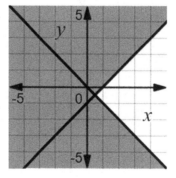

SOLVING SYSTEMS OF EQUATIONS

Systems of equations are a set of simultaneous equations that all use the same variables. A solution to a system of equations must be true for each equation in the system. **Consistent systems** are those with at least one solution. **Inconsistent systems** are systems of equations that have no solution.

> **Review Video: Systems of Equations**
> Visit mometrix.com/academy and enter code: 658153

SUBSTITUTION

To solve a system of linear equations by **substitution**, start with the easier equation and solve for one of the variables. Express this variable in terms of the other variable. Substitute this expression in the other equation, and solve for the other variable. The solution should be expressed in the form (x, y). Substitute the values into both of the original equations to check your answer. Consider the following system of equations:

$$x + 6y = 15$$
$$3x - 12y = 18$$

Solving the first equation for x: $x = 15 - 6y$

Substitute this value in place of x in the second equation, and solve for y:

$$3(15 - 6y) - 12y = 18$$
$$45 - 18y - 12y = 18$$
$$30y = 27$$
$$y = \frac{27}{30} = \frac{9}{10} = 0.9$$

Plug this value for y back into the first equation to solve for x:

$$x = 15 - 6(0.9) = 15 - 5.4 = 9.6$$

Check both equations if you have time:

$$9.6 + 6(0.9) = 15 \qquad 3(9.6) - 12(0.9) = 18$$
$$9.6 + 5.4 = 15 \qquad 28.8 - 10.8 = 18$$
$$15 = 15 \qquad 18 = 18$$

Therefore, the solution is $(9.6, 0.9)$.

ELIMINATION

To solve a system of equations using **elimination**, begin by rewriting both equations in standard form $Ax + By = C$. Check to see if the coefficients of one pair of like variables add to zero. If not, multiply one or both of the equations by a non-zero number to make one set of like variables add to zero. Add the two equations to solve for one of the variables. Substitute this value into one of the original equations to solve for the other variable. Check your work by substituting into the other equation. Now, consider solving the following system using the elimination method:

$$5x + 6y = 4$$
$$x + 2y = 4$$

If we multiply the second equation by -3, we can eliminate the y terms:

$$5x + 6y = 4$$
$$-3x - 6y = -12$$

51

Add the equations together and solve for x:

$$2x = -8$$
$$x = \frac{-8}{2} = -4$$

Plug the value for x back in to either of the original equations and solve for y:

$$-4 + 2y = 4$$
$$y = \frac{4 + 4}{2} = 4$$

Check both equations if you have time:

$$5(-4) + 6(4) = 4 \qquad\qquad -4 + 2(4) = 4$$
$$-20 + 24 = 4 \qquad\qquad -4 + 8 = 4$$
$$4 = 4 \qquad\qquad\qquad 4 = 4$$

Therefore, the solution is (-4, 4).

Review Video: <u>Substitution and Elimination for Solving Linear Systems</u>
Visit mometrix.com/academy and enter code: 958611

GRAPHICALLY

To solve a system of linear equations **graphically**, plot both equations on the same graph. The solution of the equations is the point where both lines cross. If the lines do not cross (are parallel), then there is **no solution**.

For example, consider the following system of equations:

$$y = 2x + 7$$
$$y = -x + 1$$

Since these equations are given in slope-intercept form, they are easy to graph; the y intercepts of the lines are $(0, 7)$ and $(0, 1)$. The respective slopes are 2 and –1, thus the graphs look like this:

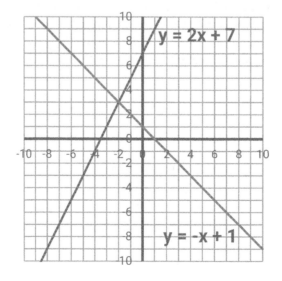

The two lines intersect at the point $(-2, 3)$, thus this is the solution to the system of equations.

Solving a system graphically is generally only practical if both coordinates of the solution are integers; otherwise the intersection will lie between gridlines on the graph and the coordinates will be difficult or impossible to determine exactly. It also helps if, as in this example, the equations are in slope-intercept form or some other form that makes them easy to graph. Otherwise, another method of solution (by substitution or elimination) is likely to be more useful.

SOLVING SYSTEMS OF EQUATIONS USING THE TRACE FEATURE

Using the **trace feature** on a calculator requires that you rewrite each equation, isolating the y-variable on one side of the equal sign. Enter both equations in the graphing calculator and plot the graphs simultaneously. Use the trace cursor to find where the two lines cross. Use the zoom feature if necessary to obtain more accurate results. Always check your answer by substituting into the original equations. The trace method is likely to be less accurate than other methods due to the resolution of graphing calculators, but is a useful tool to provide an approximate answer.

CALCULATIONS USING POINTS

Sometimes you need to perform calculations using only points on a graph as input data. Using points, you can determine what the **midpoint** and **distance** are. If you know the equation for a line you can calculate the distance between the line and the point.

To find the **midpoint** of two points (x_1, y_1) and (x_2, y_2), average the x-coordinates to get the x-coordinate of the midpoint, and average the y-coordinates to get the y-coordinate of the midpoint. The formula is: $\left(\frac{x_1 + x_2}{2}, \frac{y_1 + y_2}{2}\right)$.

The **distance** between two points is the same as the length of the hypotenuse of a right triangle with the two given points as endpoints, and the two sides of the right triangle parallel to the x-axis and y-axis, respectively. The length of the segment parallel to the x-axis is the difference between the x-coordinates of the two points. The length of the segment parallel to the y-axis is the difference between the y-coordinates of the two points. Use the Pythagorean theorem $a^2 + b^2 = c^2$ or $c = \sqrt{a^2 + b^2}$ to find the distance. The formula is $d = \sqrt{(x_2 - x_1)^2 + (y_2 - y_1)^2}$.

When a line is in the format $Ax + By + C = 0$, where A, B, and C are coefficients, you can use a point (x_1, y_1) not on the line and apply the formula $d = \frac{|Ax_1 + By_1 + C|}{\sqrt{A^2 + B^2}}$ to find the distance between the line and the point (x_1, y_1).

Mometrix

Practice

P1. Seeing the equation $2x + 4 = 4x + 7$, a student divides the first terms on each side by 2, yielding $x + 4 = 2x + 7$, and then combines like terms to get $x = -3$. However, this is incorrect, as can be seen by substituting –3 into the original equation. Explain what is wrong with the student's reasoning.

P2. Describe the steps necessary to solve the equation $2x + 1 - x = 4 + 3x + 7$.

P3. Describe the steps necessary to solve the equation $2(x + 5) = 7(4 - x)$.

P4. Find all real solutions to the equation $1 - \sqrt{x} = 2$.

P5. Find all real solutions to the equation $|x + 1| = 2x + 5$.

P6. Solve for x: $-x + 2\sqrt{x + 5} + 1 = 3$.

P7. Ray earns $10 an hour at his job. Write an equation for his earnings as a function of time spent working. Determine how long Ray has to work in order to earn $360.

P8. Simplify the following: $3x + 2 + 2y = 5y - 7 + |2x - 1|$

P9. Analyze the following inequalities:

(a) $2 - |x + 1| < 3$
(b) $2(x - 1)^2 + 7 \leq 1$

P10. Graph the following on a number line:

(a) $x \geq 3$
(b) $-2 \leq x \leq 6$
(c) $|x| < 2$

P11. Graph $y = x^2 - 3x + 2$.

P12. Solve the following systems of equations:

(a) $3x + 4y = 9$
 $-12x + 7y = 10$

(b) $-3x + 2y = -1$
 $4x - 5y = 6$

P13. Find the distance and midpoint between points (2, 4) and (8,6).

Mometrix

Practice Solutions

P1. As stated, it's easy to verify that the student's solution is incorrect: $2(-3) + 4 = -2$ and $4(-3) + 7 = -5$; clearly $-2 \neq -5$. The mistake was in the first step, which illustrates a common type of error in solving equations. The student tried to simplify the two variable terms by dividing them by 2. However, it's not valid to multiply or divide only one term on each side of an equation by a number; when multiplying or dividing, the operation must be applied to *every* term in the equation. So, dividing by 2 would yield not $x + 4 = 2x + 7$, but $x + 2 = 2x + \frac{7}{2}$. While this is now valid, that fraction is inconvenient to work with, so this may not be the best first step in solving the equation. Rather, it may have been better to first combine like terms: subtracting $4x$ from both sides yields $-2x + 4 = 7$; subtracting 4 from both sides yields $-2x = 3$; and *now* we can divide both sides by –2 to get $x = -\frac{3}{2}$.

P2. Our ultimate goal is to isolate the variable, x. To that end we first move all the terms containing x to the left side of the equation, and all the constant terms to the right side. Note that when we move a term to the other side of the equation its sign changes. We are therefore now left with $2x - x - 3x = 4 + 7 - 1$.

Next, we combine the like terms on each side of the equation, adding and subtracting the terms as appropriate. This leaves us with $-2x = 10$.

At this point, we're almost done; all that remains is to divide both sides by -2 to leave the x by itself. We now have our solution, $x = -5$. We can verify that this is a correct solution by substituting it back into the original equation.

P3. Generally, in equations that have a sum or difference of terms multiplied by another value or expression, the first step is to multiply those terms, distributing as necessary: $2(x + 5) = 2(x) + 2(5) = 2x + 10$, and $7(4 - x) = 7(4) - 7(x) = 28 - 7x$. So, the equation becomes $2x + 10 = 28 - 7x$. We can now add $7x$ to both sides to eliminate the variable from the right-hand side: $9x + 10 = 28$. Similarly, we can subtract 10 from both sides to move all the constants to the right: $9x = 18$. Finally, we can divide both sides by 9, yielding the final answer, $x = 2$.

P4. It's not hard to isolate the root: subtract one from both sides, yielding $-\sqrt{x} = 1$. Finally, multiply both sides by –1, yielding $\sqrt{x} = -1$. Squaring both sides of the equation yields $x = 1$. However, if we plug this back into the original equation, we get $1 - \sqrt{1} = 2$, which is false. Therefore $x = 1$ is a spurious solution, and the equation has no real solutions.

P5. This equation has two possibilities: $x + 1 = 2x + 5$, which simplifies to $x = -4$; or $x + 1 = -(2x + 5) = -2x - 5$, which simplifies to $x = -2$. However, if we try substituting both values back into the original equation, we see that only $x = -2$ yields a true statement. $x = -4$ is a spurious solution; $x = -2$ is the only valid solution to the equation.

P6. Start by isolating the term with the root. We can do that by moving the $-x$ and the 1 to the other side, yielding $2\sqrt{x + 5} = 3 + x - 1$, or $2\sqrt{x + 5} = x + 2$. Dividing both sides of the equation by 2 would give us a fractional term that could be messy to deal with, so we won't do that for now. Instead, we square both sides of the equation; note that on the left-hand side the 2 is outside the square root sign, so we have to square it. As a result, we get $4(x + 5) = (x + 2)^2$. Expanding both sides gives us $4x + 20 = x^2 + 4x + 4$. In this case, we see that we have $4x$ on both sides, so we can cancel the $4x$ (which is what allows us to solve this equation despite the different powers of x). We now have $20 = x^2 + 4$, or $x^2 = 16$. Since the variable is raised to an even power, we need to take

55

the positive and negative roots, so $x = \pm 4$: that is, $x = 4$ or $x = -4$. Substituting both values into the original equation, we see that $x = 4$ satisfies the equation but $x = -4$ does not; hence $x = -4$ is a spurious solution, and the only solution to the equation is $x = 4$.

P7. The number of dollars that Ray earns is dependent on the number of hours he works, so earnings will be represented by the dependent variable y and hours worked will be represented by the independent variable x. He earns 10 dollars per hour worked, so his earning can be calculated as $y = 10x$. To calculate the number of hours Ray must work in order to earn \$360, plug in 360 for y and solve for x:

$$360 = 10x$$
$$x = \frac{360}{10} = 36$$

P8. To simplify this equation, we must isolate one of its variables on one side of the equation. In this case, the x appears under an absolute value sign, which makes it difficult to isolate. The y, on the other hand, only appears without an exponent—the equation is linear in y. We will therefore choose to isolate the y. The first step, then, is to move all the terms with y to the left side of the equation, which we can do by subtracting $5y$ from both sides:

$$3x + 2 - 3y = -7 + |2x - 1|$$

We can then move all the terms that do *not* include y to the right side of the equation, by subtracting $3x$ and 2 from both sides of the equation:

$$-3y = -3x - 9 + |2x - 1|$$

Finally, we can isolate the y by dividing both sides by –3.

$$y = x + 3 - \frac{1}{3}|2x - 1|$$

This is as far as we can simplify the equation; we cannot combine the terms inside and outside the absolute value sign. We can therefore consider the equation to be solved.

P9. (a) Subtracting 2 from both sides yields $-|x + 1| < 1$; multiplying by -1—and flipping the inequality, since we're multiplying by a negative number—yields $|x + 1| > -1$. But since the absolute value cannot be negative, it's *always* greater than –1, so this inequality is true for all values of x.

(b) Subtracting 7 from both sides yields $2(x - 1)^2 \leq -6$; dividing by 2 yields $(x - 1)^2 \leq -3$. But $(x - 1)^2$ must be nonnegative, and hence cannot be less than or equal to –3; this inequality has no solution.

P10. (a) We would graph the inequality $x \geq 3$ by putting a solid circle at 3 and filling in the part of the line to the right:

(b) The inequality $-2 \leq x \leq 6$ is equivalent to "$x \geq -2$ and $x \leq 6$." To plot this compound inequality, we first put solid circles at –2 and 6, and then fill in the part of the line *between* these circles:

(c) The inequality $|x| < 2$ can be rewritten as "$x > -2$ and $x < 2$." We place hollow circles at the points –2 and 2 and fill in the part of the line between them:

P11. The equation $y = x^2 - 3x + 2$ is not linear, so we may need more points to get an idea of its shape. By substituting in different values of x, we find the points $(0, 2)$, $(1, 0)$, $(2, 0)$, and $(3, 2)$. That may be enough to give us an idea of the shape, though we can find more points if we're still not sure:

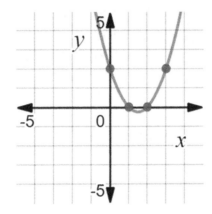

P12. (a) If we multiply the first equation by 4, we can eliminate the x terms:

$$12x + 16y = 36$$
$$-12x + 7y = 10$$

Add the equations together and solve for y:

$$23y = 46$$
$$y = 2$$

Plug the value for y back in to either of the original equations and solve for x:

$$3x + 4(2) = 10$$
$$x = \frac{10 - 8}{3} = \frac{2}{3}$$

The solution is $\left(\frac{2}{3}, 2\right)$

(b) Solving the first equation for y:

$$-3x + 2y = -1$$
$$2y = 3x - 1$$
$$y = \frac{3x - 1}{2}$$

Substitute this expression in place of y in the second equation, and solve for x:

$$4x - 5\left(\frac{3x - 1}{2}\right) = 6$$
$$4x - \frac{15x}{2} + \frac{5}{2} = 6$$
$$8x - 15x + 5 = 12$$
$$-7x = 7$$
$$x = -1$$

Plug the value for x back in to either of the original equations and solve for y:

$$-3(-1) + 2y = -1$$
$$3 + 2y = -1$$
$$2y = -4$$
$$y = -2$$

The solution is $(-1, -2)$

P13. Use the formulas for distance and midpoint:

$$\text{Distance} = \sqrt{(x_2 - x_1)^2 + (y_2 - y_1)^2}$$
$$= \sqrt{(8 - 2)^2 + (6 - 4)^2}$$
$$= \sqrt{(6)^2 + (2)^2}$$
$$= \sqrt{36 + 4}$$
$$= \sqrt{40} \text{ or } 2\sqrt{10}$$

$$\text{Midpoint} = \left(\frac{x_1 + x_2}{2}, \frac{y_1 + y_2}{2}\right)$$
$$= \left(\frac{2 + 8}{2}, \frac{4 + 6}{2}\right)$$
$$= \left(\frac{10}{2}, \frac{10}{2}\right)$$
$$= (5,5)$$

Polynomial Algebra

POLYNOMIALS

Equations are made up of monomials and polynomials. A **monomial** is a single variable or product of constants and variables, such as x, $2x$, or $\frac{2}{x}$. There will never be addition or subtraction symbols in a monomial. Like monomials have like variables, but they may have different coefficients. **Polynomials** are algebraic expressions which use addition and subtraction to combine two or more monomials. Two terms make a **binomial**, three terms make a **trinomial**, etc. The **degree of a monomial** is the sum of the exponents of the variables. The **degree of a polynomial** is the highest degree of any individual term.

> **Review Video: Polynomials**
> Visit mometrix.com/academy and enter code: 305005

SIMPLIFYING POLYNOMIALS

Simplifying polynomials requires combining like terms. The like terms in a polynomial expression are those that have the same variable raised to the same power. It is often helpful to connect the like terms with arrows or lines in order to separate them from the other monomials. Once you have determined the like terms, you can rearrange the polynomial by placing them together. Remember to include the sign that is in front of each term. Once the like terms are placed together, you can apply each operation and simplify. When adding and subtracting polynomials, only add and subtract the **coefficient**, or the number part; the variable and exponent stay the same.

THE FOIL METHOD

In general, multiplying polynomials is done by multiplying each term in one polynomial by each term in the other and adding the results. In the specific case for multiplying binomials, there is useful acronym, FOIL, that can help you make sure to cover each combination of terms. The **FOIL method** for $(Ax + By)(Cx + Dy)$ would be:

F	Multiply the *first* terms of each binomial	$(\overbrace{Ax}^{first} + By)(\overbrace{Cx}^{first} + Dy)$	ACx^2
O	Multiply the *outer* terms	$(\overbrace{Ax}^{outer} + By)(Cx + \overbrace{Dy}^{outer})$	$ADxy$
I	Multiply the *inner* terms	$(Ax + \overbrace{By}^{inner})(\overbrace{Cx}^{inner} + Dy)$	$BCxy$
L	Multiply the *last* terms of each binomial	$(Ax + \overbrace{By}^{last})(Cx + \overbrace{Dy}^{last})$	BDy^2

Then add up the result of each and combine like terms: $ACx^2 + (AD + BC)xy + BDy^2$.

For example, using the FOIL method on binomials $(x + 2)$ and $(x - 3)$:

$$\text{First:} \quad (\boxed{x} + 2)(\boxed{x} + (-3)) \rightarrow (x)(x) = x^2$$
$$\text{Outer:} \quad (\boxed{x} + 2)(x + \boxed{(-3)}) \rightarrow (x)(-3) = -3x$$
$$\text{Inner:} \quad (x + \boxed{2})(\boxed{x} + (-3)) \rightarrow (2)(x) = 2x$$
$$\text{Last:} \quad (x + \boxed{2})(x + \boxed{(-3)}) \rightarrow (2)(-3) = -6$$

59

This results in: $(x^2) + (-3x) + (2x) + (-6)$

Combine like terms: $x^2 + (-3+2)x + (-6) = x^2 - x - 6$

DIVIDING POLYNOMIALS

To divide polynomials, set up a long division problem, dividing a polynomial by either a monomial or another polynomial of equal or lesser degree.

When **dividing by a monomial**, divide each term of the polynomial by the monomial.

When **dividing by a polynomial**, begin by arranging the terms of each polynomial in order of one variable. You may arrange in ascending or descending order, but be consistent with both polynomials. To get the first term of the quotient, divide the first term of the dividend by the first term of the divisor. Multiply the first term of the quotient by the entire divisor and subtract that product from the dividend. Repeat for the second and successive terms until you either get a remainder of zero or a remainder whose degree is less than the degree of the divisor. If the quotient has a remainder, write the answer as a mixed expression in the form:

$$\text{quotient} + \frac{\text{remainder}}{\text{divisor}}$$

For example, we can evaluate the following expression in the same way as long division:

$$\frac{x^3 - 3x^2 - 2x + 5}{x - 5}$$

$$
\begin{array}{r}
x^2 + 2x + 8 \\
x - 5 \overline{)\ x^3 - 3x^2 - 2x + 5} \\
\underline{x^3 - 5x^2} \\
2x^2 - 2x \\
\underline{2x^2 - 10x} \\
8x + 5 \\
\underline{8x + 40} \\
45
\end{array}
$$

$$\frac{x^3 - 3x^2 - 2x + 5}{x - 5} = x^2 + 2x + 8 + \frac{45}{x - 5}$$

When **factoring** a polynomial, first check for a common monomial factor, that is look to see if each coefficient has a common factor or if each term has an x in it. If the factor is a trinomial but not a perfect trinomial square, look for a factorable form, such as one of these:

$$x^2 + (a+b)x + ab = (x+a)(x+b)$$
$$(ac)x^2 + (ad+bc)x + bd = (ax+b)(cx+d)$$

For factors with four terms, look for groups to factor. Once you have found the factors, write the original polynomial as the product of all the factors. Make sure all of the polynomial factors are

prime. Monomial factors may be *prime* or *composite*. Check your work by multiplying the factors to make sure you get the original polynomial.

Below are patterns of some special products to remember to help make factoring easier:

- Perfect trinomial squares: $x^2 + 2xy + y^2 = (x + y)^2$ or $x^2 - 2xy + y^2 = (x - y)^2$
- Difference between two squares: $x^2 - y^2 = (x + y)(x - y)$
- Sum of two cubes: $x^3 + y^3 = (x + y)(x^2 - xy + y^2)$
 - Note: the second factor is *not* the same as a perfect trinomial square, so do not try to factor it further.
- Difference between two cubes: $x^3 - y^3 = (x - y)(x^2 + xy + y^2)$
 - Again, the second factor is *not* the same as a perfect trinomial square.
- Perfect cubes: $x^3 + 3x^2y + 3xy^2 + y^3 = (x + y)^3$ and $x^3 - 3x^2y + 3xy^2 - y^3 = (x - y)^3$

RATIONAL EXPRESSIONS

Rational expressions are fractions with polynomials in both the numerator and the denominator; the value of the polynomial in the denominator cannot be equal to zero. Be sure to keep track of values that make the denominator of the original expression zero as the final result inherits the same restrictions. For example, a denominator of $x - 3$ indicates that the expression is not defined when $x = 3$ and as such, regardless of any operations done to the expression, it remains undefined there.

To **add or subtract** rational expressions, first find the common denominator, then rewrite each fraction as an equivalent fraction with the common denominator. Finally, add or subtract the numerators to get the numerator of the answer, and keep the common denominator as the denominator of the answer.

When **multiplying** rational expressions factor each polynomial and cancel like factors (a factor which appears in both the numerator and the denominator). Then, multiply all remaining factors in the numerator to get the numerator of the product, and multiply the remaining factors in the denominator to get the denominator of the product. Remember: cancel entire factors, not individual terms.

To **divide** rational expressions, take the reciprocal of the divisor (the rational expression you are dividing by) and multiply by the dividend.

> **Review Video: Rational Expressions**
> Visit mometrix.com/academy and enter code: 415183

SIMPLIFYING RATIONAL EXPRESSIONS

To simplify a rational expression, factor the numerator and denominator completely. Factors that are the same and appear in the numerator and denominator have a ratio of 1. For example, look at the following expression:

$$\frac{x - 1}{1 - x^2}$$

The denominator, $(1 - x^2)$, is a difference of squares. It can be factored as $(1 - x)(1 + x)$. The factor $1 - x$ and the numerator $x - 1$ are opposites and have a ratio of –1. Rewrite the numerator as $-1(1 - x)$. So, the rational expression can be simplified as follows:

$$\frac{x - 1}{1 - x^2} = \frac{-1(1 - x)}{(1 - x)(1 + x)} = \frac{-1}{1 + x}$$

Note that since the original expression is only defined for $x \neq \{-1, 1\}$, the simplified expression has the same restrictions.

Review Video: <u>Reducing Rational Expressions</u>
Visit mometrix.com/academy and enter code: 788868

SOLVING QUADRATIC EQUATIONS

Quadratic equations are a special set of trinomials of the form $y = ax^2 + bx + c$ that occur commonly in math and real world applications. The **roots** of a quadratic equation are the solutions that satisfy the equation when $y = 0$; in other words, where the graph touches the x-axis. There are several ways to determine these solutions including using the quadratic formula, factoring, completing the square, and graphing the function.

Review Video: <u>Finding the Missing Roots</u>
Visit mometrix.com/academy and enter code: 198376

Review Video: <u>Changing Constants in Graphs of Functions: Quadratic Equations</u>
Visit mometrix.com/academy and enter code: 476276

QUADRATIC FORMULA

The **quadratic formula** is used to solve quadratic equations when other methods are more difficult. To use the quadratic formula to solve a quadratic equation, begin by rewriting the equation in standard form $ax^2 + bx + c = 0$, where a, b, and c are coefficients. Once you have identified the values of the coefficients, substitute those values into the quadratic formula

$$x = \frac{-b \pm \sqrt{b^2 - 4ac}}{2a}$$

Evaluate the equation and simplify the expression. Again, check each root by substituting into the original equation. In the quadratic formula, the portion of the formula under the radical ($b^2 - 4ac$) is called the **discriminant**. If the discriminant is zero, there is only one root: $-\frac{b}{2a}$. If the discriminant is positive, there are two different real roots. If the discriminant is negative, there are no real roots, you will instead find complex roots. Often these solutions don't make sense in context and are ignored.

Review Video: <u>Using the Quadratic Formula</u>
Visit mometrix.com/academy and enter code: 163102

FACTORING

To solve a quadratic equation by factoring, begin by rewriting the equation in standard form, $x^2 + bx + c = 0$. Remember that the goal of factoring is to find numbers f and g such that

I apologize—my response experienced an error with repeated tokens. Let me provide the clean transcription:

The denominator, $(1 - x^2)$, is a difference of squares. It can be factored as $(1 - x)(1 + x)$. The factor $1 - x$ and the numerator $x - 1$ are opposites and have a ratio of –1. Rewrite the numerator as $-1(1 - x)$. So, the rational expression can be simplified as follows:

$$\frac{x - 1}{1 - x^2} = \frac{-1(1 - x)}{(1 - x)(1 + x)} = \frac{-1}{1 + x}$$

Note that since the original expression is only defined for $x \neq \{-1, 1\}$, the simplified expression has the same restrictions.

Review Video: <u>Reducing Rational Expressions</u>
Visit mometrix.com/academy and enter code: 788868

SOLVING QUADRATIC EQUATIONS

Quadratic equations are a special set of trinomials of the form $y = ax^2 + bx + c$ that occur commonly in math and real world applications. The **roots** of a quadratic equation are the solutions that satisfy the equation when $y = 0$; in other words, where the graph touches the x-axis. There are several ways to determine these solutions including using the quadratic formula, factoring, completing the square, and graphing the function.

Review Video: <u>Finding the Missing Roots</u>
Visit mometrix.com/academy and enter code: 198376

Review Video: <u>Changing Constants in Graphs of Functions: Quadratic Equations</u>
Visit mometrix.com/academy and enter code: 476276

QUADRATIC FORMULA

The **quadratic formula** is used to solve quadratic equations when other methods are more difficult. To use the quadratic formula to solve a quadratic equation, begin by rewriting the equation in standard form $ax^2 + bx + c = 0$, where a, b, and c are coefficients. Once you have identified the values of the coefficients, substitute those values into the quadratic formula

$$x = \frac{-b \pm \sqrt{b^2 - 4ac}}{2a}$$

Evaluate the equation and simplify the expression. Again, check each root by substituting into the original equation. In the quadratic formula, the portion of the formula under the radical ($b^2 - 4ac$) is called the **discriminant**. If the discriminant is zero, there is only one root: $-\frac{b}{2a}$. If the discriminant is positive, there are two different real roots. If the discriminant is negative, there are no real roots, you will instead find complex roots. Often these solutions don't make sense in context and are ignored.

Review Video: <u>Using the Quadratic Formula</u>
Visit mometrix.com/academy and enter code: 163102

FACTORING

To solve a quadratic equation by factoring, begin by rewriting the equation in standard form, $x^2 + bx + c = 0$. Remember that the goal of factoring is to find numbers f and g such that

Copyright © Mometrix Media. You have been licensed one copy of this document for personal use only. Any other reproduction or redistribution is strictly prohibited. All rights reserved.

$(x + f)(x + g) = x^2 + (f + g)x + fg$, in other words $(f + g) = b$ and $fg = c$ or . This can be a really useful method when b and c are integers. Determine the factors of c and look for pairs that could sum to b.

For example, consider finding the roots of $x^2 + 6x - 16 = 0$. The factors of -16 include, -4 and 4, -8 and 2, -2 and 8, -1 and 16, and 1 and -16. The factors that sum to 6 are -2 and 8. Write these factors as the product of two binomials, $0 = (x - 2)(x + 8)$. Finally, since these binomials multiply together to equal zero, set them each equal to zero and solve each for x. This results in $x - 2 = 0$, which simplifies to $x = 2$ and $x + 8 = 0$, which simplifies to $x = -8$. Therefore, the roots of the equation are 2 and -8.

> **Review Video: <u>Factoring Quadratic Equations</u>**
> Visit mometrix.com/academy and enter code: 336566

COMPLETING THE SQUARE

One way to find the roots of a quadratic equation is to find a way to manipulate it such that it follows the form of a perfect square $(x^2 + 2px + p^2)$ by adding and subtracting a constant. This process is called **completing the square**. In other words, if are given a quadratic that is not a perfect square, $x^2 + bx + c = 0$, you can find a constant d that could be added in to make it a perfect square:

$$x^2 + bx + c + (d - d) = 0; \ \{\text{Let } b = 2p \text{ and } c + d = p^2\}$$
$$\text{then: } x^2 + 2px + p^2 - d = 0 \text{ and } d = \frac{b^2}{4} - c$$

Once you have completed the square you can find the roots of the resulting equation:

$$x^2 + 2px + p^2 - d = 0$$
$$(x + p)^2 = d$$
$$x + p = \pm\sqrt{d}$$
$$x = -p \pm \sqrt{d}$$

It is worth noting that substituting the original expressions into this solution gives the same result as the quadratic formula where $a = 1$:

$$x = -p \pm \sqrt{d} = -\frac{b}{2} \pm \sqrt{\frac{b^2}{4} - c} = -\frac{b}{2} \pm \frac{\sqrt{b^2 - 4c}}{2} = \frac{-b \pm \sqrt{b^2 - 4c}}{2}$$

Completing the square can be seen as arranging block representations of each of the terms to be as close to a square as possible and then filling in the gaps. For example, consider the quadratic expression $x^2 + 6x + 2$:

$$x^2 + 6x + 2 \qquad = \qquad (x+3)^2 - 7$$

USING GIVEN ROOTS TO FIND QUADRATIC EQUATION

One way to find the roots of a quadratic equation is to factor the equation and use the **zero product property**, setting each factor of the equation equal to zero to find the corresponding root. We can use this technique in reverse to find an equation given its roots. Each root corresponds to a linear equation which in turn corresponds to a factor of the quadratic equation.

For example, we can find a quadratic equation whose roots are $x = 2$ and $x = -1$. The root $x = 2$ corresponds to the equation $x - 2 = 0$, and the root $x = -1$ corresponds to the equation $x + 1 = 0$.

These two equations correspond to the factors $(x - 2)$ and $(x + 1)$, from which we can derive the equation $(x - 2)(x + 1) = 0$, or $x^2 - x - 2 = 0$.

Any integer multiple of this entire equation will also yield the same roots, as the integer will simply cancel out when the equation is factored. For example, $2x^2 - 2x - 4 = 0$ factors as $2(x - 2)(x + 1) = 0$.

SOLVING A SYSTEM OF EQUATIONS CONSISTING OF A LINEAR EQUATION AND A QUADRATIC EQUATION

ALGEBRAICALLY

Generally, the simplest way to solve a system of equations consisting of a linear equation and a quadratic equation algebraically is through the method of substitution. One possible strategy is to solve the linear equation for y and then substitute that expression into the quadratic equation. After expansion and combining like terms, this will result in a new quadratic equation for x which, like all quadratic equations, may have zero, one, or two solutions. Plugging each solution for x back into one of the original equations will then produce the corresponding value of y.

For example, consider the following system of equations:

$$x + y = 1$$
$$y = (x + 3)^2 - 2$$

64

We can solve the linear equation for y to yield $y = -x + 1$. Substituting this expression into the quadratic equation produces $-x + 1 = (x + 3)^2 - 2$. We can simplify this equation:

$$-x + 1 = (x + 3)^2 - 2$$
$$-x + 1 = x^2 + 6x + 9 - 2$$
$$-x + 1 = x^2 + 6x + 7$$
$$0 = x^2 + 7x + 6$$

This quadratic equation can be factored as $(x + 1)(x + 6) = 0$. It therefore has two solutions: $x_1 = -1$ and $x_2 = -6$. Plugging each of these back into the original linear equation yields $y_1 = -x_1 + 1 = -(-1) + 1 = 2$ and $y_2 = -x_2 + 1 = -(-6) + 1 = 7$. Thus, this system of equations has two solutions, $(-1, 2)$ and $(-6, 7)$.

It may help to check your work by putting each x and y value back into the original equations and verifying that they do provide a solution.

GRAPHICALLY

To solve a system of equations consisting of a linear equation and a quadratic equation graphically, plot both equations on the same graph. The linear equation will of course produce a straight line, while the quadratic equation will produce a parabola. These two graphs will intersect at zero, one, or two points; each point of intersection is a solution of the system.

For example, consider the following system of equations:

$$y = -2x + 2$$
$$y = -2x^2 + 4x + 2$$

The linear equation describes a line with a y-intercept of $(0, 2)$ and a slope of -2.

To graph the quadratic equation, we can first find the vertex of the parabola: the x-coordinate of the vertex is $h = -\frac{b}{2a} = -\frac{4}{2(-2)} = 1$, and the y coordinate is $k = -2(1)^2 + 4(1) + 2 = 4$. Thus, the vertex lies at $(1, 4)$. To get a feel for the rest of the parabola, we can plug in a few more values of x to find more points; by putting in $x = 2$ and $x = 3$ in the quadratic equation, we find that the points $(2, 2)$ and $(3, -4)$ lie on the parabola; by symmetry thus do $(0, 2)$ and $(-1, -4)$. We can now plot both equations:

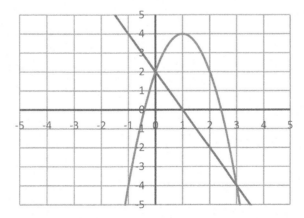

These two curves intersect at the points $(0, 2)$ and $(3, -4)$, thus these are the solutions of the equation.

Practice

P1. Expand the following polynomials:

 (a) $(x + 3)(x - 7)(2x)$

 (b) $(x + 2)^2(x - 2)^2$

 (c) $(x^2 + 5x + 5)(3x - 1)$

P2. Find the roots of $y = 2x^2 + 8x + 4$.

P3. Find a quadratic equation with roots $x = 4$ and $x = -6$.

P4. Evaluate the following rational expressions:

 (a) $\dfrac{x^3 - 2x^2 - 5x + 6}{3x + 6}$

 (b) $\dfrac{x^2 + 4x + 4}{4 - x^2}$

66

Practice Solutions

P1. (a) Apply the FOIL method and the distributive property of multiplication:

$$(x + 3)(x - 7)(2x) = (x^2 - 7x + 3x - 21)(2x)$$
$$= (x^2 - 4x - 21)(2x)$$
$$= 2x^3 - 8x^2 - 42x$$

(b) Note the difference of squares form:

$$(x + 2)^2(x - 2)^2 = (x + 2)(x + 2)(x - 2)(x - 2)$$
$$= [(x + 2)(x - 2)][(x + 2)(x - 2)]$$
$$= (x^2 - 4)(x^2 - 4)$$
$$= x^4 - 8x^2 + 16$$

(c) Multiply each pair of monomials and combine like terms:

$$(x^2 + 5x + 5)(3x - 1) = 3x^3 + 15x^2 + 15x - x^2 - 5x - 5$$
$$= 3x^3 + 14x^2 + 10x - 5$$

P2. First, substitute 0 in for y in the quadratic equation: $0 = 2x^2 + 8x + 4$

Next, try to factor the quadratic equation. Since $a \neq 1$, list the factors of ac, or 8:

$$(1, 8), (-1, -8), (2, 4), (-2, -4)$$

Look for the factors of ac that add up to b, or 8. Since none do, the equation cannot be factored with whole numbers. Substitute the values of a, b, and c into the quadratic formula, $x = \frac{-b \pm \sqrt{b^2 - 4ac}}{2a}$:

$$x = \frac{-8 \pm \sqrt{8^2 - 4(2)(4)}}{2(2)}$$

Use the order of operations to simplify:

$$x = \frac{-8 \pm \sqrt{64 - 32}}{4}$$
$$x = \frac{-8 \pm \sqrt{32}}{4}$$

Reduce and simplify:

$$x = \frac{-8 \pm \sqrt{(16)(2)}}{4}$$
$$x = \frac{-8 \pm 4\sqrt{2}}{4}$$
$$x = -2 \pm \sqrt{2}$$
$$x = \left(-2 + \sqrt{2}\right) \text{ and } \left(-2 - \sqrt{2}\right)$$

P3. The root $x = 4$ corresponds to the equation $x - 4 = 0$, and the root $x = -6$ corresponds to the equation $x + 6 = 0$. These two equations correspond to the factors $(x - 4)$ and $(x + 6)$, from which we can derive the equation $(x - 4)(x + 6) = 0$, or $x^2 - 10x - 24 = 0$.

P4. (a) Rather than trying to factor the fourth-degree polynomial, we can use long division:

$$\frac{x^3 - 2x^2 - 5x + 6}{3x + 6} = \frac{x^3 - 2x^2 - 5x + 6}{3(x + 2)}$$

$$
\begin{array}{r}
x^2 - 4x + 3 \\
x + 2 \overline{\smash{)}\; x^3 - 2x^2 - 5x + 6} \\
\underline{x^3 + 2x^2} \\
-4x^2 - 5x \\
\underline{-4x^2 - 8x} \\
3x + 6 \\
\underline{3x + 6} \\
0
\end{array}
$$

$$\frac{x^3 - 2x^2 - 5x + 6}{3(x + 2)} = \frac{x^2 - 4x + 3}{3}$$

Note that since the original expression is only defined for $x \neq \{-2\}$, the simplified expression has the same restrictions.

(b) The denominator, $(4 - x^2)$, is a difference of squares. It can be factored as $(2 - x)(2 + x)$. The numerator, $(x^2 + 4x + 4)$, is a perfect square. It can be factored as $(x + 2)(x + 2)$. So, the rational expression can be simplified as follows:

$$\frac{x^2 + 4x + 4}{4 - x^2} = \frac{(x + 2)(x + 2)}{(2 - x)(2 + x)} = \frac{(x + 2)}{(2 - x)}$$

Note that since the original expression is only defined for $x \neq \{-2, 2\}$, the simplified expression has the same restrictions.

Functions

FUNCTION AND RELATION

When expressing functional relationships, the **variables** x and y are typically used. These values are often written as the **coordinates** (x, y). The x-value is the independent variable and the y-value is the dependent variable. A **relation** is a set of data in which there is not a unique y-value for each x-value in the dataset. This means that there can be two of the same x-values assigned to different y-values. A relation is simply a relationship between the x and y-values in each coordinate but does not apply to the relationship between the values of x and y in the data set. A **function** is a relation where one quantity depends on the other. For example, the amount of money that you make depends on the number of hours that you work. In a function, each x-value in the data set has one unique y-value because the y-value depends on the x-value.

> **Review Video: <u>Definition of a Function</u>**
> Visit mometrix.com/academy and enter code: 784611

FUNCTIONS

A function has exactly one value of **output variable** (dependent variable) for each value of the **input variable** (independent variable). The set of all values for the input variable (here assumed to be x) is the domain of the function, and the set of all corresponding values of output variable (here assumed to be y) is the range of the function. When looking at a graph of an equation, the easiest way to determine if the equation is a function or not is to conduct the vertical line test. If a vertical line drawn through any value of x crosses the graph in more than one place, the equation is not a function.

DETERMINING A FUNCTION

You can determine whether an equation is a **function** by substituting different values into the equation for x. These values are called input values. All possible input values are referred to as the **domain**. The result of substituting these values into the equation is called the output, or **range**. You can display and organize these numbers in a data table. A **data table** contains the values for x and y, which you can also list as coordinates. In order for a function to exist, the table cannot contain any repeating x-values that correspond with different y-values. If each x-coordinate has a unique y-coordinate, the table contains a function. However, there can be repeating y-values that correspond with different x-values. An example of this is when the function contains an exponent. For example, if $x^2 = y$, $2^2 = 4$, and $(-2)^2 = 4$.

> **Review Video: <u>Basics of Functions</u>**
> Visit mometrix.com/academy and enter code: 822500

WRITING A FUNCTION RULE USING A TABLE

If given a set of data, place the corresponding x and y-values into a table and analyze the relationship between them. Consider what you can do to each x-value to obtain the corresponding y-value. Try adding or subtracting different numbers to and from x and then try multiplying or dividing different numbers to and from x. If none of these **operations** give you the y-value, try combining the operations. Once you find a rule that works for one pair, make sure to try it with each additional set of ordered pairs in the table. If the same operation or combination of operations satisfies each set of coordinates, then the table contains a function. The rule is then used to write the equation of the function in "$y =$" form.

69

DIRECT AND INVERSE VARIATIONS OF VARIABLES

Variables that vary directly are those that either both increase at the same rate or both decrease at the same rate. For example, in the functions $y = kx$ or $y = kx^n$, where k and n are positive, the value of y increases as the value of x increases and decreases as the value of x decreases.

Variables that vary inversely are those where one increases while the other decreases. For example, in the functions $y = \frac{k}{x}$ or $y = \frac{k}{x^n}$ where k and n are positive, the value of y increases as the value of x decreases, and decreases as the value of x increases.

In both cases, k is the constant of variation.

PROPERTIES OF FUNCTIONS

There are many different ways to classify functions based on their structure or behavior. Important features of functions include:

- **End behavior**: the behavior of the function at extreme values ($f(x)$ as $x \to \pm\infty$)
- **y-intercept**: the value of function at $f(0)$
- **Roots**: the values of x where the function equals zero ($f(x) = 0$)
- **Extrema**: minimum or maximum values of the function or where the function changes direction ($f(x) \geq k$ or $f(x) \leq k$)

CLASSIFICATION OF FUNCTIONS

An **invertible function** is defined as a function, $f(x)$, for which there is another function, $f^{-1}(x)$, such that $f^{-1}(f(x)) = x$. For example, if $f(x) = 3x - 2$ the inverse function, $f^{-1}(x)$, can be found:

$$x = 3(f^{-1}(x)) - 2$$
$$\frac{x + 2}{3} = f^{-1}(x)$$

$$f^{-1}(f(x)) = \frac{3x - 2 + 2}{3}$$
$$= \frac{3x}{3}$$
$$= x$$

Note that $f^{-1}(x)$ is a valid function over all values of x.

In a **one-to-one function**, each value of x has exactly one value for y on the coordinate plane (this is the definition of a function) and each value of y has exactly one value for x. While the vertical line test will determine if a graph is that of a function, the horizontal line test will determine if a function is a one-to-one function. If a horizontal line drawn at any value of y intersects the graph in more than one place, the graph is not that of a one-to-one function. Do not make the mistake of using the horizontal line test exclusively in determining if a graph is that of a one-to-one function. A one-to-one function must pass both the vertical line test and the horizontal line test. As such, one-to-one functions are invertible functions.

A **many-to-one function** is a function whereby the relation is a function, but the inverse of the function is not a function. In other words, each element in the domain is mapped to one and only one element in the range. However, one or more elements in the range may be mapped to the same element in the domain. A graph of a many-to-one function would pass the vertical line test, but not the horizontal line test. One result of this is the fact that many-to-one functions are not invertible.

A **monotone function** is a function whose graph either constantly increases or constantly decreases. Examples include the functions $f(x) = x$, $f(x) = -x$, or $f(x) = x^3$.

An **even function** has a graph that is symmetric with respect to the y-axis and satisfies the equation $f(x) = f(-x)$. Examples include the functions $f(x) = x^2$ and $f(x) = ax^n$, where a is any real number and n is a positive even integer.

An **odd function** has a graph that is symmetric with respect to the origin and satisfies the equation $f(x) = -f(-x)$. Examples include the functions $f(x) = x^3$ and $f(x) = ax^n$, where a is any real number and n is a positive odd integer.

Algebraic functions are those that exclusively use polynomials and roots. These would include polynomial functions, rational functions, square root functions, and all combinations of these functions, such as polynomials as the radicand. These combinations may be joined by addition, subtraction, multiplication, or division, but may not include variables as exponents.

Transcendental functions are all functions that are non-algebraic. Any function that includes logarithms, trigonometric functions, variables as exponents, or any combination that includes any of these is not algebraic in nature, even if the function includes polynomials or roots.

Constant functions are given by the equation $f(x) = b$, where b is a real number. There is no independent variable present in the equation, so the function has a constant value for all x. The graph of a constant function is a horizontal line of slope 0 that is positioned b units from the x-axis. If b is positive, the line is above the x-axis; if b is negative, the line is below the x-axis.

Identity functions are identified by the equation $f(x) = x$, where every value of the function is equal to its corresponding value of x. The only zero is the point $(0, 0)$. The graph is a line with slope of 1.

In **linear functions**, the value of the function changes in direct proportion to x. The rate of change, represented by the slope on its graph, is constant throughout. The standard form of a linear equation is $ax + cy = d$, where a, c, and d are real numbers. As a function, this equation is commonly in the form $y = mx + b$ or $f(x) = mx + b$ where $m = -\frac{a}{c}$ and $b = \frac{d}{c}$. This is known as the slope-intercept form, because the coefficients give the slope of the graphed function (m) and its y-intercept (b). Solve the equation $mx + b = 0$ for x to get $x = -\frac{b}{m}$, which is the only zero of the function. The domain and range are both the set of all real numbers.

QUADRATIC FUNCTIONS

A **quadratic function** is a function in the form $y = ax^2 + bx + c$, where a does not equal 0. While a linear function forms a line, a quadratic function forms a **parabola**, which is a u-shaped figure that either opens upward or downward. A parabola that opens upward is said to be a **positive quadratic function** and a parabola that opens downward is said to be a **negative quadratic function**. The shape of a parabola can differ, depending on the values of a, b, and c. All parabolas contain a **vertex**, which is the highest possible point, the **maximum**, or the lowest possible point, the **minimum**. This is the point where the graph begins moving in the opposite direction. A quadratic function can have zero, one, or two solutions, and therefore, zero, one, or two x-intercepts. Recall that the x-intercepts are referred to as the zeros, or roots, of a function. A quadratic function will have only one y-intercept. Understanding the basic components of a quadratic function can give you an idea of the shape of its graph.

Example graph of a positive quadratic function, $x^2 + 2x - 3$:

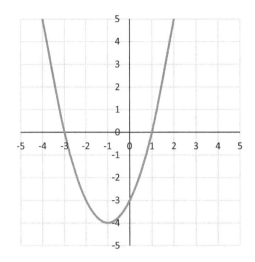

POLYNOMIAL FUNCTIONS

A **polynomial function** is a function with multiple terms and multiple powers of x, such as:

$$f(x) = a_n x^n + a_{n-1} x^{n-1} + a_{n-2} x^{n-2} + \cdots + a_1 x + a_0$$

where n is a non-negative integer that is the highest exponent in the polynomial, and $a_n \neq 0$. The domain of a polynomial function is the set of all real numbers. If the greatest exponent in the polynomial is even, the polynomial is said to be of even degree and the range is the set of real numbers that satisfy the function. If the greatest exponent in the polynomial is odd, the polynomial is said to be odd and the range, like the domain, is the set of all real numbers.

> **Review Video: Simplifying Rational Polynomial Functions**
> Visit mometrix.com/academy and enter code: 351038

RATIONAL FUNCTIONS

A **rational function** is a function that can be constructed as a ratio of two polynomial expressions: $f(x) = \frac{p(x)}{q(x)}$, where $p(x)$ and $q(x)$ are both polynomial expressions and $q(x) \neq 0$. The domain is the set of all real numbers, except any values for which $q(x) = 0$. The range is the set of real numbers that satisfies the function when the domain is applied. When you graph a rational function, you will have vertical asymptotes wherever $q(x) = 0$. If the polynomial in the numerator is of lesser degree than the polynomial in the denominator, the x-axis will also be a horizontal asymptote. If the numerator and denominator have equal degrees, there will be a horizontal asymptote not on the x-axis. If the degree of the numerator is exactly one greater than the degree of the denominator, the graph will have an oblique, or diagonal, asymptote. The asymptote will be along the line $y = \frac{p_n}{q_{n-1}} x + \frac{p_{n-1}}{q_{n-1}}$, where p_n and q_{n-1} are the coefficients of the highest degree terms in their respective polynomials.

SQUARE ROOT FUNCTIONS

A **square root function** is a function that contains a radical and is in the format $f(x) = \sqrt{ax + b}$. The domain is the set of all real numbers that yields a positive radicand or a radicand equal to zero. Because square root values are assumed to be positive unless otherwise identified, the range is all real numbers from zero to infinity. To find the zero of a square root function, set the radicand equal

72

to zero and solve for x. The graph of a square root function is always to the right of the zero and always above the x-axis.

Example graph of a square root function, $f(x) = \sqrt{2x + 1}$:

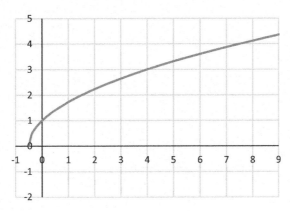

ABSOLUTE VALUE FUNCTIONS

An **absolute value function** is in the format $f(x) = |ax + b|$. Like other functions, the domain is the set of all real numbers. However, because absolute value indicates positive numbers, the range is limited to positive real numbers. To find the zero of an absolute value function, set the portion inside the absolute value sign equal to zero and solve for x.

An absolute value function is also known as a piecewise function because it must be solved in pieces – one for if the value inside the absolute value sign is positive, and one for if the value is negative. The function can be expressed as

$$f(x) = \begin{cases} ax + b \text{ if } ax + b \geq 0 \\ -(ax + b) \text{ if } ax + b < 0 \end{cases}$$

This will allow for an accurate statement of the range. The graph of an example absolute value function, $f(x) = |2x - 1|$, is below:

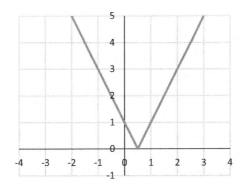

EXPONENTIAL FUNCTIONS

Exponential functions are equations that have the format $y = b^x$, where base $b > 0$ and $b \neq 1$. The exponential function can also be written $f(x) = b^x$. Recall the properties of exponents, like the product of terms with the same base is equal to the base raised to the sum of the exponents: $a^x \times a^y = a^{x+y}$ and a term with an exponent that is raised to an exponent is equal to the base of

the original term raised to the product of the exponents: $(a^x)^y = a^{xy}$. The graph of an example exponential function, $f(x) = 2^x$, is below:

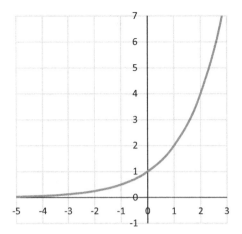

Note in the graph that the y value approaches zero to the left and infinity to the right. One of the key features of an exponential function is that there will be one end that goes off to infinity and another that asymptotically approaches a lower bound. Common forms of exponential functions include:

Geometric sequences: $a_n = a_1 \times r^{n-1}$, where a_n is the value of the nth term, a_1 is the initial value, r is the common ratio, and n is the number of terms. Note that $a_1 \times r^{1-1} = a_1 \times r^0 = a_1 \times 1 = a_1$.

Population growth: $f(t) = ae^{rt}$, where $f(t)$ is the population at time $t \geq 0$, a is the initial population, e is the mathematical constant known as Euler's number, and r is the growth rate.

Compound interest: $f(t) = P\left(1 + \dfrac{r}{n}\right)^{nt}$, where $f(t)$ is the account value at a certain number of time periods $t \geq 0$, P is the initial principle balance, r is the interest rate, and n is the number of times the interest is applied per time period.

General exponential growth or decay: $f(t) = a(1 + r)^t$, where $f(t)$ is the future count, a is the current or initial count, r is the growth or decay rate, and t is the time.

For example, suppose the initial population of a town was 1,200 people. The population growth is 5%. The current population is 2,400. To find out how much time has passed since the town was founded, we can use the following function:

$$2400 = 1200e^{0.05t}.$$

The general form for population growth may be represented as $f(t) = ae^{rt}$, where $f(t)$ represents the current population, a represents the initial population, r represents the growth rate, and t represents the time. Thus, substituting the initial population, current population, and rate into this form gives the equation above.

The number of years that have passed were found by first dividing both sides of the equation by 1,200. Doing so gives $2 = e^{0.05t}$. Taking the natural logarithm of both sides gives $\ln(2) = ln(e^{0.05t})$. Applying the power property of logarithms, the equation may be rewritten as $\ln(2) = 0.05t \times \ln(e)$, which simplifies as $\ln(2) = 0.05t$. Dividing both sides of this equation by 0.05 gives $t \approx 13.86$. Thus, approximately 13.86 years passed.

LOGARITHMIC FUNCTIONS

Logarithmic functions are equations that have the format $y = \log_b x$ or $f(x) = \log_b x$. The base b may be any number except one; however, the most common bases for logarithms are base 10 and base e. The log base e is the natural logarithm, or ln, expressed by the function $f(x) = \ln x$.

Any logarithm that does not have an assigned value of b is assumed to be base 10: $\log x = \log_{10} x$. Exponential functions and logarithmic functions are related in that one is the inverse of the other. If $f(x) = b^x$, then $f^{-1}(x) = \log_b x$. This can perhaps be expressed more clearly by the two equations: $y = b^x$ and $x = \log_b y$.

The following properties apply to logarithmic expressions:

Property	Description
$\log_b 1 = 0$	The log of 1 is equal to 0 for any base
$\log_b b = 1$	The log of the base is equal to 1
$\log_b b^p = p$	The log of the base raised to a power is equal to that power
$\log_b MN = \log_b M + \log_b N$	The log of a product is the sum of the log of each factor
$\log_b \dfrac{M}{N} = \log_b M - \log_b N$	The log of a quotient is equal to the log of the dividend minus the log of the divisor
$\log_b M^p = p \log_b M$	The log of a value raised to a power is equal to the power times the log of the value

The graph of an example logarithmic function, $f(x) = \log_2(x + 2)$, is below:

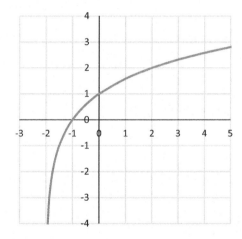

MANIPULATION OF FUNCTIONS

Translation occurs when values are added to or subtracted from the x or y values. If a constant is added to the y portion of each point, the graph shifts up. If a constant is subtracted from the y portion of each point, the graph shifts down. This is represented by the expression $f(x) \pm k$, where k is a constant. If a constant is added to the x portion of each point, the graph shifts left. If a constant is subtracted from the x portion of each point, the graph shifts right. This is represented by the expression $f(x \pm k)$, where k is a constant.

Stretching, compression, and reflection occur when different parts of a function are multiplied by different groups of constants. If the function as a whole is multiplied by a real number constant greater than 1, $(k \times f(x))$, the graph is stretched vertically. If k in the previous equation is greater than zero but less than 1, the graph is compressed vertically. If k is less than zero, the graph is reflected about the x-axis, in addition to being either stretched or compressed vertically if k is less

75

than or greater than -1, respectively. If instead, just the x-term is multiplied by a constant greater than 1 ($f(k \times x)$), the graph is compressed horizontally. If k in the previous equation is greater than zero but less than 1, the graph is stretched horizontally. If k is less than zero, the graph is reflected about the y-axis, in addition to being either stretched or compressed horizontally if k is greater than or less than -1, respectively.

ALGEBRAIC THEOREMS

According to the **fundamental theorem of algebra**, every non-constant, single variable polynomial has exactly as many roots as the polynomial's highest exponent. For example, if x^4 is the largest exponent of a term, the polynomial will have exactly 4 roots. However, some of these roots may have multiplicity or be non-real numbers. For instance, in the polynomial function $f(x) = x^4 - 4x + 3$, the only real roots are 1 and -1. The root 1 has multiplicity of 2 and there is one non-real root $(-1 - \sqrt{2}i)$.

The **remainder theorem** is useful for determining the remainder when a polynomial is divided by a binomial. The remainder theorem states that if a polynomial function $f(x)$ is divided by a binomial $x - a$, where a is a real number, the remainder of the division will be the value of $f(a)$. If $f(a) = 0$, then a is a root of the polynomial.

The **factor theorem** is related to the remainder theorem and states that if $f(a) = 0$ then $(x - a)$ is a factor of the function.

According to the **rational root theorem,** any rational root of a polynomial function $f(x) = a_n x^n + a_{n-1} x^{n-1} + \cdots + a_1 x + a_0$ with integer coefficients will, when reduced to its lowest terms, be a positive or negative fraction such that the numerator is a factor of a_0 and the denominator is a factor of a_n. For instance, if the polynomial function $f(x) = x^3 + 3x^2 - 4$ has any rational roots, the numerators of those roots can only be factors of 4 (1, 2, 4), and the denominators can only be factors of 1 (1). The function in this example has roots of 1 $\left(\text{or } \frac{1}{1}\right)$ and -2 $\left(\text{or } -\frac{2}{1}\right)$.

APPLYING THE BASIC OPERATIONS TO FUNCTIONS

For each of the basic operations, we will use these functions as examples: $f(x) = x^2$ and $g(x) = x$.

To find the sum of two functions f and g, assuming the domains are compatible, simply add the two functions together: $(f + g)(x) = f(x) + g(x) = x^2 + x$

To find the difference of two functions f and g, assuming the domains are compatible, simply subtract the second function from the first: $(f - g)(x) = f(x) - g(x) = x^2 - x$.

To find the product of two functions f and g, assuming the domains are compatible, multiply the two functions together: $(f \times g)(x) = f(x) \times g(x) = x^2 \times x = x^3$.

To find the quotient of two functions f and g, assuming the domains are compatible, divide the first function by the second: $\frac{f}{g}(x) = \frac{f(x)}{g(x)} = \frac{x^2}{x} = x \, ; x \neq 0$.

The example given in each case is fairly simple, but on a given problem, if you are looking only for the value of the sum, difference, product or quotient of two functions at a particular x-value, it may be simpler to solve the functions individually and then perform the given operation using those values.

The composite of two functions f and g, written as $(f \circ g)(x)$ simply means that the output of the second function is used as the input of the first. This can also be written as $f(g(x))$. In general, this can be solved by substituting $g(x)$ for all instances of x in $f(x)$ and simplifying. Using the example functions $f(x) = x^2 - x + 2$ and $g(x) = x + 1$, we can find that $(f \circ g)(x)$ or $f(g(x))$ is equal to $f(x + 1) = (x + 1)^2 - (x + 1) + 2$, which simplifies to $x^2 + x + 2$.

It is important to note that $(f \circ g)(x)$ is not necessarily the same as $(g \circ f)(x)$. The process is not always commutative like addition or multiplication expressions. It *can* be commutative, but most often this is not the case.

Practice

P1. A professor wishes to invest $20,000 in a CD that compounds annually. The interest rate at his bank is 1.9%. How many years will it take for his account to reach $50,000?

P2. Suppose a new strain of bacteria, after x days, shows a growth rate of 10%. The current count for the new bacteria strain is 100. How many days will pass before the count reaches 1 million bacteria?

P3. Each of the following functions cross the x- and y-axes at the same points. Identify the most likely function type of each graph

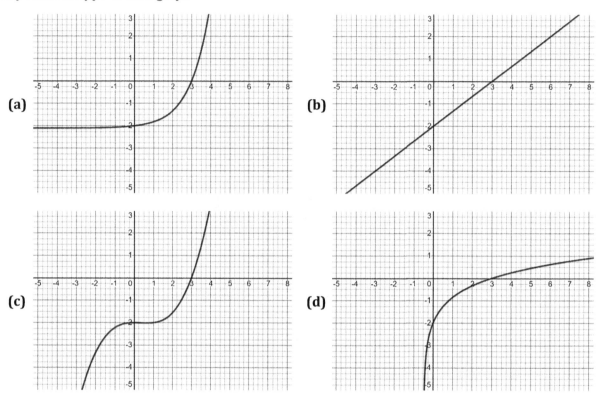

(a)

(b)

(c)

(d)

P4. Given the functions $f(x) = -3x + 3$, $g(x) = e^x + 3$, and $h(x) = x^2 - 2x + 1$, perform the following operations and write out the resulting function:

 (a) Shift $g(x)$ 4 units to the left and 1 unit up, then compress the new function by a factor of $1/2$

 (b) $\dfrac{f(x)}{h(x)}$

 (c) $h\big(g(x)\big)$

 (d) $\dfrac{f(x)+h(x)}{x-1}$

P5. Martin needs a 20% medicine solution. The pharmacy has a 5% solution and a 30% solution. He needs 50 mL of the solution. If the pharmacist must mix the two solutions, how many milliliters of 5% solution and 30% solution should be used?

78

Copyright © Mometrix Media. You have been licensed one copy of this document for personal use only. Any other reproduction or redistribution is strictly prohibited. All rights reserved.

P6. Describe two different strategies for solving the following problem:

Kevin can mow the yard in 4 hours. Mandy can mow the same yard in 5 hours. If they work together, how long will it take them to mow the yard?

P7. A car, traveling at 65 miles per hour, leaves Flagstaff and heads east on I-40. Another car, traveling at 75 miles per hour, leaves Flagstaff 2 hours later, from the same starting point and also heads east on I-40. Determine how many hours it will take the second car catch the first car by:

(a) Using a table.

(b) Using algebra.

Practice Solutions

P1. In order to solve, the compound interest formula should be evaluated for a future value of $50,000, principal of $20,000, rate of 0.019, and number of years of t. The exponential equation may then be solved by taking the logarithm of both sides. The process is shown below:

$$50{,}000 = 20{,}000\left(1 + \frac{0.019}{1}\right)^{t}$$

Dividing both sides of the equation by 20,000 gives $2.5 = 1.019^{t}$. Taking the logarithm of both sides gives $\log(2.5) = t\log(1.019)$. Dividing both sides of this equation by $\log(1.019)$ gives $t \approx 48.68$. Thus, after approximately 49 years, the professor's account will reach $50,000.

P2. The problem may be solved by writing and solving an exponential growth function, in the form, $f(x) = a(1 + r)^{x}$, where $f(x)$ represents the future count, a represents the current count, r represents the growth rate, and x represents the time. Once the function is evaluated for a future count of 1,000,000, a current count of 100, and a growth rate of 0.10, the exponential equation may be solved by taking the logarithm of both sides.

The problem may be modeled with the equation, $1{,}000{,}000 = 100 \times (1.10)^{x}$. Dividing both sides of the equation by 100 gives $10{,}000 = 1.10^{x}$. Taking the logarithm of both sides gives $\log(10{,}000) = x\log(1.10)$. Dividing both sides of this equation by $\log(1.10)$ gives $x \approx 96.6$. Thus, after approximately 97 days, the bacteria count will reach 1 million.

P3. (a) Exponential function – positive, increasing slope

(b) Linear function – positive, continuous slope.

(c) Polynomial function (odd degree) – positive, changing slope. Note that the graph goes off to infinity in opposite quadrants I and III, thus it is an odd degree.

(d) Logarithmic function – positive, decreasing slope

P4. (a) Shifting $g(x)$ to the left 4 units is the same as $g(x + 4)$ and shifting the function up one unit is $g(x) + 1$. Combining these and multiplying by ½ results in the following:

$$\frac{1}{2}(g(x + 4) + 1) = \frac{1}{2}\left((e^{x+4} + 3) + 1\right)$$
$$= \frac{e^{x+4}}{2} + 2$$

(b) Factor $h(x)$, noting that it is a perfect square, and be sure to note the constraint on x due to the original denominator of the rational expression:

$$\frac{f(x)}{h(x)} = \frac{-3x+3}{x^2-2x+1} = \frac{-3(x-1)}{(x-1)(x-1)} = \frac{-3}{(x-1)}; x \neq 1$$

(c) Evaluate the composition as follows:

$$\begin{aligned} h\big(g(x)\big) &= (e^x+3)^2 - 2(e^x+3) + 1 \\ &= (e^x)^2 + 6e^x + 9 - 2e^x - 6 + 1 \\ &= e^{2x} + 4e^x + 4 \\ &= (e^x+2)^2 \end{aligned}$$

(d) Note the constraint on x due to the original denominator of the rational expression:

$$\begin{aligned} \frac{f(x)+h(x)}{x-1} &= \frac{(-3x+3)+(x^2-2x+1)}{x-1} \\ &= \frac{-3(x-1)+(x-1)(x-1)}{x-1} \\ &= -3+(x-1) \\ &= x-4; x \neq 1 \end{aligned}$$

P5. To solve this problem, a table may be created to represent the variables, percentages, and total amount of solution. Such a table is shown below:

	mL solution	% medicine	Total mL medicine
5% solution	x	0.05	$0.05x$
30% solution	y	0.30	$0.30y$
Mixture	$x+y=50$	0.20	$(0.20)(50)=10$

The variable, x, may be rewritten as $50-y$, so the equation, $0.05(50-y)+0.30y=10$, may be written and solved for y. Doing so gives $y=30$. So, 30 mL of 30% solution are needed. Evaluating the expression, $50-y$ for an x-value of 20, shows that 20 mL of 5% solution are needed.

P6. Two possible strategies both involve the use of rational equations to solve. The first strategy involves representing the fractional part of the yard mowed by each person in one hour and setting this sum equal to the ratio of 1 to the total time needed. The appropriate equation is $1/4 + 1/5 = 1/t$, which simplifies as $9/20 = 1/t$, and finally as $t = 20/9$. So, the time it will take them to mow the yard, when working together, is a little more than 2.2 hours.

A second strategy involves representing the time needed for each person as two fractions and setting the sum equal to 1 (representing 1 yard). The appropriate equation is $t/4 + t/5 = 1$, which simplifies as $9t/20 = 1$, and finally as $t = 20/9$. This strategy also shows the total time to be a little more than 2.2 hours.

P7. (a) One strategy might involve creating a table of values for the number of hours and distances for each car. The table may be examined to find the same distance traveled and the corresponding number of hours taken. Such a table is shown below:

Car A		Car B	
x (hours)	*y* (distance)	*x* (hours)	*y* (distance)
0	0	0	
1	65	1	
2	130	2	0
3	195	3	75
4	260	4	150
5	325	5	225
6	390	6	300
7	455	7	375
8	520	8	450
9	585	9	525
10	650	10	600
11	715	11	675
12	780	12	750
13	845	13	825
14	910	14	900
15	975	15	975

The table shows that after 15 hours, the distance traveled is the same. Thus, the second car catches up with the first car after a distance of 975 miles and 15 hours.

(b) A second strategy might involve setting up and solving an algebraic equation. This situation may be modeled as $65x = 75(x - 2)$. This equation sets the distances traveled by each car equal to one another. Solving for *x* gives $x = 15$. Thus, once again, the second car will catch up with the first car after 15 hours.

Factorials

The **factorial** is a function that can be performed on any **non-negative integer**. It is represented by the ! sign written after the integer on which it is being performed. The factorial of an integer is the product of all positive integers less than or equal to the number. For example, 4! (read "4 factorial") is calculated as $4 \times 3 \times 2 \times 1 = 24$.

Since 0 is not itself a positive integer, nor does it have any positive integers less than it, 0! cannot be calculated using this method. Instead, 0! is defined by convention to equal 1. This makes sense if you consider the pattern of descending factorials:

$$5! = 120$$
$$4! = \frac{5!}{5} = \frac{120}{5} = 24$$
$$3! = \frac{4!}{4} = \frac{24}{4} = 6$$
$$2! = \frac{3!}{3} = \frac{6}{3} = 2$$
$$1! = \frac{2!}{2} = \frac{2}{2} = 1$$
$$0! = \frac{1!}{1} = \frac{1}{1} = 1$$

PERMUTATIONS

For any given set of data, the individual elements in the set may be arranged in different groups containing different numbers of elements arranged in different orders. For example, given the set of integers from one to three, inclusive, the elements of the set are 1, 2, and 3: written as {1, 2, 3}. They may be arranged as follows: 1, 2, 3, 12, 21, 13, 31, 23, 32, 123, 132, 213, 231, 312, and 321. These ordered sequences of elements from the given set of data are called **permutations**. It is important to note that in permutations, the order of the elements in the sequence is important. The sequence 123 is not the same as the sequence 213. Also, no element in the given set may be used more times as an element in a permutation than it appears as an element in the original set. For example, 223 is not a permutation in the above example because the number 2 only appears one time in the given set.

To find the number of permutations of r items from a set of n items, use the formula $_nP_r = \frac{n!}{(n-r)!}$. When using this formula, each element of r must be unique. Also, this assumes that different arrangements of the same set of elements yields different outcomes. For example, 123 is not the same as 321; order is important.

A special case arises while finding the number of possible permutations of n items from a set of n items. Because $n = r$, the equation for the number of permutations becomes simply $P = n!$ The same result is true for $r = n - 1$. Both of these cases are a result of the fact that 0! and 1! are both equal to 1.

If a set contains one or more groups of **indistinguishable or interchangeable elements** (e.g., the set {1, 2, 3, 3}, which has a group of two indistinguishable 3's), there is a different formula for finding distinct permutations of all n elements. Use the formula $P = \frac{n!}{m_1!m_2!...m_k!}$, where P is the

number of permutations, n is the total number of elements in the set, and m_1 through m_k are the number of identical elements in each group (e.g., for the set {1, 1, 2, 2, 2, 3, 3}, $m_1 = 2$, $m_2 = 3$, and $m_3 = 2$). It is important to note that each repeated number is counted as its own element for the purpose of defining n (e.g., for the set {1, 1, 2, 2, 2, 3, 3}, $n = 7$, not 3).

To find the number of possible permutations of **any number of elements** in a set of unique elements, you must apply the permutation formulas multiple times. For example, to find the total number of possible permutations of the set {1, 2, 3} first apply the permutation formula for situations where $n = r$ as follows: $P = n! = 3! = 6$. This gives the number of permutations of the three elements when all three elements are used. To find the number of permutations when only two of the three elements are used, use the formula $_nP_r = \frac{n!}{(n-r)!}$, where n is 3 and r is 2.

$$_nP_r = \frac{n!}{(n-r)!} \Rightarrow {}_3P_2 = \frac{3!}{(3-2)!} = \frac{6}{1} = 6$$

To find the number of permutations when one element is used, use the formula $_nP_r = \frac{n!}{(n-r)!}$, where n is 3 and r is 1.

$$_nP_r = \frac{n!}{(n-r)!} \Rightarrow {}_3P_1 = \frac{3!}{(3-1)!} = \frac{3!}{2!} = \frac{6}{2} = 3$$

Find the sum of the three formulas: $6 + 6 + 3 = 15$ total possible permutations.

Alternatively, the general formula for total possible permutations can be written as follows:

$$P_T = \sum_{i=1}^{n} \frac{n!}{(i-1)!}$$

COMBINATIONS

Combinations are essentially defined as permutations where the order in which the elements appear does not matter. Going back to the earlier example of the set {1, 2, 3}, the possible combinations that can be made from that set are 1, 2, 3, 12, 13, 23, and 123.

In a set containing n elements, the number of combinations of r items from the set can be found using the formula $_nC_r = \frac{n!}{r!(n-r)!}$. Notice the similarity to the formula for permutations. In effect, you are dividing the number of permutations by $r!$ to get the number of combinations, and the formula may be written $_nC_r = \frac{_nP_r}{r!}$. When finding the number of combinations, it is important to remember that the elements in the set must be unique (i.e., there must not be any duplicate items), and that no item may be used more than once in any given sequence.

> **Review Video: Probability - Permutation and Combination**
> Visit mometrix.com/academy and enter code: 907664

Practice

P1. Ichiro has 4 shirts, 1 jacket, and 5 different pairs of pants that he packed for his work trip. If wearing a jacket is optional, how many outfit combinations can he make?

P2. Determine the number of permutations and combinations of the following:

(a) Choose 3 from the set: $\{4, 5, 6, 7\}$

(b) Choose 2 from the set: $\{a, b, c, d, e\}$

(c) Choose 4 from the set: $\{a, h, m, t\}$

Practice Solutions

P1. To start with, each shirt can be matched with each pair of pants, so that would be $4 \times 5 = 20$ combinations. Since the jacket is optional each of the 20 can be either with or without the jacket, i.e. $20 \times 2 = 40$. There are 40 distinct combinations he could wear.

P2. (a) $_nP_r = \frac{n!}{(n-r)!} = \frac{4!}{(4-3)!} = \frac{4\times3\times2\times1}{1} = 24$; $_nC_r = \frac{n!}{(n-r)!r!} = \frac{4!}{(4-3)!3!} = \frac{4\times3\times2\times1}{3\times2\times1} = 4$

(b) $_nP_r = \frac{n!}{(n-r)!} = \frac{5!}{(5-2)!} = \frac{5\times4\times3\times2\times1}{3\times2\times1} = 20$; $_nC_r = \frac{n!}{(n-r)!r!} = \frac{5!}{(5-2)!2!} = \frac{5\times4\times3\times2\times1}{(3\times2\times1)\times(2\times1)} = 10$

(c) $_nP_r = \frac{n!}{(n-r)!} = \frac{4!}{(4-4)!} = \frac{4\times3\times2\times1}{1} = 24$; $_nC_r = \frac{n!}{(n-r)!r!} = \frac{4!}{(4-4)!4!} = \frac{4\times3\times2\times1}{1\times(4\times3\times2\times1)} = 1$

Linear Algebra

MATRIX BASICS

A **matrix** (plural: matrices) is a rectangular array of numbers or variables, often called **elements**, which are arranged in columns and rows. A matrix is generally represented by a capital letter, with its elements represented by the corresponding lowercase letter with two subscripts indicating the row and column of the element. For example, n_{ab} represents the element in row a column b of matrix N.

$$N = \begin{bmatrix} n_{11} & n_{12} & n_{13} \\ n_{21} & n_{22} & n_{23} \end{bmatrix}$$

A matrix can be described in terms of the number of rows and columns it contains in the format $a \times b$, where a is the number of rows and b is the number of columns. The matrix shown above is a 2×3 matrix. Any $a \times b$ matrix where $a = b$ is a square matrix. A **vector** is a matrix that has exactly one column (**column vector**) or exactly one row (**row vector**).

The **main diagonal** of a matrix is the set of elements on the diagonal from the top left to the bottom right of a matrix. Because of the way it is defined, only square matrices will have a main diagonal. For the matrix shown below, the main diagonal consists of the elements $n_{11}, n_{22}, n_{33}, n_{44}$.

$$\begin{bmatrix} n_{11} & n_{12} & n_{13} & n_{14} \\ n_{21} & n_{22} & n_{23} & n_{24} \\ n_{31} & n_{32} & n_{33} & n_{34} \\ n_{41} & n_{42} & n_{43} & n_{44} \end{bmatrix}$$

A 3×4 matrix such as the one shown below would not have a main diagonal because there is no straight line of elements between the top left corner and the bottom right corner that joins the elements.

$$\begin{bmatrix} n_{11} & n_{12} & n_{13} & n_{14} \\ n_{21} & n_{22} & n_{23} & n_{24} \\ n_{31} & n_{32} & n_{33} & n_{34} \end{bmatrix}$$

A **diagonal matrix** is a square matrix that has a zero for every element in the matrix except the elements on the main diagonal. All the elements on the main diagonal must be nonzero numbers.

$$\begin{bmatrix} n_{11} & 0 & 0 & 0 \\ 0 & n_{22} & 0 & 0 \\ 0 & 0 & n_{33} & 0 \\ 0 & 0 & 0 & n_{44} \end{bmatrix}$$

If every element on the main diagonal of a diagonal matrix is equal to one, the matrix is called an **identity matrix**. The identity matrix is often represented by the letter I.

$$I = \begin{bmatrix} 1 & 0 & 0 & 0 \\ 0 & 1 & 0 & 0 \\ 0 & 0 & 1 & 0 \\ 0 & 0 & 0 & 1 \end{bmatrix}$$

A **zero matrix** is a matrix that has zero as the value for every element in the matrix.

$$\begin{bmatrix} 0 & 0 & 0 & 0 \\ 0 & 0 & 0 & 0 \\ 0 & 0 & 0 & 0 \\ 0 & 0 & 0 & 0 \end{bmatrix}$$

The zero matrix is the *identity for matrix addition*. Do not confuse the zero matrix with the identity matrix.

The **negative of a matrix** is also known as the additive inverse of a matrix. If matrix N is the given matrix, then matrix $-N$ is its negative. This means that every element n_{ab} is equal to $-n_{ab}$ in the negative. To find the negative of a given matrix, change the sign of every element in the matrix and keep all elements in their original corresponding positions in the matrix.

If two matrices have the same order and all corresponding elements in the two matrices are the same, then the two matrices are **equal matrices**.

A matrix N may be **transposed** to matrix N^T by changing all rows into columns and changing all columns into rows. The easiest way to accomplish this is to swap the positions of the row and column notations for each element. For example, suppose the element in the second row of the third column of matrix N is $n_{23} = 6$. In the transposed matrix N^T, the transposed element would be $n_{32} = 6$, and it would be placed in the third row of the second column.

$$N = \begin{bmatrix} 1 & 2 & 3 \\ 4 & 5 & 6 \end{bmatrix}; N^T = \begin{bmatrix} 1 & 4 \\ 2 & 5 \\ 3 & 6 \end{bmatrix}$$

To quickly transpose a matrix by hand, begin with the first column and rewrite a new matrix with those same elements in the same order in the first row. Write the elements from the second column of the original matrix in the second row of the transposed matrix. Continue this process until all columns have been completed. If the original matrix is identical to the transposed matrix, the matrices are symmetric.

The **determinant** of a matrix is a scalar value that is calculated by taking into account all the elements of a square matrix. A determinant only exists for square matrices. Finding the determinant of a 2×2 matrix is as simple as remembering a simple equation. For a 2×2 matrix $M = \begin{bmatrix} m_{11} & m_{12} \\ m_{21} & m_{22} \end{bmatrix}$, the determinant is obtained by the equation $|M| = m_{11}m_{22} - m_{12}m_{21}$. Anything larger than 2×2 requires multiple steps. Take matrix $N = \begin{bmatrix} a & b & c \\ d & e & f \\ g & h & j \end{bmatrix}$. The determinant of N is calculated as $|N| = a\begin{vmatrix} e & f \\ h & j \end{vmatrix} - b\begin{vmatrix} d & f \\ g & j \end{vmatrix} + c\begin{vmatrix} d & e \\ g & h \end{vmatrix}$ or $|N| = a(ej - fh) - b(dj - fg) + c(dh - eg)$.

There is a shortcut for 3×3 matrices: add the products of each unique set of elements diagonally left-to-right and subtract the products of each unique set of elements diagonally right-to-left. In matrix N, the left-to-right diagonal elements are (a, e, j), (b, f, g), and (c, d, h). The right-to-left diagonal elements are (a, f, h), (b, d, j), and (c, e, g). $\det(N) = aej + bfg + cdh - afh - bdj - ceg$.

Calculating the determinants of matrices larger than 3×3 is rarely, if ever, done by hand.

The **inverse** of a matrix M is the matrix that, when multiplied by matrix M, yields a product that is the identity matrix. Multiplication of matrices will be explained in greater detail shortly. Not all matrices have inverses. Only a square matrix whose determinant is not zero has an inverse. If a matrix has an inverse, that inverse is unique to that matrix. For any matrix M that has an inverse, the inverse is represented by the symbol M^{-1}. To calculate the inverse of a 2×2 square matrix, use the following pattern:

$$M = \begin{bmatrix} m_{11} & m_{12} \\ m_{21} & m_{22} \end{bmatrix}; \; M^{-1} = \begin{bmatrix} \dfrac{m_{22}}{|M|} & \dfrac{-m_{12}}{|M|} \\ \dfrac{-m_{21}}{|M|} & \dfrac{m_{11}}{|M|} \end{bmatrix}$$

Another way to find the inverse of a matrix by hand is use an augmented matrix and elementary row operations. An **augmented matrix** is formed by appending the entries from one matrix onto the end of another. For example, given a 2×2 invertible matrix $N = \begin{bmatrix} a & b \\ c & d \end{bmatrix}$, you can find the inverse N^{-1} by creating an augmented matrix by appending a 2×2 identity matrix: $\begin{bmatrix} a & b & 1 & 0 \\ c & d & 0 & 1 \end{bmatrix}$. To find the inverse of the original 2×2 matrix, perform elementary row operations to convert the original matrix on the left to an identity matrix: $\begin{bmatrix} 1 & 0 & e & f \\ 0 & 1 & g & h \end{bmatrix}$. For instance, the first step might be to multiply the second row by $\frac{b}{d}$ and then subtract it from the first row to make its second column a zero. The end result is that the 2×2 section on the right will become the inverse of the original matrix: $N^{-1} = \begin{bmatrix} e & f \\ g & h \end{bmatrix}$.

ELEMENTARY ROW OPERATIONS

Elementary row operations include multiplying a row by a non-zero scalar, adding scalar multiples of two rows, and switching rows. These operations can be done using matrix multiplication with specialized transformation matrices. **Row switching** is achieved by swapping the corresponding rows in the identity matrix. For example, consider switching row 2 and row 3 in a 3×3 matrix:

$$M_{R_2 \leftrightarrow R_3} = \begin{bmatrix} 1 & 0 & 0 \\ 0 & 0 & 1 \\ 0 & 1 & 0 \end{bmatrix}$$

The transformation matrix for **row multiplication** is also based on the identity matrix with the scalar multiplication factor in place of the 1 in the corresponding row. Multiplying row 1 by -4 in a 3×3 matrix:

$$M_{-4R_1 \rightarrow R_1} = \begin{bmatrix} -4 & 0 & 0 \\ 0 & 1 & 0 \\ 0 & 0 & 1 \end{bmatrix}$$

The transformation matrix for **row addition** consists of the identity matrix with a 1 in the element corresponding to the two rows being added in the column where you want the result to go. Adding row 2 to row 1 in a 3×3 matrix:

$$M_{R_1 + R_2 \rightarrow R_1} = \begin{bmatrix} 1 & 0 & 0 \\ 1 & 1 & 0 \\ 0 & 0 & 1 \end{bmatrix}$$

BASIC OPERATIONS WITH MATRICES

There are two categories of basic operations with regard to matrices: operations between a matrix and a scalar, and operations between two matrices.

SCALAR OPERATIONS

A scalar being added to a matrix is treated as though it were being added to each element of the matrix:

$$M + \text{k} = \begin{bmatrix} m_{11} + k & m_{12} + k \\ m_{21} + k & m_{22} + k \end{bmatrix}$$

The same is true for the other three operations.

Subtraction:

$$M - k = \begin{bmatrix} m_{11} - k & m_{12} - k \\ m_{21} - k & m_{22} - k \end{bmatrix}$$

Multiplication:

$$M \times k = \begin{bmatrix} m_{11} \times k & m_{12} \times k \\ m_{21} \times k & m_{22} \times k \end{bmatrix}$$

Division:

$$M \div k = \begin{bmatrix} m_{11} \div k & m_{12} \div k \\ m_{21} \div k & m_{22} \div k \end{bmatrix}$$

MATRIX ADDITION AND SUBTRACTION

All four of the basic operations can be used with operations between matrices (although division is usually discarded in favor of multiplication by the inverse), but there are restrictions on the situations in which they can be used. Matrices that meet all the qualifications for a given operation are called **conformable matrices**. However, conformability is specific to the operation; two matrices that are conformable for addition are not necessarily conformable for multiplication.

For two matrices to be conformable for addition or subtraction, they must be of the same dimension; otherwise the operation is not defined. If matrix M is a 3×2 matrix and matrix N is a 2×3 matrix, the operations $M + N$ and $M - N$ are meaningless. If matrices M and N are the same size, the operation is as simple as adding or subtracting all of the corresponding elements:

$$\begin{bmatrix} m_{11} & m_{12} \\ m_{21} & m_{22} \end{bmatrix} + \begin{bmatrix} n_{11} & n_{12} \\ n_{21} & n_{22} \end{bmatrix} = \begin{bmatrix} m_{11} + n_{11} & m_{12} + n_{12} \\ m_{21} + n_{21} & m_{22} + n_{22} \end{bmatrix}$$

$$\begin{bmatrix} m_{11} & m_{12} \\ m_{21} & m_{22} \end{bmatrix} - \begin{bmatrix} n_{11} & n_{12} \\ n_{21} & n_{22} \end{bmatrix} = \begin{bmatrix} m_{11} - n_{11} & m_{12} - n_{12} \\ m_{21} - n_{21} & m_{22} - n_{22} \end{bmatrix}$$

The result of addition or subtraction is a matrix of the same dimension as the two original matrices involved in the operation.

MATRIX MULTIPLICATION

The first thing it is necessary to understand about matrix multiplication is that it is not commutative. In scalar multiplication, the operation is commutative, meaning that $a \times b = b \times a$. For matrix multiplication, this is not the case: $A \times B \neq B \times A$. The terminology must be specific when describing matrix multiplication. The operation $A \times B$ can be described as A multiplied (or **post-multiplied**) by B, or B **pre-multiplied** by A.

Copyright © Mometrix Media. You have been licensed one copy of this document for personal use only. Any other reproduction or redistribution is strictly prohibited. All rights reserved.

For two matrices to be conformable for multiplication, they need not be of the same dimension, but specific dimensions must correspond. Taking the example of two matrices M and N to be multiplied $M \times N$, matrix M must have the same number of columns as matrix N has rows. Put another way, if matrix M has the dimensions $a \times b$ and matrix N has the dimensions $c \times d$, b must equal c if the two matrices are to be conformable for this multiplication. The matrix that results from the multiplication will have the dimensions $a \times d$. If a and d are both equal to 1, the product is simply a scalar. Square matrices of the same dimensions are always conformable for multiplication, and their product is always a matrix of the same size.

The simplest type of matrix multiplication is a 1×2 matrix (a row vector) times a 2×1 matrix (a column vector). These will multiply in the following way:

$$[m_{11} \quad m_{12}] \times \begin{bmatrix} n_{11} \\ n_{21} \end{bmatrix} = m_{11}n_{11} + m_{12}n_{21}$$

The two matrices are conformable for multiplication because matrix M has the same number of columns as matrix N has rows. Because the other dimensions are both 1, the result is a scalar. Expanding our matrices to 1×3 and 3×1, the process is the same:

$$[m_{11} \quad m_{12} \quad m_{13}] \times \begin{bmatrix} n_{11} \\ n_{21} \\ n_{31} \end{bmatrix} = m_{11}n_{11} + m_{12}n_{21} + m_{13}n_{31}$$

Once again, the result is a scalar. This type of basic matrix multiplication is the building block for the multiplication of larger matrices.

To multiply larger matrices, treat each **row from the first matrix** and each **column from the second matrix** as individual vectors and follow the pattern for multiplying vectors. The scalar value found from multiplying the first-row vector by the first column vector is placed in the first row, first column of the new matrix. The scalar value found from multiplying the second-row vector by the first column vector is placed in the second row, first column of the new matrix. Continue this pattern until each row of the first matrix has been multiplied by each column of the second vector.

Below is an example of the multiplication of a 3×2 matrix and a 2×3 matrix.

$$\begin{bmatrix} m_{11} & m_{12} \\ m_{21} & m_{22} \\ m_{31} & m_{32} \end{bmatrix} \times \begin{bmatrix} n_{11} & n_{12} & n_{13} \\ n_{21} & n_{22} & n_{23} \end{bmatrix} = \begin{bmatrix} m_{11}n_{11} + m_{12}n_{21} & m_{11}n_{12} + m_{12}n_{22} & m_{11}n_{13} + m_{12}n_{23} \\ m_{21}n_{11} + m_{22}n_{21} & m_{21}n_{12} + m_{22}n_{22} & m_{21}n_{13} + m_{22}n_{23} \\ m_{31}n_{11} + m_{32}n_{21} & m_{31}n_{12} + m_{32}n_{22} & m_{31}n_{13} + m_{32}n_{23} \end{bmatrix}$$

This process starts by taking the first column of the second matrix and running it through each row of the first matrix. Removing all but the first M row and first N column, we would see only the following:

$$[m_{11} \quad m_{12}] \times \begin{bmatrix} n_{11} \\ n_{21} \end{bmatrix} = m_{11}n_{11} + m_{12}n_{21}$$

The first product would then be $m_{11}n_{11} + m_{12}n_{21}$. This process will be continued for each column of the N matrix to find the first full row of the product matrix, as shown below.

$$[m_{11}n_{11} + m_{12}n_{21} \quad m_{11}n_{12} + m_{12}n_{22} \quad m_{11}n_{13} + m_{12}n_{23}]$$

After completing the first row, the next step would be to simply move to the second row of the M matrix and repeat the process until all of the rows have been finished. The result is a 3 × 3 matrix.

$$\begin{bmatrix} m_{11} & m_{12} \\ m_{21} & m_{22} \\ m_{31} & m_{32} \end{bmatrix} \times \begin{bmatrix} n_{11} & n_{12} & n_{13} \\ n_{21} & n_{22} & n_{23} \end{bmatrix} = \begin{bmatrix} m_{11}n_{11}+m_{12}n_{21} & m_{11}n_{12}+m_{12}n_{22} & m_{11}n_{13}+m_{12}n_{23} \\ m_{21}n_{11}+m_{22}n_{21} & m_{21}n_{12}+m_{22}n_{22} & m_{21}n_{13}+m_{22}n_{23} \\ m_{31}n_{11}+m_{32}n_{21} & m_{31}n_{12}+m_{32}n_{22} & m_{31}n_{13}+m_{32}n_{23} \end{bmatrix}$$

If the operation were done in reverse ($N \times M$), the result would be a 2 × 2 matrix.

$$\begin{bmatrix} n_{11} & n_{12} & n_{13} \\ n_{21} & n_{22} & n_{23} \end{bmatrix} \times \begin{bmatrix} m_{11} & m_{12} \\ m_{21} & m_{22} \\ m_{31} & m_{32} \end{bmatrix} = \begin{bmatrix} m_{11}n_{11}+m_{21}n_{12}+m_{31}n_{13} & m_{12}n_{11}+m_{22}n_{12}+m_{32}n_{13} \\ m_{11}n_{21}+m_{21}n_{22}+m_{31}n_{23} & m_{12}n_{21}+m_{22}n_{22}+m_{32}n_{23} \end{bmatrix}$$

SOLVING SYSTEMS OF EQUATIONS

Matrices can be used to represent the coefficients of a system of linear equations and can be very useful in solving those systems. Take for instance three equations with three variables where all a, b, c, and d are known constants:

$$a_1 x + b_1 y + c_1 z = d_1$$
$$a_2 x + b_2 y + c_2 z = d_2$$
$$a_3 x + b_3 y + c_3 z = d_3$$

To solve this system, define three matrices:

$$A = \begin{bmatrix} a_1 & b_1 & c_1 \\ a_2 & b_2 & c_2 \\ a_3 & b_3 & c_3 \end{bmatrix}; D = \begin{bmatrix} d_1 \\ d_2 \\ d_3 \end{bmatrix}; X = \begin{bmatrix} x \\ y \\ z \end{bmatrix}$$

The three equations in our system can be fully represented by a single matrix equation:

$$AX = D$$

We know that the identity matrix times X is equal to X, and we know that any matrix multiplied by its inverse is equal to the identity matrix.

$$A^{-1}AX = IX = X; \text{thus } X = A^{-1}D$$

Our goal then is to find the inverse of A, or A^{-1}. Once we have that, we can pre-multiply matrix D by A^{-1} (post-multiplying here is an undefined operation) to find matrix X.

Systems of equations can also be solved using the transformation of an augmented matrix in a process similar to that for finding a matrix inverse. Begin by arranging each equation of the system in the following format:

$$a_1 x + b_1 y + c_1 z = d_1$$
$$a_2 x + b_2 y + c_2 z = d_2$$
$$a_3 x + b_3 y + c_3 z = d_3$$

Define matrices A and D and combine them into augmented matrix A_a:

$$A = \begin{bmatrix} a_1 & b_1 & c_1 \\ a_2 & b_2 & c_2 \\ a_3 & b_3 & c_3 \end{bmatrix}; D = \begin{bmatrix} d_1 \\ d_2 \\ d_3 \end{bmatrix}; A_a = \begin{bmatrix} a_1 & b_1 & c_1 & d_1 \\ a_2 & b_2 & c_2 & d_2 \\ a_3 & b_3 & c_3 & d_3 \end{bmatrix}$$

To solve the augmented matrix and the system of equations, use elementary row operations to form an identity matrix in the first 3×3 section. When this is complete, the values in the last column are the solutions to the system of equations:

$$\begin{bmatrix} 1 & 0 & 0 & x \\ 0 & 1 & 0 & y \\ 0 & 0 & 1 & z \end{bmatrix}$$

If an identity matrix is not possible, the system of equations has no unique solution. Sometimes only a partial solution will be possible. The following are partial solutions you may find:

$\begin{bmatrix} 1 & 0 & k_1 & x_0 \\ 0 & 1 & k_2 & y_0 \\ 0 & 0 & 0 & 0 \end{bmatrix}$ gives the non-unique solution $x = x_0 - k_1 z$; $y = y_0 - k_2 z$

$\begin{bmatrix} 1 & j_1 & k_1 & x_0 \\ 0 & 0 & 0 & 0 \\ 0 & 0 & 0 & 0 \end{bmatrix}$ gives the non-unique solution $x = x_0 - j_1 y - k_1 z$

This process can be used to solve systems of equations with any number of variables, but three is the upper limit for practical purposes. Anything more ought to be done with a graphing calculator.

REDUCED ROW-ECHELON FORMS

When a system of equations has a solution, finding the transformation of the augmented matrix will result in one of three reduced row-echelon forms. Only one of these forms will give a unique solution to the system of equations, however. The following examples show the solutions indicated by particular results:

$\begin{bmatrix} 1 & 0 & 0 & x_0 \\ 0 & 1 & 0 & y_0 \\ 0 & 0 & 1 & z_0 \end{bmatrix}$ gives the unique solution $x = x_0$; $y = y_0$; $z = z_0$

$\begin{bmatrix} 1 & 0 & k_1 & x_0 \\ 0 & 1 & k_2 & y_0 \\ 0 & 0 & 0 & 0 \end{bmatrix}$ gives a non-unique solution $x = x_0 - k_1 z$; $y = y_0 - k_2 z$

$\begin{bmatrix} 1 & j_1 & k_1 & x_0 \\ 0 & 0 & 0 & 0 \\ 0 & 0 & 0 & 0 \end{bmatrix}$ gives a non-unique solution $x = x_0 - j_1 y - k_1 z$

GEOMETRIC TRANSFORMATIONS

The four *geometric transformations* are **translations**, **reflections**, **rotations**, and **dilations**. When geometric transformations are expressed as matrices, the process of performing the transformations is simplified. For calculations of the geometric transformations of a planar figure, make a $2 \times n$ matrix, where n is the number of vertices in the planar figure. Each column represents the rectangular coordinates of one vertex of the figure, with the top row containing the values of the x-coordinates and the bottom row containing the values of the y-coordinates. For example, given a planar triangular figure with coordinates (x_1, y_1), (x_2, y_2), and (x_3, y_3), the corresponding matrix is $\begin{bmatrix} x_1 & x_2 & x_3 \\ y_1 & y_2 & y_3 \end{bmatrix}$. You can then perform the necessary transformations on this matrix to determine the coordinates of the resulting figure.

TRANSLATION

A **translation** moves a figure along the x-axis, the y-axis, or both axes without changing the size or shape of the figure. To calculate the new coordinates of a planar figure following a translation, set up a matrix of the coordinates and a matrix of the translation values and add the two matrices.

$$\begin{bmatrix} h & h & h \\ v & v & v \end{bmatrix} + \begin{bmatrix} x_1 & x_2 & x_3 \\ y_1 & y_2 & y_3 \end{bmatrix} = \begin{bmatrix} h + x_1 & h + x_2 & h + x_3 \\ v + y_1 & v + y_2 & v + y_3 \end{bmatrix}$$

where h is the number of units the figure is moved along the x-axis (horizontally) and v is the number of units the figure is moved along the y-axis (vertically).

REFLECTION

To find the **reflection** of a planar figure over the x-axis, set up a matrix of the coordinates of the vertices and pre-multiply the matrix by the 2 × 2 matrix $\begin{bmatrix} 1 & 0 \\ 0 & -1 \end{bmatrix}$ so that $\begin{bmatrix} 1 & 0 \\ 0 & -1 \end{bmatrix} \begin{bmatrix} x_1 & x_2 & x_3 \\ y_1 & y_2 & y_3 \end{bmatrix} =$ $\begin{bmatrix} x_1 & x_2 & x_3 \\ -y_1 & -y_2 & -y_3 \end{bmatrix}$. To find the reflection of a planar figure over the y-axis, set up a matrix of the coordinates of the vertices and pre-multiply the matrix by the 2 × 2 matrix $\begin{bmatrix} -1 & 0 \\ 0 & 1 \end{bmatrix}$ so that $\begin{bmatrix} -1 & 0 \\ 0 & 1 \end{bmatrix} \begin{bmatrix} x_1 & x_2 & x_3 \\ y_1 & y_2 & y_3 \end{bmatrix} = \begin{bmatrix} -x_1 & -x_2 & -x_3 \\ y_1 & y_2 & y_3 \end{bmatrix}$. To find the reflection of a planar figure over the line y = x, set up a matrix of the coordinates of the vertices and pre-multiply the matrix by the 2 × 2 matrix $\begin{bmatrix} 0 & 1 \\ 1 & 0 \end{bmatrix}$ so that $\begin{bmatrix} 0 & 1 \\ 1 & 0 \end{bmatrix} \begin{bmatrix} x_1 & x_2 & x_3 \\ y_1 & y_2 & y_3 \end{bmatrix} = \begin{bmatrix} y_1 & y_2 & y_3 \\ x_1 & x_2 & x_3 \end{bmatrix}$. Remember that the order of multiplication is important when multiplying matrices. The commutative property does not apply.

ROTATION

To find the coordinates of the figure formed by rotating a planar figure about the origin θ degrees in a counterclockwise direction, set up a matrix of the coordinates of the vertices and pre-multiply the matrix by the 2 × 2 matrix $\begin{bmatrix} \cos\theta & \sin\theta \\ -\sin\theta & \cos\theta \end{bmatrix}$. For example, if you want to rotate a figure 90° clockwise around the origin, you would have to convert the degree measure to 270° counterclockwise and solve the 2 × 2 matrix you have set as the pre-multiplier: $\begin{bmatrix} \cos 270° & \sin 270° \\ -\sin 270° & \cos 270° \end{bmatrix} = \begin{bmatrix} 0 & -1 \\ 1 & 0 \end{bmatrix}$. Use this as the pre-multiplier for the matrix $\begin{bmatrix} x_1 & x_2 & x_3 \\ y_1 & y_2 & y_3 \end{bmatrix}$ and solve to find the new coordinates.

DILATION

To find the **dilation** of a planar figure by a scale factor of k, set up a matrix of the coordinates of the vertices of the planar figure and pre-multiply the matrix by the 2 × 2 matrix $\begin{bmatrix} k & 0 \\ 0 & k \end{bmatrix}$ so that $\begin{bmatrix} k & 0 \\ 0 & k \end{bmatrix} \begin{bmatrix} x_1 & x_2 & x_3 \\ y_1 & y_2 & y_3 \end{bmatrix} = \begin{bmatrix} kx_1 & kx_2 & kx_3 \\ ky_1 & ky_2 & ky_3 \end{bmatrix}$. This is effectively the same as multiplying the matrix by the scalar k, but the matrix equation would still be necessary if the figure were being dilated by different factors in vertical and horizontal directions. The scale factor k will be greater than 1 if the figure is being enlarged, and between 0 and 1 if the figure is being shrunk. Again, remember that when multiplying matrices, the order of the matrices is important. The commutative property does not apply, and the matrix with the coordinates of the figure must be the second matrix.

Mⓥmetrix

Practice

P1. A sporting-goods store sells baseballs, volleyballs, and basketballs.

$$\begin{array}{ll} \textbf{Baseballs} & \$3 \text{ each} \\ \textbf{Volleyballs} & \$8 \text{ each} \\ \textbf{Basketballs} & \$15 \text{ each} \end{array}$$

Here are the same store's sales numbers for one weekend:

	Baseballs	Volleyballs	Basketballs
Friday	5	4	4
Saturday	7	3	10
Sunday	4	3	6

Find the total sales for each day by multiplying matrices.

P2. Given the following matrices, perform the operations if possible:

$$A = \begin{bmatrix} 3 & 5 \\ -4 & -2 \end{bmatrix}, \quad B = \begin{bmatrix} -4 & -9 \\ 1 & 1 \\ 8 & -2 \end{bmatrix}, \quad C = \begin{bmatrix} -3 & 6 & -9 \\ 1 & 2 & 5 \end{bmatrix}, \quad D = \begin{bmatrix} -1 \\ -5 \\ -2 \end{bmatrix}$$

(a) $\det A$

(b) AB

(c) AC

(d) $\det(CD)$

(e) BA

(f) $BACD$

P3. Solve the following system of equations using an augmented matrix and elementary row operations:

$$4x + 6y + 5z = 1$$

$$-2x - 5y = z$$

$$x + -3y + 5z = 1$$

94

Mometrix

Practice Solutions

P1. The first table can be represented by the following column-vector: $\begin{bmatrix} 3 \\ 8 \\ 15 \end{bmatrix}$

And the second table can be represented by this matrix: $\begin{bmatrix} 5 & 4 & 4 \\ 7 & 3 & 10 \\ 4 & 3 & 6 \end{bmatrix}$

Multiplying the second matrix by the first will result in a column vector showing the total sales for each day:

$$\begin{bmatrix} 5 & 4 & 4 \\ 7 & 3 & 10 \\ 4 & 3 & 6 \end{bmatrix} \times \begin{bmatrix} 3 \\ 8 \\ 15 \end{bmatrix} = \begin{bmatrix} 3\times5+8\times4+15\times4 \\ 3\times7+8\times3+15\times10 \\ 3\times4+8\times3+15\times6 \end{bmatrix} = \begin{bmatrix} 15+32+60 \\ 21+24+150 \\ 12+24+90 \end{bmatrix} = \begin{bmatrix} 107 \\ 195 \\ 126 \end{bmatrix}$$

From this, we can see that Friday's sales were \$107, Saturday's sales were \$195, and Sunday's sales were \$126.

P2. (a) $\det\left(\begin{bmatrix} 3 & 5 \\ -4 & -2 \end{bmatrix}\right) = 3(-2) - 5(-4) = -6 + 20 = 14$

(b) $AB = \begin{bmatrix} 3 & 5 \\ -4 & -2 \end{bmatrix} \times \begin{bmatrix} -4 & -9 \\ 1 & 1 \\ 8 & -2 \end{bmatrix} = undefined$, since columns in $A \neq$ rows in B

(c) $AC = \begin{bmatrix} 3 & 5 \\ -4 & -2 \end{bmatrix} \times \begin{bmatrix} -3 & 6 & -9 \\ 1 & 2 & 5 \end{bmatrix} = \begin{bmatrix} 3(-3)+5(1) & 3(6)+5(2) & 3(-9)+5(5) \\ -4(-3)+-2(1) & -4(6)+-2(2) & -4(-9)+-2(5) \end{bmatrix}$

$$= \begin{bmatrix} -4 & 28 & -2 \\ 10 & -28 & 26 \end{bmatrix}$$

(d) $CD = \begin{bmatrix} -3 & 6 & -9 \\ 1 & 2 & 5 \end{bmatrix} \times \begin{bmatrix} -1 \\ -5 \\ -2 \end{bmatrix} = \begin{bmatrix} -3(-1)+6(-5)+-9(-2) \\ 1(-1)+2(-5)+5(-2) \end{bmatrix} = \begin{bmatrix} -9 \\ -21 \end{bmatrix}$

The determinant is not defined for a non-square matrix. $\det(CD) = undefined$

(e) $BA = \begin{bmatrix} -4 & -9 \\ 1 & 1 \\ 8 & -2 \end{bmatrix} \times \begin{bmatrix} 3 & 5 \\ -4 & -2 \end{bmatrix} = \begin{bmatrix} -4(3)+-9(-4) & -4(5)+-9(-2) \\ 1(3)+1(-4) & 1(5)+1(-2) \\ 8(3)+-2(-4) & 8(5)+-2(-2) \end{bmatrix} = \begin{bmatrix} 24 & -2 \\ -1 & 3 \\ 32 & 44 \end{bmatrix}$

(f) $BACD = BA \times CD = \begin{bmatrix} 24 & -2 \\ -1 & 3 \\ 32 & 44 \end{bmatrix} \times \begin{bmatrix} -9 \\ -21 \end{bmatrix} = \begin{bmatrix} 24(-9)+-2(-21) \\ -1(-9)+3(-21) \\ 32(-9)+44(-21) \end{bmatrix} = \begin{bmatrix} -174 \\ -54 \\ -1212 \end{bmatrix}$

Recall that for matrix multiplication the order of terms matters, but not the grouping. That means $BACD = BA \times CD = B(A(CD)) = (BAC)D$ or any grouping that maintains the order will give the same result.

95

P3. Begin by setting up the augmented matrix: $\begin{bmatrix} 4 & 6 & 5 & 1 \\ -2 & -5 & -1 & 0 \\ 1 & -3 & 5 & 1 \end{bmatrix}$

Using elementary row operations, there are many ways to arrive at the answer. Here is one way (note that the row operations refer to the values in the row from the previous matrix):

$$\begin{matrix} 2R_2 \rightarrow R_2 = \\ -4R_3 \rightarrow R_3 \end{matrix} \begin{bmatrix} 4 & 6 & 5 & 1 \\ -4 & -10 & -2 & 0 \\ -4 & 12 & -20 & -4 \end{bmatrix}, \qquad \begin{matrix} R_2 + R_1 \rightarrow R_2 = \\ R_3 + R_1 \rightarrow R_3 \end{matrix} \begin{bmatrix} 4 & 6 & 5 & 1 \\ 0 & -4 & 3 & 1 \\ 0 & 18 & -15 & -3 \end{bmatrix}$$

$$\begin{matrix} = \\ 4.5R_2 + R_3 \rightarrow R_3 \end{matrix} \begin{bmatrix} 4 & 6 & 5 & 1 \\ 0 & -4 & 3 & 1 \\ 0 & 0 & -1.5 & 1.5 \end{bmatrix}, \qquad \begin{matrix} 2R_3 + R_2 \rightarrow R_2 = \\ R_3/(-1.5) \rightarrow R_3 \end{matrix} \begin{bmatrix} 4 & 6 & 5 & 1 \\ 0 & -4 & 0 & 4 \\ 0 & 0 & 1 & -1 \end{bmatrix}$$

$$\begin{matrix} 1.5R_2 + 5R_3 + R_1 \rightarrow R_1 \\ R_2/(-4) \rightarrow R_2 = \end{matrix} \begin{bmatrix} 4 & 0 & 0 & 12 \\ 0 & 1 & 0 & -1 \\ 0 & 0 & 1 & -1 \end{bmatrix}, \qquad \begin{matrix} R_1/(4) \rightarrow R_1 \\ = \end{matrix} \begin{bmatrix} 1 & 0 & 0 & 3 \\ 0 & 1 & 0 & -1 \\ 0 & 0 & 1 & -1 \end{bmatrix}$$

This reduced row echelon form indicates that the values that satisfy the original system of equations are $x = 3, y = -1,$ and $z = -1$.

Measurement

PRECISION, ACCURACY, AND ERROR

Precision: How reliable and repeatable a measurement is. The more consistent the data is with repeated testing, the more precise it is. For example, hitting a target consistently in the same spot, which may or may not be the center of the target, is precision.

Accuracy: How close the data is to the correct data. For example, hitting a target consistently in the center area of the target, whether or not the hits are all in the same spot, is accuracy.

Note: it is possible for data to be precise without being accurate. If a scale is off balance, the data will be precise, but will not be accurate. For data to have precision and accuracy, it must be repeatable and correct.

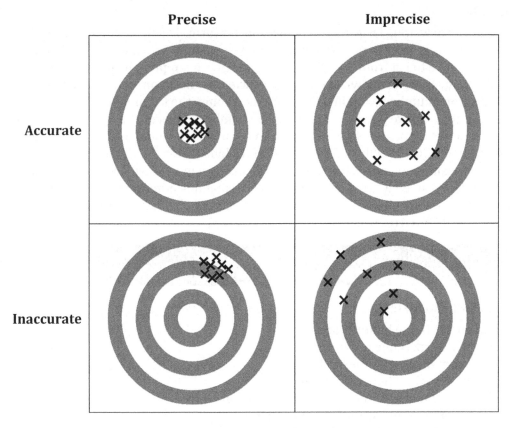

Approximate error: The amount of error in a physical measurement. Approximate error is often reported as the measurement, followed by the ± symbol and the amount of the approximate error.

Maximum possible error: Half the magnitude of the smallest unit used in the measurement. For example, if the unit of measurement is 1 centimeter, the maximum possible error is $\frac{1}{2}$ cm, written as ± 0.5 cm following the measurement. It is important to apply significant figures in reporting maximum possible error. Do not make the answer appear more accurate than the least accurate of your measurements.

ROUNDING AND ESTIMATION

Rounding is reducing the digits in a number while still trying to keep the value similar. The result will be less accurate, but will be in a simpler form, and will be easier to use. Whole numbers can be rounded to the nearest ten, hundred or thousand.

When you are asked to estimate the solution to a problem, you will need to provide only an approximate figure or **estimation** for your answer. In this situation, you will need to round each number in the calculation to the level indicated (nearest hundred, nearest thousand, etc.) or to a level that makes sense for the numbers involved. When estimating a sum **all numbers must be rounded to the same level**. You cannot round one number to the nearest thousand while rounding another to the nearest hundred.

> **Review Video: Rounding and Estimation**
> Visit mometrix.com/academy and enter code: 126243

SCIENTIFIC NOTATION

Scientific notation is a way of writing large numbers in a shorter form. The form $a \times 10^n$ is used in scientific notation, where a is greater than or equal to 1, but less than 10, and n is the number of places the decimal must move to get from the original number to a. Example: The number 230,400,000 is cumbersome to write. To write the value in scientific notation, place a decimal point between the first and second numbers, and include all digits through the last non-zero digit ($a = 2.304$). To find the appropriate power of 10, count the number of places the decimal point had to move ($n = 8$). The number is positive if the decimal moved to the left, and negative if it moved to the right. We can then write 230,400,000 as 2.304×10^8. If we look instead at the number 0.00002304, we have the same value for a, but this time the decimal moved 5 places to the right ($n = -5$). Thus, 0.00002304 can be written as 2.304×10^{-5}. Using this notation makes it simple to compare very large or very small numbers. By comparing exponents, it is easy to see that 3.28×10^4 is smaller than 1.51×10^5, because 4 is less than 5.

> **Review Video: Scientific Notation**
> Visit mometrix.com/academy and enter code: 976454

METRIC MEASUREMENT PREFIXES

Giga-: one billion (1 *giga*watt is one billion watts)
Mega-: one million (1 *mega*hertz is one million hertz)
Kilo-: one thousand (1 *kilo*gram is one thousand grams)
Deci-: one tenth (1 *deci*meter is one tenth of a meter)
Centi-: one hundredth (1 *centi*meter is one hundredth of a meter)
Milli-: one thousandth (1 *milli*liter is one thousandth of a liter)
Micro-: one millionth (1 *micro*gram is one millionth of a gram)

MEASUREMENT CONVERSION

When converting between units, the goal is to maintain the same meaning but change the way it is displayed. In order to go from a larger unit to a smaller unit, multiply the number of the known amount by the equivalent amount. When going from a smaller unit to a larger unit, divide the number of the known amount by the equivalent amount.

For complicated conversions, it may be helpful to set up conversion fractions. In these fractions, one fraction is the **conversion factor**. The other fraction has the unknown amount in the numerator.

So, the known value is placed in the denominator. Sometimes the second fraction has the known value from the problem in the numerator, and the unknown in the denominator. Multiply the two fractions to get the converted measurement. Note that since the numerator and the denominator of the factor are equivalent, the value of the fraction is 1. That is why we can say that the result in the new units is equal to the result in the old units even though they have different numbers.

It can often be necessary to chain known conversion factors together. As an example, consider converting 512 square inches to square meters. We know that there are 2.54 centimeters in an inch, 100 centimeters in a meter, and that squaring each of these factors is necessary to maintain equality.

$$\frac{512 \text{ in}^2}{1} \times \left(\frac{2.54 \text{ cm}}{1 \text{ in}}\right)^2 \times \left(\frac{1 \text{ m}}{100 \text{ cm}}\right)^2 = \frac{512 \text{ in}^2}{1} \times \left(\frac{6.4516 \text{ cm}^2}{1 \text{ in}^2}\right) \times \left(\frac{1 \text{ m}^2}{10000 \text{ cm}^2}\right) = 0.330 \text{ m}^2$$

COMMON UNITS AND EQUIVALENTS

METRIC EQUIVALENTS

1000 µg (microgram)	1 mg
1000 mg (milligram)	1 g
1000 g (gram)	1 kg
1000 kg (kilogram)	1 metric ton
1000 mL (milliliter)	1 L
1000 µm (micrometer)	1 mm
1000 mm (millimeter)	1 m
100 cm (centimeter)	1 m
1000 m (meter)	1 km

DISTANCE AND AREA MEASUREMENT

Unit	Abbreviation	U.S. equivalent	Metric equivalent
Inch	in	1 inch	2.54 centimeters
Foot	ft	12 inches	0.305 meters
Yard	yd	3 feet	0.914 meters
Mile	mi	5280 feet	1.609 kilometers
Acre	ac	4840 square yards	0.405 hectares
Square Mile	mi^2	640 acres	2.590 square kilometers

CAPACITY MEASUREMENTS

Unit	Abbreviation	U.S. equivalent	Metric equivalent
Fluid Ounce	fl oz	8 fluid drams	29.573 milliliters
Cup	cp	8 fluid ounces	0.237 liter
Pint	pt	16 fluid ounces	0.473 liter
Quart	qt	2 pints	0.946 liter
Gallon	gal	4 quarts	3.785 liters
Teaspoon	t or tsp	1 fluid dram	5 milliliters
Tablespoon	T or tbsp	4 fluid drams	15 or 16 milliliters
Cubic Centimeter	cc or cm^3	0.271 drams	1 milliliter

WEIGHT MEASUREMENTS

Unit	Abbreviation	U.S. equivalent	Metric equivalent
Ounce	oz	16 drams	28.35 grams
Pound	lb	16 ounces	453.6 grams
Ton	t	2,000 pounds	907.2 kilograms

VOLUME AND WEIGHT MEASUREMENT CLARIFICATIONS

Always be careful when using ounces and fluid ounces. They are not equivalent.

$$1 \text{ pint} = 16 \text{ fluid ounces} \qquad 1 \text{ fluid ounce} \neq 1 \text{ ounce}$$
$$1 \text{ pound} = 16 \text{ ounces} \qquad\qquad 1 \text{ pint} \neq 1 \text{ pound}$$

Having one pint of something does not mean you have one pound of it. In the same way, just because something weighs one pound does not mean that its volume is one pint.

In the United States, the word "ton" by itself refers to a short ton or a net ton. Do not confuse this with a long ton (also called a gross ton) or a metric ton (also spelled *tonne*), which have different measurement equivalents.

$$1 \text{ U.S. ton} = 2000 \text{ pounds} \qquad \neq \qquad 1 \text{ metric ton} = 1000 \text{ kilograms}$$

Practice

P1. Round each number to the indicated degree:

 (a) Round to the nearest ten: 11; 47; 118

 (b) Round to the nearest hundred: 78; 980; 248

 (c) Round each number to the nearest thousand: 302; 1274; 3756

P2. Estimate the solution to 345,932 + 96,369 by rounding each number to the nearest ten thousand.

P3. A runner's heart beats 422 times over the course of six minutes. About how many times did the runner's heart beat during each minute?

P4. Perform the following conversions:

 (a) 1.4 meters to centimeters

 (b) 218 centimeters to meters

 (c) 42 inches to feet

 (d) 15 kilograms to pounds

 (e) 80 ounces to pounds

 (f) 2 miles to kilometers

 (g) 5 feet to centimeters

 (h) 15.14 liters to gallons

 (i) 8 quarts to liters

 (j) 13.2 pounds to grams

Mometrix

Practice Solutions

P1. (a) When rounding to the nearest ten, anything ending in 5 or greater rounds up. So, 11 rounds to 10, 47 rounds to 50, and 118 rounds to 120.

(b) When rounding to the nearest hundred, anything ending in 50 or greater rounds up. So, 78 rounds to 100, 980 rounds to 1000, and 248 rounds to 200.

(c) When rounding to the nearest thousand, anything ending in 500 or greater rounds up. So, 302 rounds to 0, 1274 rounds to 1000, and 3756 rounds to 4000.

P2. Start by rounding each number to the nearest ten thousand: 345,932 becomes 350,000, and 96,369 becomes 100,000. Then, add the rounded numbers: $350,000 + 100,000 = 450,000$. So, the answer is approximately 450,000. The exact answer would be $345,932 + 96,369 = 442,301$. So, the estimate of 450,000 is a similar value to the exact answer.

P3. "About how many" indicates that you need to estimate the solution. In this case, look at the numbers you are given. 422 can be rounded down to 420, which is easily divisible by 6. A good estimate is $420 \div 6 = 70$ beats per minute. More accurately, the patient's heart rate was just over 70 beats per minute since his heart actually beat a little more than 420 times in six minutes.

P4. (a) $\frac{100 \text{ cm}}{1 \text{ m}} = \frac{x \text{ cm}}{1.4 \text{ m}}$ Cross multiply to get $x = 140$

(b) $\frac{100 \text{ cm}}{1 \text{ m}} = \frac{218 \text{ cm}}{x \text{ m}}$ Cross multiply to get $100x = 218$, or $x = 2.18$

(c) $\frac{12 \text{ in}}{1 \text{ ft}} = \frac{42 \text{ in}}{x \text{ ft}}$ Cross multiply to get $12x = 42$, or $x = 3.5$

(d) 15 kilograms $\times \frac{2.2 \text{ pounds}}{1 \text{ kilogram}} = 33$ pounds

(e) 80 ounces $\times \frac{1 \text{ pound}}{16 \text{ ounces}} = 5$ pounds

(f) 2 miles $\times \frac{1.609 \text{ kilometers}}{1 \text{ mile}} = 3.218$ kilometers

(g) 5 feet $\times \frac{12 \text{ inches}}{1 \text{ foot}} \times \frac{2.54 \text{ centimeters}}{1 \text{ inch}} = 152.4$ centimeters

(h) 15.14 liters $\times \frac{1 \text{ gallon}}{3.785 \text{ liters}} = 4$ gallons

(i) 8 quarts $\times \frac{1 \text{ gallon}}{4 \text{ quarts}} \times \frac{3.785 \text{ liters}}{1 \text{ gallon}} = 7.57$ liters

(j) 13.2 pounds $\times \frac{1 \text{ kilogram}}{2.2 \text{ pounds}} \times \frac{1000 \text{ grams}}{1 \text{ kilogram}} = 6000$ grams

Geometry

LINES AND PLANES

A **point** is a fixed location in space; has no size or dimensions; commonly represented by a dot. A **line** is a set of points that extends infinitely in two opposite directions. It has length, but no width or depth. A line can be defined by any two distinct points that it contains. A **line segment** is a portion of a line that has definite endpoints. A **ray** is a portion of a line that extends from a single point on that line in one direction along the line. It has a definite beginning, but no ending.

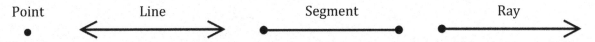

Intersecting lines are lines that have exactly one point in common. **Concurrent lines** are multiple lines that intersect at a single point. **Perpendicular lines** are lines that intersect at right angles. They are represented by the symbol \perp. The shortest distance from a line to a point not on the line is a perpendicular segment from the point to the line. **Parallel lines** are lines in the same plane that have no points in common and never meet. It is possible for lines to be in different planes, have no points in common, and never meet, but they are not parallel because they are in different planes.

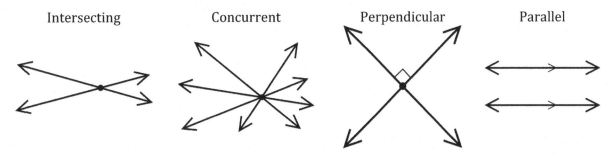

A **transversal** is a line that intersects at least two other lines, which may or may not be parallel to one another. A transversal that intersects parallel lines is a common occurrence in geometry. A **bisector** is a line or line segment that divides another line segment into two equal lengths. A **perpendicular bisector** of a line segment is composed of points that are equidistant from the endpoints of the segment it is dividing.

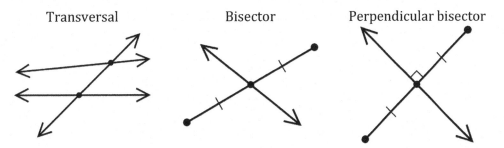

The **projection of a point on a line** is the point at which a perpendicular line drawn from the given point to the given line intersects the line. This is also the shortest distance from the given point to the line. The **projection of a segment on a line** is a segment whose endpoints are the points

formed when perpendicular lines are drawn from the endpoints of the given segment to the given line. This is similar to the length a diagonal line appears to be when viewed from above.

Projection of a point on a line Projection of a segment on a line

A **plane** is a two-dimensional flat surface defined by three non-collinear points. A plane extends an infinite distance in all directions in those two dimensions. It contains an infinite number of points, parallel lines and segments, intersecting lines and segments, as well as parallel or intersecting rays. A plane will never contain a three-dimensional figure or skew lines, lines that don't intersect and are not parallel. Two given planes are either parallel or they intersect at a line. A plane may intersect a circular conic surface to form **conic sections**, such as a parabola, hyperbola, circle or ellipse.

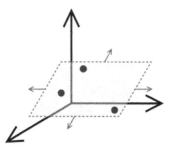

ANGLES

An **angle** is formed when two lines or line segments meet at a common point. It may be a common starting point for a pair of segments or rays, or it may be the intersection of lines. Angles are represented by the symbol ∠.

The **vertex** is the point at which two segments or rays meet to form an angle. If the angle is formed by intersecting rays, lines, and/or line segments, the vertex is the point at which four angles are formed. The pairs of angles opposite one another are called vertical angles, and their measures are equal.

- An **acute** angle is an angle with a degree measure less than 90°.
- A **right** angle is an angle with a degree measure of exactly 90°.
- An **obtuse** angle is an angle with a degree measure greater than 90° but less than 180°.
- A **straight angle** is an angle with a degree measure of exactly 180°. This is also a semicircle.
- A **reflex angle** is an angle with a degree measure greater than 180° but less than 360°.
- A **full angle** is an angle with a degree measure of exactly 360°.

> **Review Video: Geometric Symbols: Angles**
> Visit mometrix.com/academy and enter code: 452738

Two angles whose sum is exactly 90° are said to be **complementary**. The two angles may or may not be adjacent. In a right triangle, the two acute angles are complementary.

Two angles whose sum is exactly 180° are said to be **supplementary**. The two angles may or may not be adjacent. Two intersecting lines always form two pairs of supplementary angles. Adjacent supplementary angles will always form a straight line.

Two angles that have the same vertex and share a side are said to be **adjacent**. Vertical angles are not adjacent because they share a vertex but no common side.

Adjacent
Share vertex and side

Not adjacent
Share part of side, but not vertex

When two parallel lines are cut by a transversal, the angles that are between the two parallel lines are **interior angles**. In the diagram below, angles 3, 4, 5, and 6 are interior angles.

When two parallel lines are cut by a transversal, the angles that are outside the parallel lines are **exterior angles**. In the diagram below, angles 1, 2, 7, and 8 are exterior angles.

When two parallel lines are cut by a transversal, the angles that are in the same position relative to the transversal and a parallel line are **corresponding angles**. The diagram below has four pairs of corresponding angles: angles 1 and 5; angles 2 and 6; angles 3 and 7; and angles 4 and 8. Corresponding angles formed by parallel lines are congruent.

When two parallel lines are cut by a transversal, the two interior angles that are on opposite sides of the transversal are called **alternate interior angles**. In the diagram below, there are two pairs of alternate interior angles: angles 3 and 6, and angles 4 and 5. Alternate interior angles formed by parallel lines are congruent.

When two parallel lines are cut by a transversal, the two exterior angles that are on opposite sides of the transversal are called **alternate exterior angles**.

In the diagram below, there are two pairs of alternate exterior angles: angles 1 and 8, and angles 2 and 7. Alternate exterior angles formed by parallel lines are congruent.

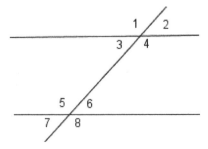

105

When two lines intersect, four angles are formed. The non-adjacent angles at this vertex are called vertical angles. Vertical angles are congruent. In the diagram, $\angle ABD \cong \angle CBE$ and $\angle ABC \cong \angle DBE$.

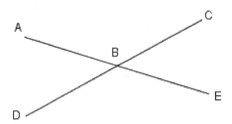

TRANSFORMATIONS

A **rotation** is a transformation that turns a figure around a point called the **center of rotation**, which can lie anywhere in the plane. If a line is drawn from a point on a figure to the center of rotation, and another line is drawn from the center to the rotated image of that point, the angle between the two lines is the **angle of rotation**. The vertex of the angle of rotation is the center of rotation.

A **translation** is a transformation which slides a figure from one position in the plane to another position in the plane. The original figure and the translated figure have the same size, shape, and orientation. A **dilation** is a transformation which proportionally stretches or shrinks a figure by a **scale factor**. The dilated image is the same shape and orientation as the original image but a different size. A polygon and its dilated image are similar.

Translation

Dilation

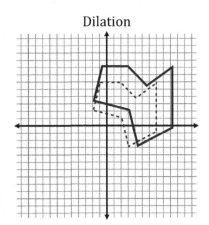

A **reflection of a figure over a line** (a "flip") creates a congruent image that is the same distance from the line as the original figure but on the opposite side. The **line of reflection** is the perpendicular bisector of any line segment drawn from a point on the original figure to its reflected image (unless the point and its reflected image happen to be the same point, which happens when a figure is reflected over one of its own sides). A **reflection of a figure over a point** (an inversion) in two dimensions is the same as the rotation of the figure 180° about that point. The image of the figure is congruent to the original figure. The **point of reflection** is the midpoint of a line segment which connects a point in the figure to its image (unless the point and its reflected image happen to be the same point, which happens when a figure is reflected in one of its own points).

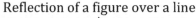

Reflection of a figure over a line

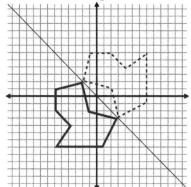

Reflection of a figure over a point

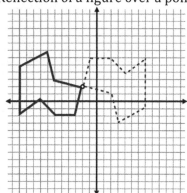

Review Video: Rotation
Visit mometrix.com/academy and enter code: 602600
Review Video: Translation
Visit mometrix.com/academy and enter code: 718628
Review Video: Dilation
Visit mometrix.com/academy and enter code: 471630
Review Video: Reflection
Visit mometrix.com/academy and enter code: 955068

POLYGONS

A **polygon** is a closed, two-dimensional figure with three or more straight line segments called **sides**. The point at which two sides of a polygon intersect is called the **vertex**. In a polygon, the number of sides is always equal to the number of vertices. A polygon with all sides congruent and all angles equal is called a **regular polygon**. Common polygons are:

Triangle = 3 sides
Quadrilateral = 4 sides
Pentagon = 5 sides
Hexagon = 6 sides
Heptagon = 7 sides
Octagon = 8 sides
Nonagon = 9 sides
Decagon = 10 sides
Dodecagon = 12 sides

More generally, an *n*-gon is a polygon that has *n* angles and *n* sides.

The sum of the interior angles of an n-sided polygon is $(n - 2) \times 180°$. For example, in a triangle $n = 3$. So, the sum of the interior angles is $(3 - 2) \times 180° = 180°$. In a quadrilateral, $n = 4$, and the sum of the angles is $(4 - 2) \times 180° = 360°$.

A line segment from the center of a polygon that is perpendicular to a side of the polygon is called the **apothem**. A line segment from the center of a polygon to a vertex of the polygon is called a **radius**. In a regular polygon, the apothem can be used to find the area of the polygon using the formula $A = \frac{1}{2}ap$, where a is the apothem, and p is the perimeter.

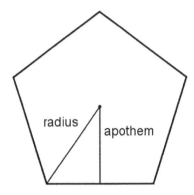

A **diagonal** is a line segment that joins two non-adjacent vertices of a polygon. The number of diagonals a polygon has can be found by using the formula:

$$\text{number of diagonals} = \frac{n(n - 3)}{2}$$

Note that n is the number of sides in the polygon. This formula works for all polygons, not just regular polygons.

A **convex polygon** is a polygon whose diagonals all lie within the interior of the polygon. A **concave polygon** is a polygon with a least one diagonal that is outside the polygon. In the diagram below, quadrilateral $ABCD$ is concave because diagonal \overline{AC} lies outside the polygon and quadrilateral $EFGH$ is convex because both diagonals lie inside the polygon

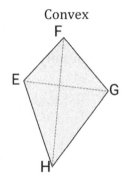

Congruent figures are geometric figures that have the same size and shape. All corresponding angles are equal, and all corresponding sides are equal. It is indicated by the symbol ≅.

Congruent polygons

Similar figures are geometric figures that have the same shape, but do not necessarily have the same size. All corresponding angles are equal, and all corresponding sides are proportional, but they do not have to be equal. It is indicated by the symbol ~.

Similar polygons

Note that all congruent figures are also similar, but not all similar figures are congruent.

Review Video: Polygons, Similarity, and Congruence
Visit mometrix.com/academy and enter code: 686174

Review Video: Polygons
Visit mometrix.com/academy and enter code: 271869

LINE OF SYMMETRY

A line that divides a figure or object into congruent parts is called a **line of symmetry**. An object may have no lines of symmetry, one line of symmetry, or multiple (i.e., more than one) lines of symmetry.

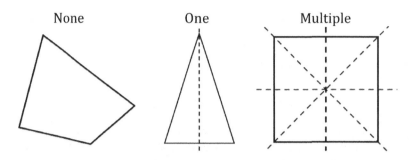

None One Multiple

QUADRILATERALS

A **quadrilateral** is a closed two-dimensional geometric figure that has four straight sides. The sum of the interior angles of any quadrilateral is 360°.

A **kite** is a quadrilateral with two pairs of adjacent sides that are congruent. A result of this is perpendicular diagonals. A kite can be concave or convex and has one line of symmetry.

110

Trapezoid: A trapezoid is defined as a quadrilateral that has at least one pair of parallel sides. There are no rules for the second pair of sides. So, there are no rules for the diagonals and no lines of symmetry for a trapezoid.

The **area of a trapezoid** is found by the formula $A = \frac{1}{2}h(b_1 + b_2)$, where h is the height (segment joining and perpendicular to the parallel bases), and b_1 and b_2 are the two parallel sides (bases). Do not use one of the other two sides as the height unless that side is also perpendicular to the parallel bases.

The **perimeter of a trapezoid** is found by the formula $P = a + b_1 + c + b_2$, where a, b_1, c, and b_2 are the four sides of the trapezoid.

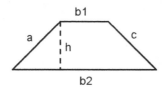

Review Video: Area and Perimeter of a Trapezoid
Visit mometrix.com/academy and enter code: 587523

Parallelogram: A quadrilateral that has two pairs of opposite parallel sides. As such it is a special type of trapezoid. The sides that are parallel are also congruent. The opposite interior angles are always congruent, and the consecutive interior angles are supplementary. The diagonals of a parallelogram divide each other. Each diagonal divides the parallelogram into two congruent triangles. A parallelogram has no line of symmetry, but does have 180-degree rotational symmetry about the midpoint.

The **area of a parallelogram** is found by the formula $A = bh$, where b is the length of the base, and h is the height. Note that the base and height correspond to the length and width in a rectangle, so this formula would apply to rectangles as well. Do not confuse the height of a parallelogram with the length of the second side. The two are only the same measure in the case of a rectangle.

The **perimeter of a parallelogram** is found by the formula $P = 2a + 2b$ or $P = 2(a + b)$, where a and b are the lengths of the two sides.

Review Video: Parallelogram
Visit mometrix.com/academy and enter code: 129981

Isosceles trapezoid: A trapezoid with equal base angles. This gives rise to other properties including: the two nonparallel sides have the same length, the two non-base angles are also equal, and there is one line of symmetry through the midpoints of the parallel sides.

Rectangle: A quadrilateral with four right angles. All rectangles are parallelograms and trapezoids, but not all parallelograms or trapezoids are rectangles. The diagonals of a rectangle are congruent. Rectangles have 2 lines of symmetry (through each pair of opposing midpoints) and 180-degree rotational symmetry about the midpoint.

The **area of a rectangle** is found by the formula $A = lw$, where A is the area of the rectangle, l is the length (usually considered to be the longer side) and w is the width (usually considered to be the shorter side). The numbers for l and w are interchangeable.

The **perimeter of a rectangle** is found by the formula $P = 2l + 2w$ or $P = 2(l + w)$, where l is the length, and w is the width. It may be easier to add the length and width first and then double the result, as in the second formula.

Rhombus: A quadrilateral with four congruent sides. All rhombuses are parallelograms and kites; thus, they inherit all the properties of both types of quadrilaterals. The diagonals of a rhombus are perpendicular to each other. Rhombi have 2 lines of symmetry (along each of the diagonals) and 180-degree rotational symmetry. The **area of a rhombus** is half the product of the diagonals: $A = \frac{d_1 d_2}{2}$ and the perimeter of a rhombus is: $P = 2\sqrt{(d_1)^2 + (d_2)^2}$

Square: A quadrilateral with four right angles and four congruent sides. Squares satisfy the criteria of all other types of quadrilaterals. The diagonals of a square are congruent and perpendicular to each other. Squares have 4 lines of symmetry (through each pair of opposing midpoints and along each of the diagonals) as well as 90-degree rotational symmetry about the midpoint.

The **area of a square** is found by using the formula $A = s^2$, where s is the length of one side. The **perimeter of a square** is found by using the formula $P = 4s$, where s is the length of one side. Because all four sides are equal in a square, it is faster to multiply the length of one side by 4 than to add the same number four times. You could use the formulas for rectangles and get the same answer.

The hierarchy of quadrilaterals can be shown as follows:

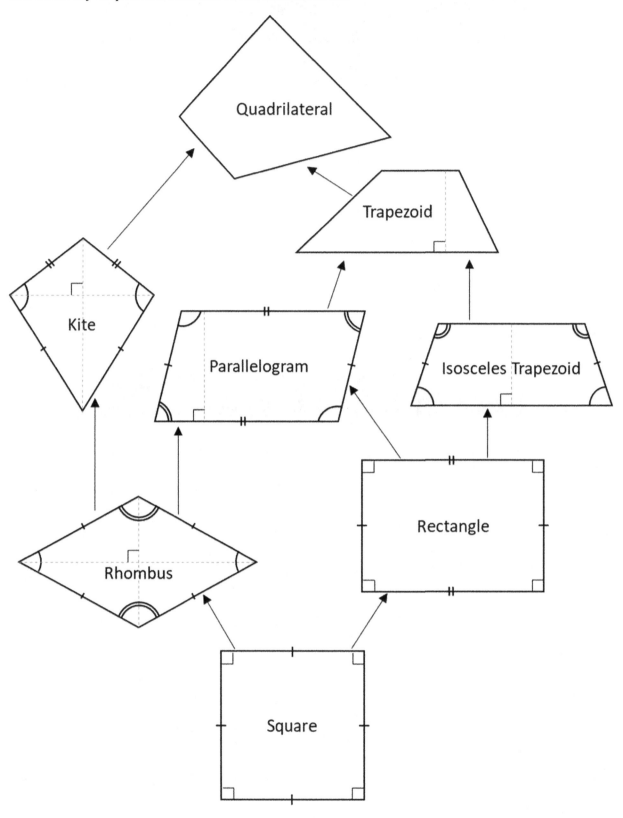

SOLIDS

The **surface area of a solid object** is the area of all sides or exterior surfaces. For objects such as prisms and pyramids, a further distinction is made between base surface area (B) and lateral surface area (LA). For a prism, the total surface area (SA) is $SA = LA + 2B$. For a pyramid or cone, the total surface area is $SA = LA + B$.

The **surface area of a sphere** can be found by the formula $A = 4\pi r^2$, where r is the radius. The volume is given by the formula $V = \frac{4}{3}\pi r^3$, where r is the radius. Both quantities are generally given in terms of π.

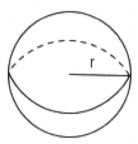

The **volume of any prism** is found by the formula $V = Bh$, where B is the area of the base, and h is the height (perpendicular distance between the bases). The surface area of any prism is the sum of the areas of both bases and all sides. It can be calculated as $SA = 2B + Ph$, where P is the perimeter of the base.

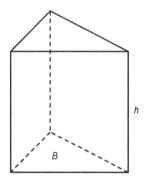

For a **rectangular prism**, the volume can be found by the formula $V = lwh$, where V is the volume, l is the length, w is the width, and h is the height. The surface area can be calculated as $SA = 2lw + 2hl + 2wh$ or $SA = 2(lw + hl + wh)$.

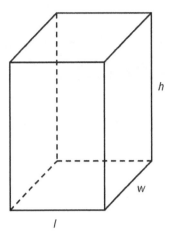

The **volume of a cube** can be found by the formula $V = s^3$, where s is the length of a side. The surface area of a cube is calculated as $SA = 6s^2$, where SA is the total surface area and s is the length of a side. These formulas are the same as the ones used for the volume and surface area of a rectangular prism, but simplified since all three quantities (length, width, and height) are the same.

> **Review Video: <u>Volume and Surface Area of a Cube</u>**
> Visit mometrix.com/academy and enter code: 664455

The **volume of a cylinder** can be calculated by the formula $V = \pi r^2 h$, where r is the radius, and h is the height. The surface area of a cylinder can be found by the formula $SA = 2\pi r^2 + 2\pi rh$. The first term is the base area multiplied by two, and the second term is the perimeter of the base multiplied by the height.

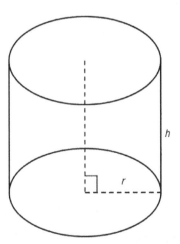

> **Review Video: <u>Volume and Surface Area of a Right Circular Cylinder</u>**
> Visit mometrix.com/academy and enter code: 226463

The **volume of a pyramid** is found by the formula $V = \frac{1}{3}Bh$, where B is the area of the base, and h is the height (perpendicular distance from the vertex to the base). Notice this formula is the same as $\frac{1}{3}$ times the volume of a prism. Like a prism, the base of a pyramid can be any shape.

Finding the **surface area of a pyramid** is not as simple as the other shapes we've looked at thus far. If the pyramid is a right pyramid, meaning the base is a regular polygon and the vertex is directly over the center of that polygon, the surface area can be calculated as $SA = B + \frac{1}{2}Ph_s$, where P is the perimeter of the base, and h_s is the slant height (distance from the vertex to the midpoint of one side of the base). If the pyramid is irregular, the area of each triangle side must be calculated individually and then summed, along with the base.

Review Video: <u>Volume and Surface Area of a Pyramid</u>
Visit mometrix.com/academy and enter code: 621932

The **volume of a cone** is found by the formula $V = \frac{1}{3}\pi r^2 h$, where r is the radius, and h is the height. Notice this is the same as $\frac{1}{3}$ times the volume of a cylinder. The surface area can be calculated as $SA = \pi r^2 + \pi rs$, where s is the slant height. The slant height can be calculated using the pythagorean thereom to be $\sqrt{r^2 + h^2}$, so the surface area formula can also be written as $SA = \pi r^2 + \pi r\sqrt{r^2 + h^2}$.

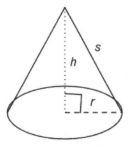

Review Video: <u>Volume and Surface Area of a Right Circular Cone</u>
Visit mometrix.com/academy and enter code: 573574

Practice

P1. Find the measure of angles **(a)**, **(b)**, and **(c)** based on the figure with two parallel lines, two perpendicular lines and one transversal:

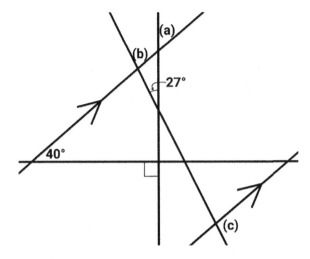

P2. Use the coordinate plane to reflect the figure below across the y-axis.

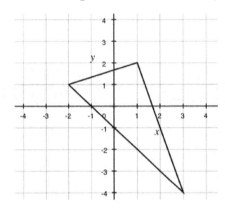

P3. Use the coordinate plane to enlarge the figure below by a factor of 2.

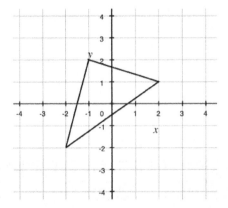

P4. Find the area and perimeter of the following quadrilaterals:

 (a) A square with side length 2.5 cm.

 (b) A parallelogram with height 3 m, base 4 m, and other side 6 m.

 (c) A rhombus with diagonals 15 in and 20 in.

P5. Find the surface area and volume of the following solids:

 (a) A cylinder with radius 5 m and height 0.5 m.

 (b) A trapezoidal prism with base area of 254 mm², base perimeter 74 mm, and height 10 mm.

 (c) A half sphere (radius 5 yds) on the base of an inverted cone with the same radius and a height of 7 yds.

Practice Solutions

P1. (a) The vertical angle paired with (a) is part of a right triangle with the 40° angle. Thus the measure can be found:

$$90° = 40° + a$$
$$a = 50°$$

(b) The triangle formed by the supplementary angle to (b) is part of a triangle with the vertical angle paired with (a) and the given angle of 27°. Since $a = 50°$:

$$180° = (180° - b) + 50° + 27°$$
$$103° = 180° - b$$
$$-77° = -b$$
$$77° = b$$

(c) As they are part of a transversal crossing parallel lines, angles (b) and (c) are supplementary. Thus $c = 103°$

P2. To reflect the image across the y-axis, replace each x-coordinate of the points that are the vertex of the triangle, x, with its negative, $-x$.

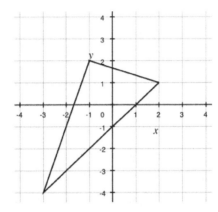

P3. An enlargement can be found by multiplying each coordinate of the coordinate pairs located at the triangle's vertices by 2. The original coordinates were $(-1, 2), (2, 1), (-2, -2)$, so the new coordinates are $(-2, 4), (4, 2), (-4, -4)$:

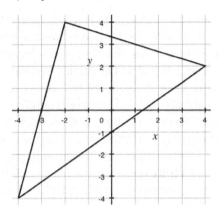

P4. (a) $A = s^2 = (2.5 \text{ cm})^2 = 6.25 \text{ cm}^2; P = 4s = 4 \times 2.5 \text{ cm} = 10 \text{ cm}$

(b) $A = bh = (3 \text{ m})(4 \text{ m}) = 12 \text{ m}^2; P = 2a + 2b = 2 \times 6 \text{ m} + 2 \times 4 \text{ m} = 20 \text{ m}$

(c) $A = \frac{d_1 d_2}{2} = \frac{(15 \text{ in})(20 \text{ in})}{2} = 150 \text{ in}^2;$
$P = 2\sqrt{(d_1)^2 + (d_2)^2} = 2\sqrt{(15 \text{ in})^2 + (20 \text{ in})^2} = 2\sqrt{625 \text{ in}^2} = 50 \text{ in}$

P5. (a) $SA = 2\pi r^2 + 2\pi rh = 2\pi(5 \text{ m})^2 + 2\pi(5 \text{ m})(0.5 \text{ m}) = 55\pi \text{ m}^2 \cong 172.79 \text{ m}^2;$
$V = \pi r^2 h = \pi(5 \text{ m})^2(0.5 \text{ m}) = 12.5\pi \text{ m}^3 \cong 39.27 \text{ m}^3$

(b) $SA = 2B + Ph = 2(254 \text{ mm}^2) + (74 \text{ mm})(10 \text{ mm}) = 1248 \text{ mm}^2;$
$V = Bh = (254 \text{ mm}^2)(10 \text{ mm}) = 2540 \text{ mm}^3$

(c) We can find s, the slant height using Pythagoras' theorem, and since this solid is made of parts of simple solids, we can combine the formulas to find surface area and volume:
$$s = \sqrt{r^2 + h^2} = \sqrt{(5 \text{ yd})^2 + (7 \text{ yd})^2} = \sqrt{74} \text{ yd}$$
$$SA = \frac{4\pi r^2}{2} + \pi rs = \frac{4\pi(5 \text{ yd})^2}{2} + \pi(5 \text{ yd})(\sqrt{74} \text{ yd}) = \left(5\pi + 5\pi\sqrt{74}\right) \text{ yd}^2 \cong 150.83 \text{ yd}^2$$
$$V = \frac{1}{3}\pi r^2 h = \frac{1}{3}\pi(5 \text{ yd})^2(7 \text{ yd}) = \frac{35\pi}{3} \text{ yd}^3 \cong 36.65 \text{ yd}^3$$

Triangles

A **scalene triangle** is a triangle with no congruent sides. A scalene triangle will also have three angles of different measures. The angle with the largest measure is opposite the longest side, and the angle with the smallest measure is opposite the shortest side. An **acute triangle** is a triangle whose three angles are all less than 90°. If two of the angles are equal, the acute triangle is also an **isosceles triangle**. An isosceles triangle will also have two congruent angles opposite the two congruent sides.If the three angles are all equal, the acute triangle is also an **equilateral triangle**. An equilateral triangle will also have three congruent angles, each 60°. All equilateral triangles are also acute triangles. An **obtuse triangle** is a triangle with exactly one angle greater than 90°. The other two angles may or may not be equal. If the two remaining angles are equal, the obtuse triangle is also an isosceles triangle. A **right triangle** is a triangle with exactly one angle equal to 90°. All right triangles follow the Pythagorean theorem. A right triangle can never be acute or obtuse.

The table below illustrates how each descriptor places a different restriction on the triangle:

Angles / Sides	Acute: All angles < 90°	Obtuse: One angle > 90°	Right: One angle = 90°
Scalene: No equal side lengths	$90° > \angle a > \angle b > \angle c$ $x > y > z$	$\angle a > 90° > \angle b > \angle c$ $x > y > z$	$90° = \angle a > \angle b > \angle c$ $x > y > z$
Isosceles: Two equal side lengths	$90° > \angle a, \angle b, or \angle c$ $\angle b = \angle c, \quad y = z$	$\angle a > 90° > \angle b = \angle c$ $x > y = z$	$\angle a = 90°, \angle b = \angle c = 45°$ $x > y = z$
Equilateral: Three equal side lengths	$60° = \angle a = \angle b = \angle c$ $x = y = z$		

PARTS OF A TRIANGLE

An **altitude** of a triangle is a line segment drawn from one vertex perpendicular to the opposite side. In the diagram below, \overline{BE}, \overline{AD}, and \overline{CF} are altitudes. The length of an altitude is also called the height of the triangle. The three altitudes in a triangle are always concurrent. The point of concurrency of the altitudes of a triangle, O, is called the **orthocenter**. Note that in an obtuse triangle, the orthocenter will be outside the triangle, and in a right triangle, the orthocenter is the vertex of the right angle.

A **median** of a triangle is a line segment drawn from one vertex to the midpoint of the opposite side. In the diagram below, \overline{BH}, \overline{AG}, and \overline{CI} are medians. This is not the same as the altitude, except the altitude to the base of an isosceles triangle and all three altitudes of an equilateral triangle. The point of concurrency of the medians of a triangle, T, is called the **centroid**. This is the same point as the orthocenter only in an equilateral triangle. Unlike the orthocenter, the centroid is always inside the triangle. The centroid can also be considered the exact center of the triangle. Any shape triangle can be perfectly balanced on a tip placed at the centroid. The centroid is also the point that is two-thirds the distance from the vertex to the opposite side.

 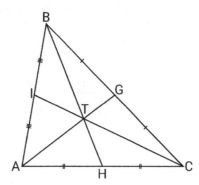

AREA AND PERIMETER OF A TRIANGLE

The **perimeter of any triangle** is found by summing the three side lengths; $P = a + b + c$. For an equilateral triangle, this is the same as $P = 3a$, where a is any side length, since all three sides are the same length.

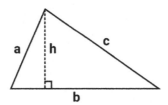

The **area of any triangle** can be found by taking half the product of one side length referred to as the base often given the variable b and the perpendicular distance from that side to the opposite vertex called the altitude or height and given the variable h. In equation form that is $A = \frac{1}{2}bh$.

Another formula that works for any triangle is $A = \sqrt{s(s-a)(s-b)(s-c)}$, where s is the semiperimeter: $\frac{a+b+c}{2}$, and a, b, and c are the lengths of the three sides. Special cases include

isosceles triangles: $A = \frac{1}{2}b\sqrt{a^2 - \frac{b^2}{4}}$, where b is the unique side and a is the length of one of the two

congruent sides, and equilateral triangles: $A = \frac{\sqrt{3}}{4}a^2$, where a is the length of a side.

SIMILARITY AND CONGRUENCE RULES

Similar triangles are triangles whose corresponding angles are equal and whose corresponding sides are proportional. Represented by AAA. Similar triangles whose corresponding sides are congruent are also congruent triangles.

The triangles can be shown to be **congruent** in 5 ways:

- **SSS**: Three sides of one triangle are congruent to the three corresponding sides of the second triangle.
- **SAS**: Two sides and the included angle (the angle formed by those two sides) of one triangle are congruent to the corresponding two sides and included angle of the second triangle.
- **ASA**: Two angles and the included side (the side that joins the two angles) of one triangle are congruent to the corresponding two angles and included side of the second triangle.
- **AAS**: Two angles and a non-included side of one triangle are congruent to the corresponding two angles and non-included side of the second triangle.
- **HL**: The hypotenuse and leg of one right triangle are congruent to the corresponding hypotenuse and leg of the second right triangle.

GENERAL RULES FOR TRIANGLES

The **triangle inequality theorem** states that the sum of the measures of any two sides of a triangle is always greater than the measure of the third side. If the sum of the measures of two sides were equal to the third side, a triangle would be impossible because the two sides would lie flat across the third side and there would be no vertex. If the sum of the measures of two of the sides was less than the third side, a closed figure would be impossible because the two shortest sides would never meet. In other words, for a triangle with sides lengths A, B, and C: $A + B > C$, $B + C > A$, and $A + C > B$

The sum of the measures of the interior angles of a triangle is always 180°. Therefore, a triangle can never have more than one angle greater than or equal to 90°.

In any triangle, the angles opposite congruent sides are congruent, and the sides opposite congruent angles are congruent. The largest angle is always opposite the longest side, and the smallest angle is always opposite the shortest side.

The line segment that joins the midpoints of any two sides of a triangle is always parallel to the third side and exactly half the length of the third side.

PYTHAGOREAN THEOREM

The side of a triangle opposite the right angle is called the **hypotenuse**. The other two sides are called the legs. The Pythagorean theorem states a relationship among the legs and hypotenuse of a

right triangle: $a^2 + b^2 = c^2$, where a and b are the lengths of the legs of a right triangle, and c is the length of the hypotenuse. Note that this formula will only work with right triangles.

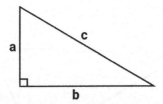

TRIGONOMETRIC FORMULAS

In the diagram below, angle C is the right angle, and side c is the hypotenuse. Side a is the side opposite to angle A and side b is the side opposite to angle B. Using ratios of side lengths as a means to calculate the sine, cosine, and tangent of an acute angle only works for right triangles.

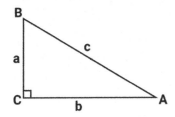

$$\sin A = \frac{\text{opposite side}}{\text{hypotenuse}} = \frac{a}{c} \qquad \csc A = \frac{1}{\sin A} = \frac{\text{hypotenuse}}{\text{opposite side}} = \frac{c}{a}$$

$$\cos A = \frac{\text{adjacent side}}{\text{hypotenuse}} = \frac{b}{c} \qquad \sec A = \frac{1}{\cos A} = \frac{\text{hypotenuse}}{\text{adjacent side}} = \frac{c}{b}$$

$$\tan A = \frac{\text{opposite side}}{\text{adjacent side}} = \frac{a}{b} \qquad \cot A = \frac{1}{\tan A} = \frac{\text{adjacent side}}{\text{opposite side}} = \frac{b}{a}$$

LAWS OF SINES AND COSINES

The **law of sines** states that $\frac{\sin A}{a} = \frac{\sin B}{b} = \frac{\sin C}{c}$, where A, B, and C are the angles of a triangle, and a, b, and c are the sides opposite their respective angles. This formula will work with all triangles, not just right triangles.

The **law of cosines** is given by the formula $c^2 = a^2 + b^2 - 2ab(\cos C)$, where a, b, and c are the sides of a triangle, and C is the angle opposite side c. This is a generalized form of the Pythagorean theorem that can be used on any triangle.

Practice

P1. Given the following pairs of triangles, determine whether they are similar, congruent, or neither (note that the figures are not drawn to scale):

(a).

(b).

(c).

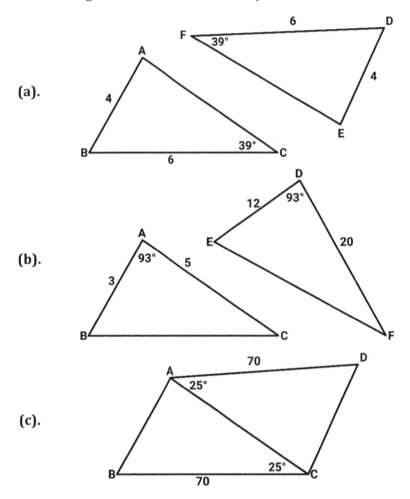

P2. Calculate the area of a triangle with side lengths of 7 ft, 8 ft, and 9 ft.

P3. Calculate the following values based on triangle MNO:

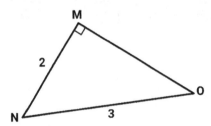

 (a) length of \overline{MO}

 (b) $\sin(\angle NOM)$

 (c) area of the triangle, if the units of the measurements are in miles

Practice Solutions

P1. (a). Neither: We are given that two sides lengths and an angle are equal, however, the angle given is not between the given side lengths. That means there are two possible triangles that could satisfy the given measurements. Thus, we cannot be certain of congruence:

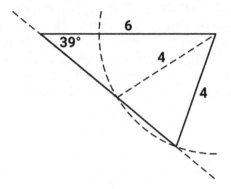

(b) Similar: Since we are given a side-angle-side of each triangle and the side lengths given are scaled evenly $\left(\frac{3}{5} \times \frac{4}{4} = \frac{12}{20}\right)$ and the angles are equal. Thus, $\triangle ABC \sim \triangle DEF$. If the side lengths were equal, then they would be congruent.

(c) Congruent: Even though we aren't given a measurement for the shared side of the figure, since it is shared it is equal. So, this is a case of SAS. Thus, $\triangle ABC \cong \triangle CDA$

P2. Given only side lengths, we can use the semi perimeter to the find the area based on the formula, $A = \sqrt{s(s-a)(s-b)(s-c)}$, where s is the semiperimeter, $\frac{a+b+c}{2} = \frac{7+8+9}{2} = 12$ ft:

$$A = \sqrt{12(12-7)(12-8)(12-9)}$$
$$= \sqrt{(12)(5)(4)(3)}$$
$$= 12\sqrt{5} \text{ ft}^2$$

P3. (a) Since triangle MNO is a right triangle, we can use the simple form of Pythagoras theorem to find the missing side length:

$$\left(\overline{MO}\right)^2 + 2^2 = 3^2$$
$$\left(\overline{MO}\right)^2 = 9 - 4$$
$$\overline{MO} = \sqrt{5}$$

(b) Recall that sine of an angle in a right triangle is the ratio of the opposite side to the hypotenuse. So, $\sin(\angle NOM) = 2/3$

(c) Since triangle MNO is a right triangle, we can use either of the legs as the height and the other as the base in the simple formula for area of a triangle:

$$A = \frac{bh}{2}$$
$$= \frac{(2 \text{ mi})(\sqrt{5} \text{ mi})}{2}$$
$$= \sqrt{5} \text{ mi}^2$$

Circles and Conic Sections

CIRCLES

The **center** of a circle is the single point from which every point on the circle is **equidistant**. The **radius** is a line segment that joins the center of the circle and any one point on the circle. All radii of a circle are equal. Circles that have the same center, but not the same length of radii are **concentric**. The **diameter** is a line segment that passes through the center of the circle and has both endpoints on the circle. The length of the diameter is exactly twice the length of the radius. Point O in the diagram below is the center of the circle, segments \overline{OX}, \overline{OY}, and \overline{OZ} are radii, and segment \overline{XZ} is a diamter.

The **area of a circle** is found by the formula $A = \pi r^2$, where r is the length of the radius. If the diameter of the circle is given, remember to divide it in half to get the length of the radius before proceeding.

The **circumference** of a circle is found by the formula $C = 2\pi r$, where r is the radius. Again, remember to convert the diameter if you are given that measure rather than the radius.

An **arc** is a portion of a circle. Specifically, an arc is the set of points between and including two points on a circle. An arc does not contain any points inside the circle. When a segment is drawn from the endpoints of an arc to the center of the circle, a sector is formed. A **minor arc** is an arc that has a measure less than 180°. A **major arc** is an arc having a measure of at least 180°. Every minor arc has a corresponding major arc that can be found by subtracting the measure of the minor arc from 360°. A **semicircle** is an arc whose endpoints are the endpoints of the diameter of a circle. A semicircle is exactly half of a circle.

A **central angle** is an angle whose vertex is the center of a circle and whose legs intercept an arc of the circle. The measure of a central angle is equal to the measure of the minor arc it intercepts.

An **inscribed angle** is an angle whose vertex lies on a circle and whose legs contain chords of that circle. The portion of the circle intercepted by the legs of the angle is called the intercepted arc. The

128

measure of the intercepted arc is exactly twice the measure of the inscribed angle. In the following diagram, angle ABC is an inscribed angle. $\widehat{AC} = 2(m\angle ABC)$

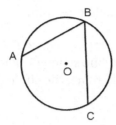

Any angle inscribed in a semicircle is a right angle. The intercepted arc is 180°, making the inscribed angle half that, or 90°. In the diagram below, angle ABC is inscribed in semicircle ABC, making angle ABC equal to 90°.

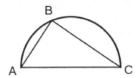

A **secant** is a line that intersects a circle in two points. The segment of a secant line that is contained within the circle is called a **chord**. Two secants may intersect inside the circle, on the circle, or outside the circle. When the two secants intersect on the circle, an inscribed angle is formed. When two secants intersect inside a circle, the measure of each of two vertical angles is equal to half the sum of the two intercepted arcs. Consider the following diagram where $m\angle AEB = \frac{1}{2}(\widehat{AB} + \widehat{CD})$ and $m\angle BEC = \frac{1}{2}(\widehat{BC} + \widehat{AD})$.

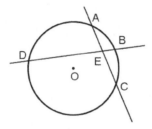

When two secants intersect outside a circle, the measure of the angle formed is equal to half the difference of the two arcs that lie between the two secants. In the diagram below, $m\angle AEB = \frac{1}{2}(\widehat{AB} - \widehat{CD})$.

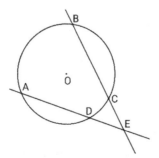

A **tangent** is a line in the same plane as a circle that touches the circle in exactly one point. The point at which a tangent touches a circle is called the **point of tangency**. While a line segment can be tangent to a circle as part of a line that is tangent, it is improper to say a tangent can be simply a line segment that touches the circle in exactly one point.

In the diagram below, \overleftrightarrow{EB} is a secant and contains chord \overline{EB} and \overleftrightarrow{CD} is tangent to circle A. Notice that \overline{FB} is not tangent to the circle. \overline{FB} is a line segment that touches the circle in exactly one point, but if the segment were extended, it would touch the circle in a second point. In the diagram below, point B is the point of tangency.

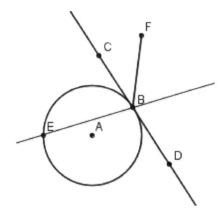

The **arc length** is the length of that portion of the circumference between two points on the circle. The formula for arc length is $s = \frac{\pi r \theta}{180°}$ where s is the arc length, r is the length of the radius, and θ is the angular measure of the arc in degrees, or $s = r\theta$, where θ is the angular measure of the arc in radians (2π radians $= 360$ degrees).

A **sector** is the portion of a circle formed by two radii and their intercepted arc. While the arc length is exclusively the points that are also on the circumference of the circle, the sector is the entire area bounded by the arc and the two radii.

The **area of a sector** of a circle is found by the formula, $A = \frac{\theta r^2}{2}$, where A is the area, θ is the measure of the central angle in radians, and r is the radius. To find the area with the central angle in degrees, use the formula, $A = \frac{\theta \pi r^2}{360}$, where θ is the measure of the central angle and r is the radius.

INSCRIBED AND CIRCUMSCRIBED FIGURES

These terms can be both used to describe a given arrangement of figures, depending on perspective. If each of the vertices of figure A lie on figure B, then it can be said that figure A is **inscribed** in figure B, but it can also be said that figure B is **circumscribed** about figure A. The following table and examples help to illustrate the concept. Note that the figures cannot both be circles, as they would be completely overlapping and neither would be inscribed or circumscribed.

Given	Description	Equivalent Description	Figures
Each of the sides of a pentagon is tangent to a circle	The circle is inscribed in the pentagon	The pentagon is circumscribed about the circle	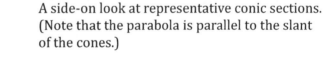
Each of the vertices of a pentagon lie on a circle	The pentagon is inscribed in the circle	The circle is circumscribed about the pentagon	

CONIC SECTIONS

Conic sections are a family of shapes that can be thought of as cross sections of a pair of infinite, right cones stacked vertex to vertex. This is easiest to see with a visual representation:

A three-dimensional look at representative conic sections. (Note that a hyperbola intersects both cones.)

A side-on look at representative conic sections. (Note that the parabola is parallel to the slant of the cones.)

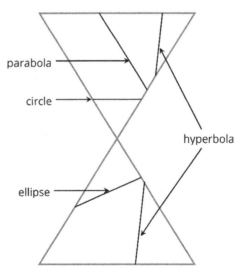

In short, a circle is a horizontal cross section, a parabola is a cross section parallel to the slant of the cone, an ellipse is a cross section at an angle *less than* the slant of the cone, and a hyperbola is a cross section at an angle *greater than* the slant of the cone.

ELLIPSE

An **ellipse** is the set of all points in a plane, whose total distance from two fixed points called the **foci** (singular: focus) is constant, and whose center is the midpoint between the foci.

The standard equation of an ellipse that is taller than it is wide is $\frac{(x-h)^2}{a^2} + \frac{(y-k)^2}{b^2} = 1$, where a and b are coefficients. The center is the point (h, k) and the foci are the points $(h, k + c)$ and $(h, k - c)$, where $c^2 = a^2 - b^2$ and $a^2 > b^2$.

The major axis has length $2a$, and the minor axis has length $2b$.

Eccentricity (e) is a measure of how elongated an ellipse is, and is the ratio of the distance between the foci to the length of the major axis. Eccentricity will have a value between 0 and 1. The closer to 1 the eccentricity is, the closer the ellipse is to being a circle. The formula for eccentricity is $= \frac{c}{a}$.

PARABOLA

A **parabola** is the set of all points in a plane that are equidistant from a fixed line, called the **directrix**, and a fixed point not on the line, called the **focus**. The **axis** is the line perpendicular to the directrix that passes through the focus.

For parabolas that open up or down, the standard equation is $(x - h)^2 = 4c(y - k)$, where h, c, and k are coefficients. If c is positive, the parabola opens up. If c is negative, the parabola opens down. The vertex is the point (h, k). The directrix is the line having the equation $y = -c + k$, and the focus is the point $(h, c + k)$.

For parabolas that open left or right, the standard equation is $(y - k)^2 = 4c(x - h)$, where k, c, and h are coefficients. If c is positive, the parabola opens to the right. If c is negative, the parabola opens to the left. The vertex is the point (h, k). The directrix is the line having the equation $x = -c + h$, and the focus is the point $(c + h, k)$.

HYPERBOLA

A **hyperbola** is the set of all points in a plane, whose distance from two fixed points, called foci, has a constant difference.

The standard equation of a horizontal hyperbola is $\frac{(x-h)^2}{a^2} - \frac{(y-k)^2}{b^2} = 1$, where a, b, h, and k are real numbers. The center is the point (h, k), the vertices are the points $(h + a, k)$ and $(h - a, k)$, and the foci are the points that every point on one of the parabolic curves is equidistant from. The foci are found using the formulas $(h + c, k)$ and $(h - c, k)$, where $c^2 = a^2 + b^2$. The asymptotes are two lines the graph of the hyperbola approaches but never reaches, and are given by the equations $y = \left(\frac{b}{a}\right)(x - h) + k$ and $y = -\left(\frac{b}{a}\right)(x - h) + k$.

The standard equation of a vertical hyperbola is $\frac{(y-k)^2}{a^2} - \frac{(x-h)^2}{b^2} = 1$, where a, b, k, and h are real numbers. The center is the point (h, k), the vertices are the points $(h, k + a)$ and $(h, k - a)$, and the foci are the points that every point on one of the hyperbolic curves is equidistant from and are found using the formulas $(h, k + c)$ and $(h, k - c)$, where $c^2 = a^2 + b^2$. The asymptotes are two lines the graph of the hyperbola approaches but never reach, and are given by the equations $y = \left(\frac{a}{b}\right)(x - h) + k$ and $y = -\left(\frac{a}{b}\right)(x - h) + k$.

Practice

P1. Given that $\angle DEB = 80°$ and $\widehat{BC} = 90°$, determine the following values based on the figure:

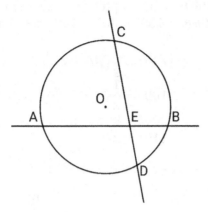

(a) \widehat{AD}

(b) $\widehat{DB} + \widehat{CA}$

P2. Given that $\angle OCB = 50°$, \overleftrightarrow{EF} is tangent to the circle at B, and $\overline{CB} = 6$ km, determine the following values abased on the figure:

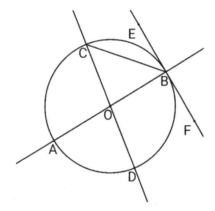

(a) The angle made between \overleftrightarrow{CD} and a line tangent to the circle at A.

(b) The area of the sector of the circle between C and B.

P3. Square ABCD is inscribed in a circle with radius 20 m. What is the area of the part of the circle outside of the square?

Practice Solutions

P1. (a). Recall that when two secants intersect inside of a circle, the measure of each of two vertical angles is equal to half the sum of the two intercepted arcs. Also, since $\angle DEB$ and $\angle CEB$ are supplementary, the measure of $\angle CEB = 180° - 80° = 100°$ In other words:

$$\angle CEB = \frac{1}{2}\left(\widehat{BC} + \widehat{AD}\right)$$
$$100° = \frac{1}{2}\left(90° + \widehat{AD}\right)$$
$$200° = 90° + \widehat{AD}$$
$$110° = \widehat{AD}$$

(b) Note that the whole circle is divided into four arcs. Thus,

$$\widehat{AD} + \widehat{DB} + \widehat{BC} + \widehat{CA} = 360°$$
$$110° + \widehat{DB} + 90° + \widehat{CA} = 360°$$
$$\widehat{DB} + \widehat{CA} = 160°$$

P2. (a) A line tangent to the circle at A creates a right triangle with one vertex at O, one at A, and the final vertex where \overleftrightarrow{CD} intersects the tangent line, let us call that point G.

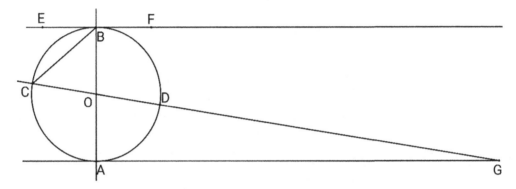

Since AB is a diameter, the line tangent at A is perpendicular to AB, so $\angle OAG = 90°$. The triangle COB has two legs that are the radius of the circle and so must be isosceles. So, $50° \times 2 + \angle COB = 180°$, which means that $\angle COB$ and the vertical angle $\angle GOA$ both equal 80°. Knowing this we can find $\angle AGO$:

$$80° + 90° + \angle AGO = 180°$$
$$\angle AGO = 10°$$

(b) We know $\angle OCB = 50°$ and that triangle COB is isosceles with two legs equal to the radius, so a perpendicular bisector of the triangle as shown will create a right triangle:

Recall that cosine of an angle in a right triangle is the ratio of the adjacent side to the hypotenuse. Thus, we can find r:

$$\cos 50° = \frac{3}{r}$$
$$r = \frac{3}{\cos 50°}$$

As noted in part (a), $\angle COB = 80°$ so, the area of the sector is:

$$A = \frac{\theta \pi r^2}{360°}$$
$$= \frac{80°\pi \left(\frac{3}{\cos 50°}\right)^2}{360°}$$
$$= \frac{2\pi \left(\frac{9}{\cos^2 50°}\right)}{9}$$
$$= \frac{2\pi}{\cos^2 50°} \cong 15.2 \text{ km}^2$$

P3. Begin by drawing a diagram of the situation, where we want to find the shaded area:

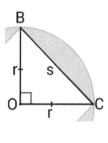

The area of the square is s^2, so the area we want to find is: $\pi r^2 - s^2$. Since the inscribed figure is a square, the triangle BCO is a 45-45-90 right triangle. Now, we can find $s^2 = r^2 + r^2 = 2r^2$. So, the shaded area is:

$$A = \pi r^2 - s^2$$
$$= \pi r^2 - 2r^2$$
$$= (\pi - 2)r^2$$
$$= (\pi - 2) \times 400$$
$$\cong 456.6 \text{ m}^2$$

Trigonometry

DEGREES, RADIANS, AND THE UNIT CIRCLE

It is important to understand the deep connection between trigonometry and circles. Specifically, the two main units, **degrees** (°) and **radians** (rad), that are used to measure angles are related this way: 360° in one full circle and 2π radians in one full circle: $360° = 2\pi$ rad. The conversion factor relating the two is often stated as $\frac{180°}{\pi}$. For example, to convert $\frac{3\pi}{2}$ radians to degrees, multiply by the conversion factor: $\frac{3\pi}{2} \times \frac{180°}{\pi} = 270°$. As another example, to convert 60° to radians, divide by the conversion factor or multiply by the reciprocal: $60° \times \frac{\pi}{180°} = \frac{\pi}{3}$ radians.

Recall that the standard equation for a circle is $(x - h)^2 + (y - k)^2 = r^2$. A **unit circle** is a circle with a radius of 1 ($r = 1$) that has its center at the origin ($h = 0, k = 0$). Thus, the equation for the unit circle simplifies from the standard equation down to $x^2 + y^2 = 1$.

Standard position is the position of an angle of measure θ whose vertex is at the origin, the initial side crosses the unit circle at the point $(1, 0)$, and the terminal side crosses the unit circle at some other point (a, b). In the standard position, $\sin\theta = b$, $\cos\theta = a$, and $\tan\theta = \frac{b}{a}$.

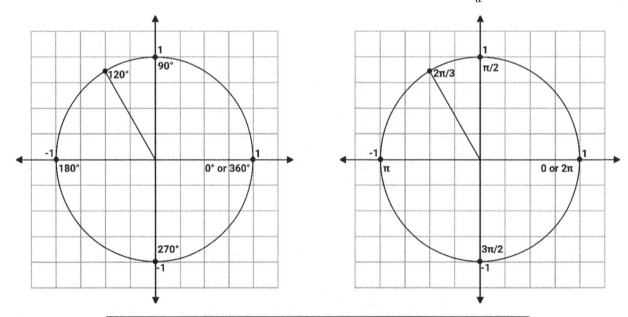

Review Video: Unit Circles and Standard Position
Visit mometrix.com/academy and enter code: 333922

BASIC TRIGONOMETRIC FUNCTIONS

SINE

The **sine** (sin) function has a period of 360° or 2π radians. This means that its graph makes one complete cycle every 360° or 2π. Because $\sin 0 = 0$, the graph of $y = \sin x$ begins at the origin, with the x-axis representing the angle measure, and the y-axis representing the sine of the angle. The graph of the sine function is a smooth curve that begins at the origin, peaks at the point $\left(\frac{\pi}{2}, 1\right)$,

136

crosses the x-axis at $(\pi, 0)$, has its lowest point at $\left(\frac{3\pi}{2}, -1\right)$, and returns to the x-axis to complete one cycle at $(2\pi, 0)$.

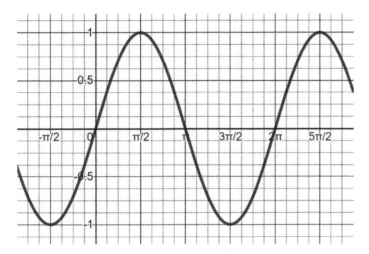

COSINE

The **cosine** (cos) function also has a period of 360° or 2π radians, which means that its graph also makes one complete cycle every 360° or 2π. Because $\cos 0° = 1$, the graph of $y = \cos x$ begins at the point $(0, 1)$, with the x-axis representing the angle measure, and the y-axis representing the cosine of the angle. The graph of the cosine function is a smooth curve that begins at the point $(0, 1)$, crosses the x-axis at the point $\left(\frac{\pi}{2}, 0\right)$, has its lowest point at $(\pi, -1)$, crosses the x-axis again at the point $\left(\frac{3\pi}{2}, 0\right)$, and returns to a peak at the point $(2\pi, 1)$ to complete one cycle.

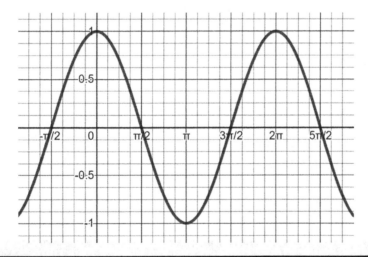

Review Video: Cosine
Visit mometrix.com/academy and enter code: 361120

TANGENT

The **tangent** (tan) function has a period of 180° or π radians, which means that its graph makes one complete cycle every 180° or π radians. The x-axis represents the angle measure, and the y-axis represents the tangent of the angle. The graph of the tangent function is a series of smooth curves that cross the x-axis at every 180° or π radians and have an asymptote every $k \times 90°$ or $\frac{k\pi}{2}$ radians,

where k is an odd integer. This can be explained by the fact that the tangent is calculated by dividing the sine by the cosine, since the cosine equals zero at those asymptote points.

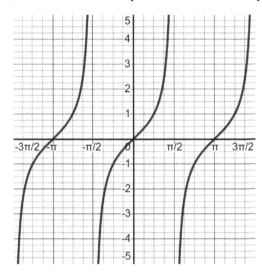

DEFINED AND RECIPROCAL FUNCTIONS

The tangent function is defined as the ratio of the sine to the cosine: $\tan x = \frac{\sin x}{\cos x}$

To take the reciprocal of a number means to place that number as the denominator of a fraction with a numerator of 1. The reciprocal functions are thus defined quite simply.

Cosecant	csc x	$\frac{1}{\sin x}$
Secant	sec x	$\frac{1}{\cos x}$
Cotangent	cot x	$\frac{1}{\tan x}$

It is important to know these reciprocal functions, but they are not as commonly used as the three basic functions.

INVERSE FUNCTIONS

Each of the trigonometric functions accepts an angular measure, either degrees or radians, and gives a numerical value as the output. The inverse functions do the opposite; they accept a numerical value and give an angular measure as the output. The inverse of sine, or arcsine, commonly written as either $\sin^{-1} x$ or $\arcsin x$, gives the angle whose sine is x. Similarly:

The inverse of $\cos x$ is written as $\cos^{-1} x$ or $\arccos x$ and means the angle whose cosine is x.

138

The inverse of tan x is written as $\tan^{-1} x$ or arctan x and means the angle whose tangent is x.
The inverse of csc x is written as $\csc^{-1} x$ or arccsc x and means the angle whose cosecant is x.
The inverse of sec x is written as $\sec^{-1} x$ or arcsec x and means the angle whose secant is x.
The inverse of cot x is written as $\cot^{-1} x$ or arccot x and means the angle whose cotangent is x.

> **Review Video: Inverse of a Cosine**
> Visit mometrix.com/academy and enter code: 156054
>
> **Review Video: Inverse of a Tangent**
> Visit mometrix.com/academy and enter code: 229055

IMPORTANT NOTE ABOUT SOLVING TRIGONOMETRIC EQUATIONS

Trigonometric and algebraic equations are solved following the same rules, but while algebraic expressions have one unique solution, trigonometric equations could have multiple solutions, and you must find them all. When solving for an angle with a known trigonometric value, you must consider the sign and include all angles with that value. Your calculator will probably only give one value as an answer, typically in the following ranges:

- For $\sin^{-1} x$, $\left[-\frac{\pi}{2}, \frac{\pi}{2}\right]$ or $[-90°, 90°]$
- For $\cos^{-1} x$, $[0, \pi]$ or $[0°, 180°]$
- For $\tan^{-1} x$, $\left[-\frac{\pi}{2}, \frac{\pi}{2}\right]$ or $[-90°, 90°]$

It is important to determine if there is another angle in a different quadrant that also satisfies the problem. To do this, find the other quadrant(s) with the same sign for that trigonometric function and find the angle that has the same reference angle. Then check whether this angle is also a solution.

- In the first quadrant, all six trigonometric functions are positive.
- In the second quadrant, sin and csc are positive.
- In the third quadrant, tan and cot are positive.
- In the fourth quadrant, cos and sec are positive.

If you remember the phrase, "ALL Students Take Classes," you will be able to remember the sign of each trigonometric function in each quadrant. ALL represents all the signs in the first quadrant. The "S" in "Students" represents the sine function and its reciprocal in the second quadrant. The "T" in "Take" represents the tangent function and its reciprocal in the third quadrant. The "C" in "Classes" represents the cosine function and its reciprocal.

DOMAIN, RANGE, AND ASYMPTOTES IN TRIGONOMETRY

The domain is the set of all possible real number values of x on the graph of a trigonometric function. Some graphs will impose limits on the values of x.

The range is the set of all possible real number values of y on the graph of a trigonometric function. Some graphs will impose limits on the values of y.

Asymptotes are lines which the graph of a trigonometric function approaches but never reaches. Asymptotes exist for values of x in the graphs of the tangent, cotangent, secant, and cosecant. The sine and cosine graphs do not have any asymptotes.

Mometrix

DOMAIN, RANGE, AND ASYMPTOTES OF THE SIX TRIGONOMETRIC FUNCTIONS

The domain, range, and asymptotes for each of the trigonometric functions are as follows:

- In the **sine** function, the domain is all real numbers, the range is $-1 \leq y \leq 1$, and there are no asymptotes.
- In the **cosine** function, the domain is all real numbers; the range is $-1 \leq y \leq 1$, and there are no asymptotes.
- In the **tangent** function, the domain is $x \in$ all real numbers; $x \neq \frac{\pi}{2} + k\pi$, the range is all real numbers; and the asymptotes are the lines $x = \frac{\pi}{2} + k\pi$.
- In the **cosecant** function, the domain is $x \in$ all real numbers; $x \neq k\pi$, the range is $(-\infty, -1]$ and $[1, \infty)$, and the asymptotes are the lines $x = k\pi$.
- In the **secant** function, the domain is $x \in$ all real numbers; $x \neq \frac{\pi}{2} + k\pi$, the range is $(-\infty, 1]$ and $[1, \infty)$, and the asymptotes are the lines $x = \frac{\pi}{2} + k\pi$.
- In the **cotangent** function, the domain is $x \in$ all real numbers; $x \neq k\pi$, the range is all real numbers, and the asymptotes are the lines $x = k\pi$.

In each of the above cases, k represents any integer.

TRIGONOMETRIC IDENTITIES

SUM AND DIFFERENCE

To find the sine, cosine, or tangent of the sum or difference of two angles, use one of the following formulas where α and β are two angles with known sine, cosine, or tangent values as needed:

$$\sin(\alpha \pm \beta) = \sin \alpha \cos \beta \pm \cos \alpha \sin \beta$$
$$\cos(\alpha \pm \beta) = \cos \alpha \cos \beta \mp \sin \alpha \sin \beta$$
$$\tan(\alpha \pm \beta) = \frac{\tan \alpha \pm \tan \beta}{1 \mp \tan \alpha \tan \beta}$$

HALF ANGLE

To find the sine or cosine of half of a known angle, use the following formulas where θ is an angle with a known exact cosine value:

$$\sin(\theta/2) = \pm\sqrt{(1 - \cos\theta)/2}$$
$$\cos(\theta/2) = \pm\sqrt{(1 + \cos\theta)/2}$$

To determine the sign of the answer, you must recognize which quadrant the given angle is in and apply the correct sign for the trigonometric function you are using. If you need to find an expression for the exact sine or cosine of an angle that you do not know, such as sine 22.5°, you can rewrite the given angle as a half angle, such as $\sin\left(\frac{45°}{2}\right)$, and use the formula above:

$$\sin\left(\frac{45°}{2}\right) = \pm\sqrt{(1 - \cos(45°))/2} = \pm\sqrt{\left(1 - \frac{\sqrt{2}}{2}\right)/2} = \pm\sqrt{(2 - \sqrt{2})/4} = \pm\frac{1}{2}\sqrt{(2 - \sqrt{2})}$$

To find the tangent or cotangent of half of a known angle, use the following formulas where θ is an angle with known exact sine and cosine values:

$$\tan\frac{\theta}{2} = \frac{\sin\theta}{1 + \cos\theta}$$
$$\cot\frac{\theta}{2} = \frac{\sin\theta}{1 - \cos\theta}$$

These formulas will work for finding the tangent or cotangent of half of any angle unless the cosine of θ happens to make the denominator of the identity equal to 0.

The Pythagorean theorem states that $a^2 + b^2 = c^2$ for all right triangles. The trigonometric identity that derives from this principle is stated in this way: $\sin^2\theta + \cos^2\theta = 1$

Dividing each term by either $\sin^2\theta$ or $\cos^2\theta$ yields two other identities, respectively:

$$1 + \cot^2\theta = \csc^2\theta$$
$$\tan^2\theta + 1 = \sec^2\theta$$

DOUBLE ANGLES

In each case, use one of the double angle formulas. To find the sine or cosine of twice a known angle, use one of the following formulas:

$$\sin(2\theta) = 2\sin\theta\cos\theta$$

$$\cos(2\theta) = \cos^2\theta - \sin^2\theta$$
$$= 2\cos^2\theta - 1$$
$$= 1 - 2\sin^2\theta$$

To find the tangent or cotangent of twice a known angle, use the formulas where θ is an angle with known exact sine, cosine, tangent, and cotangent values:

$$\tan(2\theta) = \frac{2\tan\theta}{1 - \tan^2\theta}$$
$$\cot(2\theta) = \frac{\cot\theta - \tan\theta}{2}$$

PRODUCTS

To find the product of the sines and cosines of two different angles, use one of the following formulas where α and β are two unique angles:

$$\sin\alpha\sin\beta = \frac{1}{2}[\cos(\alpha - \beta) - \cos(\alpha + \beta)]$$
$$\cos\alpha\cos\beta = \frac{1}{2}[\cos(\alpha + \beta) + \cos(\alpha - \beta)]$$
$$\sin\alpha\cos\beta = \frac{1}{2}[\sin(\alpha + \beta) + \sin(\alpha - \beta)]$$
$$\cos\alpha\sin\beta = \frac{1}{2}[\sin(\alpha + \beta) - \sin(\alpha - \beta)]$$

COMPLEMENTARY

The trigonometric cofunction identities use the trigonometric relationships of complementary angles (angles whose sum is 90°). These are:

$$\cos x = \sin(90° - x)$$
$$\csc x = \sec(90° - x)$$
$$\cot x = \tan(90° - x)$$

Review Video: Complementary Angles
Visit mometrix.com/academy and enter code: 919405

TABLE OF COMMONLY ENCOUNTERED ANGLES

$0° = 0$ radians, $30° = \frac{\pi}{6}$ radians, $45° = \frac{\pi}{4}$ radians, $60° = \frac{\pi}{3}$ radians, and $90° = \frac{\pi}{2}$ radians

$\sin 0° = 0$	$\cos 0° = 1$	$\tan 0° = 0$
$\sin 30° = \frac{1}{2}$	$\cos 30° = \frac{\sqrt{3}}{2}$	$\tan 30° = \frac{\sqrt{3}}{3}$
$\sin 45° = \frac{\sqrt{2}}{2}$	$\cos 45° = \frac{\sqrt{2}}{2}$	$\tan 45° = 1$
$\sin 60° = \frac{\sqrt{3}}{2}$	$\cos 60° = \frac{1}{2}$	$\tan 60° = \sqrt{3}$
$\sin 90° = 1$	$\cos 90° = 0$	$\tan 90° = $ undefined
$\csc 0° = $ undefined	$\sec 0° = 1$	$\cot 0° = $ undefined
$\csc 30° = 2$	$\sec 30° = \frac{2\sqrt{3}}{3}$	$\cot 30° = \sqrt{3}$
$\csc 45° = \sqrt{2}$	$\sec 45° = \sqrt{2}$	$\cot 45° = 1$
$\csc 60° = \frac{2\sqrt{3}}{3}$	$\sec 60° = 2$	$\cot 60° = \frac{\sqrt{3}}{3}$
$\csc 90° = 1$	$\sec 90° = $ undefined	$\cot 90° = 0$

The values in the upper half of this table are values you should have memorized or be able to find quickly and those in the lower half can easily be determined as the reciprocal of the corresponding function.

Review Video: Commonly Encountered Angles
Visit mometrix.com/academy and enter code: 204098

RECTANGULAR AND POLAR COORDINATES

Rectangular coordinates are those that lie on the square grids of the Cartesian plane. They should be quite familiar to you. The polar coordinate system is based on a circular graph, rather than the square grid of the Cartesian system. Points in the polar coordinate system are in the format (r, θ), where r is the distance from the origin (think radius of the circle) and θ is the smallest positive angle (moving counterclockwise around the circle) made with the positive horizontal axis.

142

To convert a point from rectangular (x, y) format to polar (r, θ) format, use the formula (x, y) to $(r, \theta) \Rightarrow r = \sqrt{x^2 + y^2}; \theta = \arctan\frac{y}{x}$ when $x \neq 0$

If x is positive, use the positive square root value for r. If x is negative, use the negative square root value for r. If $x = 0$, use the following rules:

- If $y = 0$, then $\theta = 0$
- If $y > 0$, then $\theta = \frac{\pi}{2}$
- If $y < 0$, then $\theta = \frac{3\pi}{2}$

To convert a point from polar (r, θ) format to rectangular (x, y) format, use the formula (r, θ) to $(x, y) \Rightarrow x = r\cos\theta; y = r\sin\theta$

DE MOIVRE'S THEOREM

De Moivre's theorem is used to find the powers of complex numbers (numbers that contain the imaginary number i) written in polar form. Given a trigonometric expression that contains i, such as $z = r\cos x + ir\sin x$, where r is a real number and x is an angle measurement in polar form, use the formula $z^n = r^n(\cos nx + i\sin nx)$, where r and n are real numbers, x is the angle measure in polar form, and i is the imaginary number $i = \sqrt{-1}$. The expression $\cos x + i\sin x$ can be written cis x, making the formula appear in the format $z^n = r^n$ cis nx.

Note that De Moivre's theorem is only for angles in polar form. If you are given an angle in degrees, you must convert to polar form before using the formula.

Practice

P1. Convert the following angles from degrees to radians:

 (a) 56°

 (b) 12°

 (c) 199°

P2. Convert the following angles from radians to degrees:

 (a) 3

 (b) 3π

 (c) 33

P3. Simplify the following trigonometric expressions:

 (a) $\dfrac{\sin x \tan x + \cos x}{\sec x}$

 (b) $\dfrac{4\cos 2x}{\sin^2 2x} + \sec^2 x$

Practice Solutions

P1. Multiply each by the conversion factor $\frac{\pi}{180°}$:

(a) $56° \times \frac{\pi}{180°} \cong 0.977$

(b) $12° \times \frac{\pi}{180°} \cong 0.209$

(c) $199° \times \frac{\pi}{180°} \cong 3.473$

P2. Multiply each by the conversion factor $\frac{180°}{\pi}$:

(a) $3 \times \frac{180°}{\pi} \cong 171.9°$

(b) $3\pi \times \frac{180°}{\pi} = 540° = 180°$

(c) $33 \times \frac{180°}{\pi} \cong 1890.8° \cong 90.8°$

P3. (a) Utilize trigonometric identities and definitions to simplify. Specifically, $\tan x = \frac{\sin x}{\cos x}$, $\sec x = \frac{1}{\cos x}$, and $\sin^2 x + \cos^2 x = 1$:

$$\frac{\sin x \tan x + \cos x}{\sec x} = \left(\sin x \frac{\sin x}{\cos x} + \cos x\right)\cos x$$
$$= \frac{\sin^2 x}{\cos x}\cos x + \cos^2 x$$
$$= \sin^2 x + \cos^2 x$$
$$= 1$$

(b) Utilize trigonometric identities and definitions to simplify. Specifically, double angle formulas, $\sin^2 x = (\sin x)^2$, and $\sin^2 x + \cos^2 x = 1$:

$$\frac{4\cos 2x}{\sin^2 2x} + \sec^2 x = \frac{4(\cos^2 x - \sin^2 x)}{4\sin^2 x \cos^2 x} + \sec^2 x$$
$$= \frac{\cos^2 x - \sin^2 x}{\sin^2 x \cos^2 x} + \sec^2 x$$
$$= \frac{\cos^2 x}{\sin^2 x \cos^2 x} - \frac{\sin^2 x}{\sin^2 x \cos^2 x} + \sec^2 x$$
$$= \frac{1}{\sin^2 x} - \frac{1}{\cos^2 x} + \sec^2 x$$
$$= \csc^2 x - \sec^2 x + \sec^2 x$$
$$= \csc^2 x$$

Probability

Probability is the likelihood of a certain outcome occurring for a given event. An **event** is a situation that produces a result; that could be something as simple as flipping a coin or as complex as launching a rocket. Determining the probability of an outcome for an event can be equally simple or complex. As such there are specific terms used in the study of probability that need to be understood:

- **Compound event** – event that involves two or more independent events (rolling a pair of dice and taking the sum)
- **Desired outcome** (or success) – an outcome that meets a particular set of criteria (a roll of 1 or 2 if we are looking for numbers less than 3)
- **Independent events** – two or more events whose outcomes do not affect one another (two coins tossed at the same time)
- **Dependent events** – two or more events whose outcomes affect one another (two cards drawn consecutively from the same deck)
- **Certain outcome** – probability of outcome is 100% or 1
- **Impossible outcome** – probability of outcome is 0% or 0
- **Mutually exclusive outcomes** – two or more outcomes whose criteria cannot all be satisfied in a single event (a coin coming up heads and tails on the same toss)
- **Random variable** – refers to all possible outcomes of a single event which may be discrete or continuous.

Review Video: Intro to Probability
Visit mometrix.com/academy and enter code: 212374

THEORETICAL AND EXPERIMENTAL PROBABILITY

Theoretical probability can usually be determined without actually performing the event. The likelihood of a outcome occurring, or the probability of an outcome occurring, is given by the formula:

$$P(A) = \frac{\text{Number of acceptable outcomes}}{\text{Number of possible outcomes}}$$

Note that $P(A)$ is the probability of an outcome A occurring, and each outcome is just as likely to occur as any other outcome. If each outcome has the same probability of occurring as every other possible outcome, the outcomes are said to be equally likely to occur. The total number of acceptable outcomes must be less than or equal to the total number of possible outcomes. If the two are equal, then the outcome is certain to occur and the probability is 1. If the number of acceptable outcomes is zero, then the outcome is impossible and the probability is 0. For example, if there are 20 marbles in a bag and 5 are red, then the theoretical probability of randomly selecting a red marble is 5 out of 20, ($\frac{5}{20} = \frac{1}{4}$, 0.25, or 25%).

If the theoretical probability is unknown or too complicated to calculate, it can be estimated by an experimental probability. **Experimental probability**, also called empirical probability, is an estimate of the likelihood of a certain outcome based on repeated experiments or collected data. In other words, while theoretical probability is based on what *should* happen, experimental probability is based on what *has* happened. Experimental probability is calculated in the same way

146

as theoretical, except that actual outcomes are used instead of possible outcomes. The more experiments performed or datapoints gathered, the better the estimate should be.

Theoretical and experimental probability do not always line up with one another. Theoretical probability says that out of 20 coin-tosses, 10 should be heads. However, if we were actually to toss 20 coins, we might record just 5 heads. This doesn't mean that our theoretical probability is incorrect; it just means that this particular experiment had results that were different from what was predicted. A practical application of empirical probability is the insurance industry. There are no set functions that define lifespan, health, or safety. Insurance companies look at factors from hundreds of thousands of individuals to find patterns that they then use to set the formulas for insurance premiums.

> **Review Video: Empirical Probability**
> Visit mometrix.com/academy and enter code: 513468

OBJECTIVE AND SUBJECTIVE PROBABILITY

Objective probability is based on mathematical formulas and documented evidence. Examples of objective probability include raffles or lottery drawings where there is a pre-determined number of possible outcomes and a predetermined number of outcomes that correspond to an event. Other cases of objective probability include probabilities of rolling dice, flipping coins, or drawing cards. Most gambling games are based on objective probability.

In contrast, **subjective probability** is based on personal or professional feelings and judgments. Often, there is a lot of guesswork following extensive research. Areas where subjective probability is applicable include sales trends and business expenses. Attractions set admission prices based on subjective probabilities of attendance based on varying admission rates in an effort to maximize their profit.

SAMPLE SPACE

The total set of all possible results of a test or experiment is called a **sample space**, or sometimes a universal sample space. The sample space, represented by one of the variables S, Ω, or U (for universal sample space) has individual elements called outcomes. Other terms for outcome that may be used interchangeably include elementary outcome, simple event, or sample point. The number of outcomes in a given sample space could be infinite or finite, and some tests may yield multiple unique sample sets. For example, tests conducted by drawing playing cards from a standard deck would have one sample space of the card values, another sample space of the card suits, and a third sample space of suit-denomination combinations. For most tests, the sample spaces considered will be finite.

An **event**, represented by the variable E, is a portion of a sample space. It may be one outcome or a group of outcomes from the same sample space. If an event occurs, then the test or experiment will generate an outcome that satisfies the requirement of that event. For example, given a standard deck of 52 playing cards as the sample space, and defining the event as the collection of face cards, then the event will occur if the card drawn is a J, Q, or K. If any other card is drawn, the event is said to have not occurred.

For every sample space, each possible outcome has a specific likelihood, or probability, that it will occur. The probability measure, also called the **distribution**, is a function that assigns a real number probability, from zero to one, to each outcome. For a probability measure to be accurate, every outcome must have a real number probability measure that is greater than or equal to zero

and less than or equal to one. Also, the probability measure of the sample space must equal one, and the probability measure of the union of multiple outcomes must equal the sum of the individual probability measures.

Probabilities of events are expressed as real numbers from zero to one. They give a numerical value to the chance that a particular event will occur. The probability of an event occurring is the sum of the probabilities of the individual elements of that event. For example, in a standard deck of 52 playing cards as the sample space and the collection of face cards as the event, the probability of drawing a specific face card is $\frac{1}{52} = 0.019$, but the probability of drawing any one of the twelve face cards is $12(0.019) = 0.228$. Note that rounding of numbers can generate different results. If you multiplied 12 by the fraction $\frac{1}{52}$ before converting to a decimal, you would get the answer $\frac{12}{52} = 0.231$.

TREE DIAGRAM

For a simple sample space, possible outcomes may be determined by using a **tree diagram** or an organized chart. In either case, you can easily draw or list out the possible outcomes. For example, to determine all the possible ways three objects can be ordered, you can draw a tree diagram:

You can also make a chart to list all the possibilities:

First object	Second object	Third object
●	X	O
●	O	X
O	●	X
O	X	●
X	●	O
X	O	●

Either way, you can easily see there are six possible ways the three objects can be ordered.

If two events have no outcomes in common, they are said to be **mutually exclusive**. For example, in a standard deck of 52 playing cards, the event of all card suits is mutually exclusive to the event of all card values. If two events have no bearing on each other so that one event occurring has no influence on the probability of another event occurring, the two events are said to be independent. For example, rolling a standard six-sided die multiple times does not change that probability that a particular number will be rolled from one roll to the next. If the outcome of one event does affect the probability of the second event, the two events are said to be dependent. For example, if cards are drawn from a deck, the probability of drawing an ace after an ace has been drawn is different than the probability of drawing an ace if no ace (or no other card, for that matter) has been drawn.

In probability, the **odds in favor of an event** are the number of times the event will occur compared to the number of times the event will not occur. To calculate the odds in favor of an

event, use the formula $\frac{P(A)}{1-P(A)}$, where $P(A)$ is the probability that the event will occur. Many times, odds in favor is given as a ratio in the form $\frac{a}{b}$ or $a{:}b$, where a is the probability of the event occurring and b is the complement of the event, the probability of the event not occurring. If the odds in favor are given as 2:5, that means that you can expect the event to occur two times for every 5 times that it does not occur. In other words, the probability that the event will occur is $\frac{2}{2+5}=\frac{2}{7}$.

In probability, the **odds against an event** are the number of times the event will not occur compared to the number of times the event will occur. To calculate the odds against an event, use the formula $\frac{1-P(A)}{P(A)}$, where $P(A)$ is the probability that the event will occur. Many times, odds against is given as a ratio in the form $\frac{b}{a}$ or $b{:}a$, where b is the probability the event will not occur (the complement of the event) and a is the probability the event will occur. If the odds against an event are given as 3:1, that means that you can expect the event to not occur 3 times for every one time it does occur. In other words, 3 out of every 4 trials will fail.

PERMUTATIONS AND COMBINATIONS

When trying to calculate the probability of an event using the $\frac{\text{desired outcomes}}{\text{total outcomes}}$ formula, you may frequently find that there are too many outcomes to individually count them. **Permutation** and **combination formulas** offer a shortcut to counting outcomes. A permutation is an arrangement of a specific number of a set of objects in a specific order. The number of **permutations** of r items given a set of n items can be calculated as $_nP_r=\frac{n!}{(n-r)!}$. Combinations are similar to permutations, except there are no restrictions regarding the order of the elements. While ABC is considered a different permutation than BCA, ABC and BCA are considered the same combination. The number of **combinations** of r items given a set of n items can be calculated as $_nC_r=\frac{n!}{r!(n-r)!}$ or $_nC_r=\frac{_nP_r}{r!}$.

Suppose you want to calculate how many different 5-card hands can be drawn from a deck of 52 cards. This is a combination since the order of the cards in a hand does not matter. There are 52 cards available, and 5 to be selected. Thus, the number of different hands is $_{52}C_5=\frac{52!}{5!\times47!}=$ 2,598,960.

COMPLEMENT OF AN EVENT

Sometimes it may be easier to calculate the possibility of something not happening, or the **complement of an event**. Represented by the symbol \bar{A}, the complement of A is the probability that event A does not happen. When you know the probability of event A occurring, you can use the formula $P(\bar{A})=1-P(A)$, where $P(\bar{A})$ is the probability of event A not occurring, and $P(A)$ is the probability of event A occurring.

ADDITION RULE

The **addition rule** for probability is used for finding the probability of a compound event. Use the formula $P(A\text{ or }B)=P(A)+P(B)-P(A\text{ and }B)$, where $P(A\text{ and }B)$ is the probability of both events occurring to find the probability of a compound event. The probability of both events occurring at the same time must be subtracted to eliminate any overlap in the first two probabilities.

CONDITIONAL PROBABILITY

Conditional probability is the probability of an event occurring once another event has already occurred. Given event A and dependent event B, the probability of event B occurring when event A

149

has already occurred is represented by the notation $P(A|B)$. To find the probability of event B occurring, take into account the fact that event A has already occurred and adjust the total number of possible outcomes. For example, suppose you have ten balls numbered 1–10 and you want ball number 7 to be pulled in two pulls. On the first pull, the probability of getting the 7 is $\frac{1}{10}$ because there is one ball with a 7 on it and 10 balls to choose from. Assuming the first pull did not yield a 7, the probability of pulling a 7 on the second pull is now $\frac{1}{9}$ because there are only 9 balls remaining for the second pull.

MULTIPLICATION RULE

The **multiplication rule** can be used to find the probability of two independent events occurring using the formula $P(A \text{ and } B) = P(A) \times P(B)$, where $P(A \text{ and } B)$ is the probability of two independent events occurring, $P(A)$ is the probability of the first event occurring, and $P(B)$ is the probability of the second event occurring.

The multiplication rule can also be used to find the probability of two dependent events occurring using the formula $P(A \text{ and } B) = P(A) \times P(B|A)$, where $P(A \text{ and } B)$ is the probability of two dependent events occurring and $P(B|A)$ is the probability of the second event occurring after the first event has already occurred. Before using the multiplication rule, you MUST first determine whether the two events are *dependent* or *independent*.

Use a **combination of the multiplication** rule and the rule of complements to find the probability that at least one outcome of the element will occur. This given by the general formula $P(\text{at least one event occurring}) = 1 - P(\text{no outcomes occurring})$. For example, to find the probability that at least one even number will show when a pair of dice is rolled, find the probability that two odd numbers will be rolled (no even numbers) and subtract from one. You can always use a tree diagram or make a chart to list the possible outcomes when the sample space is small, such as in the dice-rolling example, but in most cases it will be much faster to use the multiplication and complement formulas.

EXPECTED VALUE

Expected value is a method of determining expected outcome in a random situation. It is really a sum of the weighted probabilities of the possible outcomes. Multiply the probability of an event occurring by the weight assigned to that probability (such as the amount of money won or lost). A practical application of the expected value is to determine whether a game of chance is really fair. If the sum of the weighted probabilities is equal to zero, the game is generally considered fair because the player has a fair chance to at least break even. If the expected value is less than zero, then players lose more than they win. For example, a lottery drawing might allow the player to choose any three-digit number, 000–999. The probability of choosing the winning number is 1:1000. If it costs \$1 to play, and a winning number receives \$500, the expected value is $\left(-\$1 \times \frac{999}{1,000}\right) + \left(\$499 \times \frac{1}{1,000}\right) = -\0.50. You can expect to lose on average 50 cents for every dollar you spend.

> **Review Video: Expected Value**
> Visit mometrix.com/academy and enter code: 643554

EXPECTED VALUE AND SIMULATORS

A die roll simulator will show the results of n rolls of a die. The result of each die roll may be recorded. For example, suppose a die is rolled 100 times. All results may be recorded. The numbers of 1s, 2s, 3s, 4s, 5s, and 6s, may be counted. The experimental probability of rolling each number

will equal the ratio of the frequency of the rolled number to the total number of rolls. As the number of rolls increases, or approaches infinity, the experimental probability will approach the theoretical probability of 1/6. Thus, the expected value for the roll of a die is shown to be $(1 \times 1/6) + (2 \times 1/6) + (3 \times 1/6) + (4 \times 1/6) + (5 \times 1/6) + (6 \times 1/6)$, or 3.5.

Practice

P1. Determine the theoretical probability of the following events:

(a) Rolling an even number on a regular 6-sided die.

(b) Not getting a red ball when selecting one from a bag of 3 red balls, 4 black balls, and 2 green balls.

(c) Rolling a standard die and then selecting a card from a standard deck that is less than the value rolled.

P2. There is a game of chance involving a standard deck of cards that has been shuffled and then laid on a table. The player wins $10 if they can turn over 2 cards of matching color (black or red), $50 for 2 cards with matching value (A-K), and $100 for 2 cards with both matching color and value. What is the expected value of playing this game?

Mⓥmetrix

Practice Solutions

P1. (a). The values on the faces of a regular die are 1, 2, 3, 4, 5, and 6. Since three of these are even numbers (2, 4, 6), The probability of rolling an even number is $\frac{3}{6} = \frac{1}{2} = 0.5 = 50\%$.

(b) The bag contains a total of 9 balls, 6 of which are not red, so the probability of selecting one non-red ball would be $\frac{6}{9} = \frac{2}{3} \cong 0.667 \cong 66.7\%$.

(c) In this scenario, we need to determine how many cards could satisfy the condition for each possible value of the die roll. If a one is rolled, there is no way to achieve the desired outcome, since no cards in a standard deck are less than 1. If a two is rolled, then any of the four aces would achieve the desired result. If a three is rolled, then either an ace or a two would satisfy the condition, and so on. Note that any value on the die is equally likely to occur, meaning that the probability of each roll is $\frac{1}{6}$. Putting all this in a table can help:

Roll	Cards < Roll	Probability of Card	Probability of Event
1	-	$\frac{0}{52} = 0$	$\frac{1}{6} \times 0 = 0$
2	1	$\frac{4}{52} = \frac{1}{13}$	$\frac{1}{6} \times \frac{1}{13} = \frac{1}{78}$
3	1,2	$\frac{8}{52} = \frac{2}{13}$	$\frac{1}{6} \times \frac{2}{13} = \frac{2}{78}$
4	1,2,3	$\frac{12}{52} = \frac{3}{13}$	$\frac{1}{6} \times \frac{3}{13} = \frac{3}{78}$
5	1,2,3,4	$\frac{16}{52} = \frac{4}{13}$	$\frac{1}{6} \times \frac{4}{13} = \frac{4}{78}$
6	1,2,3,4,5	$\frac{20}{52} = \frac{5}{13}$	$\frac{1}{6} \times \frac{5}{13} = \frac{5}{78}$

Assuming that each value of the die is equally likely, then the probability is the sum of the probabilities of each way to achieve the desired outcome: $\frac{0+1+2+3+4+5}{78} = \frac{15}{78} = \frac{5}{26} \cong 0.192 \cong 19.2\%$.

P2. First, determine the probability of each way of winning each way. In each case, the fist card simply determines which of the remaining 51 cards in the deck correspond to a win. For the color of the cards to match, there are 25 cards of those remaining in the deck that match the color of the first, but one of the 25 also matches the value, so only 24 are left in this category. For the value of the cards to match, there are 3 cards of the remaining cards in the deck that match the value of the first, but one of the three also matches the color, so only 2 are left in this category. For the cards to match both color and value, there is only one card in the deck that will work. Finally, there are 24 cards left that don't match at all.

153

Now we can find the expected value of playing the game, where we multiply the value of each event by the probability it will occur and sum over all of them:

$$\$10 \times \frac{24}{51} = \$4.71$$
$$\$50 \times \frac{2}{51} = \$1.96$$
$$\$100 \times \frac{1}{51} = \$1.96$$
$$\$0 \times \frac{24}{51} = \$0$$

$$\$4.71 + \$1.96 + \$1.96 = \$8.63$$

This game therefore has an expected value of \$8.63 each time you play, which means if the cost to play is less than \$8.63 then you would, on average, *gain* money. However, if the cost to play is more than \$8.63, then you would, on average, *lose* money.

Statistics

Statistics is the branch of mathematics that deals with collecting, recording, interpreting, illustrating, and analyzing large amounts of **data**. The following terms are often used in the discussion of data and **statistics**:

- **Data** – the collective name for pieces of information (singular is datum).
- **Quantitative data** – measurements (such as length, mass, and speed) that provide information about quantities in numbers
- **Qualitative data** – information (such as colors, scents, tastes, and shapes) that cannot be measured using numbers
- **Discrete data** – information that can be expressed only by a specific value, such as whole or half numbers. For example, since people can be counted only in whole numbers, a population count would be discrete data.
- **Continuous data** – information (such as time and temperature) that can be expressed by any value within a given range
- **Primary data** – information that has been collected directly from a survey, investigation, or experiment, such as a questionnaire or the recording of daily temperatures. Primary data that has not yet been organized or analyzed is called **raw data**.
- **Secondary data** – information that has been collected, sorted, and processed by the researcher
- **Ordinal data** – information that can be placed in numerical order, such as age or weight
- **Nominal data** – information that *cannot* be placed in numerical order, such as names or places.

DATA COLLECTION

POPULATION

In statistics, the **population** is the entire collection of people, plants, etc., that data can be collected from. For example, a study to determine how well students in the area schools perform on a standardized test would have a population of all the students enrolled in those schools, although a study may include just a small sample of students from each school. A **parameter** is a numerical value that gives information about the population, such as the mean, median, mode, or standard deviation. Remember that the symbol for the mean of a population is μ and the symbol for the standard deviation of a population is σ.

SAMPLE

A **sample** is a portion of the entire population. Whereas a parameter helped describe the population, a **statistic** is a numerical value that gives information about the sample, such as mean, median, mode, or standard deviation. Keep in mind that the symbols for mean and standard deviation are different when they are referring to a sample rather than the entire population. For a sample, the symbol for mean is \bar{x} and the symbol for standard deviation is s. The mean and standard deviation of a sample may or may not be identical to that of the entire population due to a sample only being a subset of the population. However, if the sample is random and large enough, statistically significant values can be attained. Samples are generally used when the population is too large to justify including every element or when acquiring data for the entire population is impossible.

155

INFERENTIAL STATISTICS

Inferential statistics is the branch of statistics that uses samples to make predictions about an entire population. This type of statistics is often seen in political polls, where a sample of the population is questioned about a particular topic or politician to gain an understanding about the attitudes of the entire population of the country. Often, exit polls are conducted on election days using this method. Inferential statistics can have a large margin of error if you do not have a valid sample.

SAMPLING DISTRIBUTION

Statistical values calculated from various samples of the same size make up the **sampling distribution**. For example, if several samples of identical size are randomly selected from a large population and then the mean of each sample is calculated, the distribution of values of the means would be a sampling distribution.

The **sampling distribution of the mean** is the distribution of the sample mean, \bar{x}, derived from random samples of a given size. It has three important characteristics. First, the mean of the sampling distribution of the mean is equal to the mean of the population that was sampled. Second, assuming the standard deviation is non-zero, the standard deviation of the sampling distribution of the mean equals the standard deviation of the sampled population divided by the square root of the sample size. This is sometimes called the standard error. Finally, as the sample size gets larger, the sampling distribution of the mean gets closer to a normal distribution via the central limit theorem.

SURVEY STUDY

A **survey study** is a method of gathering information from a small group in an attempt to gain enough information to make accurate general assumptions about the population. Once a survey study is completed, the results are then put into a summary report.

Survey studies are generally in the format of surveys, interviews, or questionnaires as part of an effort to find opinions of a particular group or to find facts about a group.

It is important to note that the findings from a survey study are only as accurate as the sample chosen from the population.

CORRELATIONAL STUDIES

Correlational studies seek to determine how much one variable is affected by changes in a second variable. For example, correlational studies may look for a relationship between the amount of time a student spends studying for a test and the grade that student earned on the test or between student scores on college admissions tests and student grades in college.

It is important to note that correlational studies cannot show a cause and effect, but rather can show only that two variables are or are not potentially correlated.

EXPERIMENTAL STUDIES

Experimental studies take correlational studies one step farther, in that they attempt to prove or disprove a cause-and-effect relationship. These studies are performed by conducting a series of experiments to test the hypothesis. For a study to be scientifically accurate, it must have both an experimental group that receives the specified treatment and a control group that does not get the treatment. This is the type of study pharmaceutical companies do as part of drug trials for new medications. Experimental studies are only valid when proper scientific method has been followed. In other words, the experiment must be well-planned and executed without bias in the testing

process, all subjects must be selected at random, and the process of determining which subject is in which of the two groups must also be completely random.

OBSERVATIONAL STUDIES

Observational studies are the opposite of experimental studies. In observational studies, the tester cannot change or in any way control all of the variables in the test. For example, a study to determine which gender does better in math classes in school is strictly observational. You cannot change a person's gender, and you cannot change the subject being studied. The big downfall of observational studies is that you have no way of proving a cause-and-effect relationship because you cannot control outside influences. Events outside of school can influence a student's performance in school, and observational studies cannot take that into consideration.

RANDOM SAMPLES

For most studies, a **random sample** is necessary to produce valid results. Random samples should not have any particular influence to cause sampled subjects to behave one way or another. The goal is for the random sample to be a **representative sample**, or a sample whose characteristics give an accurate picture of the characteristics of the entire population. To accomplish this, you must make sure you have a proper **sample size**, or an appropriate number of elements in the sample.

BIASES

In statistical studies, biases must be avoided. **Bias** is an error that causes the study to favor one set of results over another. For example, if a survey to determine how the country views the president's job performance only speaks to registered voters in the president's party, the results will be skewed because a disproportionately large number of responders would tend to show approval, while a disproportionately large number of people in the opposite party would tend to express disapproval. **Extraneous variables** are, as the name implies, outside influences that can affect the outcome of a study. They are not always avoidable, but could trigger bias in the result.

MEASURES OF CENTRAL TENDENCY

A **measure of central tendency** is a statistical value that gives a reasonable estimate for the center of a group of data. There are several different ways of describing the measure of central tendency. Each one has a unique way it is calculated, and each one gives a slightly different perspective on the data set. Whenever you give a measure of central tendency, always make sure the units are the same. If the data has different units, such as hours, minutes, and seconds, convert all the data to the same unit, and use the same unit in the measure of central tendency. If no units are given in the data, do not give units for the measure of central tendency.

MEAN

The **statistical mean** of a group of data is the same as the arithmetic average of that group. To find the mean of a set of data, first convert each value to the same units, if necessary. Then find the sum of all the values, and count the total number of data values, making sure you take into consideration each individual value. If a value appears more than once, count it more than once. Divide the sum of the values by the total number of values and apply the units, if any. Note that the mean does not have to be one of the data values in the set, and may not divide evenly.

$$\text{mean} = \frac{\text{sum of the data values}}{\text{quantity of data values}}$$

For instance, the mean of the data set {88, 72, 61, 90, 97, 68, 88, 79, 86, 93, 97, 71, 80, 84, 89} would be the sum of the fifteen numbers divided by 15:

$$\frac{88 + 72 + 61 + 90 + 97 + 68 + 88 + 79 + 86 + 93 + 97 + 71 + 80 + 84 + 88}{15} = \frac{1242}{15}$$
$$= 82.8$$

While the mean is relatively easy to calculate and averages are understood by most people, the mean can be very misleading if used as the sole measure of central tendency. If the data set has outliers (data values that are unusually high or unusually low compared to the rest of the data values), the mean can be very distorted, especially if the data set has a small number of values. If unusually high values are countered with unusually low values, the mean is not affected as much. For example, if five of twenty students in a class get a 100 on a test, but the other 15 students have an average of 60 on the same test, the class average would appear as 70. Whenever the mean is skewed by outliers, it is always a good idea to include the median as an alternate measure of central tendency.

A **weighted mean**, or weighted average, is a mean that uses "weighted" values. The formula is weighted mean $= \frac{w_1x_1+w_2x_2+w_3x_3\ldots+w_nx_n}{w_1+w_2+w_3+\cdots+w_n}$. Weighted values, such as $w_1, w_2, w_3, \ldots w_n$ are assigned to each member of the set $x_1, x_2, x_3, \ldots x_n$. If calculating weighted mean, make sure a weight value for each member of the set is used.

MEDIAN

The **statistical median** is the value in the middle of the set of data. To find the median, list all data values in order from smallest to largest or from largest to smallest. Any value that is repeated in the set must be listed the number of times it appears. If there are an odd number of data values, the median is the value in the middle of the list. If there is an even number of data values, the median is the arithmetic mean of the two middle values.

For example, the median of the data set {88, 72, 61, 90, 97, 68, 88, 79, 86, 93, 97, 71, 80, 84, 88} is 86 since the ordered set is {61, 68, 71, 72, 79, 80, 84, **86**, 88, 88, 88, 90, 93, 97, 97}.

The big disadvantage of using the median as a measure of central tendency is that is relies solely on a value's relative size as compared to the other values in the set. When the individual values in a set of data are evenly dispersed, the median can be an accurate tool. However, if there is a group of rather large values or a group of rather small values that are not offset by a different group of values, the information that can be inferred from the median may not be accurate because the distribution of values is skewed.

MODE

The **statistical mode** is the data value that occurs the greatest number of times in the data set. It is possible to have exactly one mode, more than one mode, or no mode. To find the mode of a set of data, arrange the data like you do to find the median (all values in order, listing all multiples of data values). Count the number of times each value appears in the data set. If all values appear an equal number of times, there is no mode. If one value appears more than any other value, that value is the mode. If two or more values appear the same number of times, but there are other values that appear fewer times and no values that appear more times, all of those values are the modes.

For example, the mode of the data set {**88**, 72, 61, 90, 97, 68, **88**, 79, 86, 93, 97, 71, 80, 84, **88**} is 88.

The main disadvantage of the mode is that the values of the other data in the set have no bearing on the mode. The mode may be the largest value, the smallest value, or a value anywhere in between in the set. The mode only tells which value or values, if any, occurred the greatest number of times. It does not give any suggestions about the remaining values in the set.

> **Review Video: Mean, Median, and Mode**
> Visit mometrix.com/academy and enter code: 286207

DISPERSION

The **measure of dispersion** is a single value that helps to "interpret" the measure of central tendency by providing more information about how the data values in the set are distributed about the measure of central tendency. The measure of dispersion helps to eliminate or reduce the disadvantages of using the mean, median, or mode as a single measure of central tendency, and give a more accurate picture of the dataset as a whole. To have a measure of dispersion, you must know or calculate the range, standard deviation, or variance of the data set.

RANGE

The **range** of a set of data is the difference between the greatest and lowest values of the data in the set. To calculate the range, you must first make sure the units for all data values are the same, and then identify the greatest and lowest values. If there are multiple data values that are equal for the highest or lowest, just use one of the values in the formula. Write the answer with the same units as the data values you used to do the calculations.

STANDARD DEVIATION

Standard deviation is a measure of dispersion that compares all the data values in the set to the mean of the set to give a more accurate picture. To find the standard deviation of a sample, use the formula

$$s = \sqrt{\frac{\sum_{i=1}^{n}(x_i - \bar{x})^2}{n-1}}$$

Note that s is the standard deviation of a sample, x represents the individual values in the data set, \bar{x} is the mean of the data values in the set, and n is the number of data values in the set. The higher the value of the standard deviation is, the greater the variance of the data values from the mean. The units associated with the standard deviation are the same as the units of the data values.

VARIANCE

The **variance** of a sample, or just variance, is the square of the standard deviation of that sample. While the mean of a set of data gives the average of the set and gives information about where a specific data value lies in relation to the average, the variance of the sample gives information about the degree to which the data values are spread out and tell you how close an individual value is to the average compared to the other values. The units associated with variance are the same as the units of the data values squared.

PERCENTILE

Percentiles and quartiles are other methods of describing data within a set. **Percentiles** tell what percentage of the data in the set fall below a specific point. For example, achievement test scores are often given in percentiles. A score at the 80th percentile is one which is equal to or higher than

80 percent of the scores in the set. In other words, 80 percent of the scores were lower than that score.

Quartiles are percentile groups that make up quarter sections of the data set. The first quartile is the 25th percentile. The second quartile is the 50th percentile; this is also the median of the dataset. The third quartile is the 75th percentile.

SKEWNESS

Skewness is a way to describe the symmetry or asymmetry of the distribution of values in a dataset. If the distribution of values is symmetrical, there is no skew. In general the closer the mean of a data set is to the median of the data set, the less skew there is. Generally, if the mean is to the right of the median, the data set is *positively skewed*, or right-skewed, and if the mean is to the left of the median, the data set is *negatively skewed*, or left-skewed. However, this rule of thumb is not infallible. When the data values are graphed on a curve, a set with no skew will be a perfect bell curve.

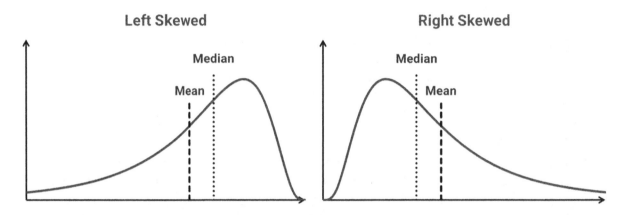

To estimate skew, use the formula:

$$\text{skew} = \frac{\sqrt{n(n-1)}}{n-2}\left(\frac{\frac{1}{n}\sum_{i=1}^{n}(x_i - \bar{x})^3}{\left(\frac{1}{n}\sum_{i=1}^{n}(x_i - \bar{x})^2\right)^{\frac{3}{2}}}\right)$$

Note that n is the datapoints in the set, x_i is the ith value in the set, and \bar{x} is the mean of the set.

UNIMODAL VS. BIMODAL

If a distribution has a single peak, it would be considered **unimodal**. If it has two discernible peaks it would be considered **bimodal**. Bimodal distributions may be an indication that the set of data being considered is actually the combination of two sets of data with significant differences. A **uniform distribution** is a distribution in which there is *no distinct peak or variation* in the data. No values or ranges are particularly more common than any other values or ranges.

OUTLIER

An outlier is an extremely high or extremely low value in the data set. It may be the result of measurement error, in which case, the outlier is not a valid member of the data set. However, it may also be a valid member of the distribution. Unless a measurement error is identified, the experimenter cannot know for certain if an outlier is or is not a member of the distribution. There

are arbitrary methods that can be employed to designate an extreme value as an outlier. One method designates an outlier (or possible outlier) to be any value less than $Q_1 - 1.5(IQR)$ or any value greater than $Q_3 + 1.5(IQR)$.

DATA ANALYSIS

SIMPLE REGRESSION

In statistics, **simple regression** is using an equation to represent a relation between an independent and a dependent variable. The independent variable is also referred to as the explanatory variable or the predictor, and is generally represented by the variable x in the equation. The dependent variable, usually represented by the variable y, is also referred to as the response variable. The equation may be any type of function – linear, quadratic, exponential, etc. The best way to handle this task is to use the regression feature of your graphing calculator. This will easily give you the curve of best fit and provide you with the coefficients and other information you need to derive an equation.

LINE OF BEST FIT

In a scatter plot, the **line of best fit** is the line that best shows the trends of the data. The line of best fit is given by the equation $\hat{y} = ax + b$, where a and b are the regression coefficients. The regression coefficient a is also the slope of the line of best fit, and b is also the y-coordinate of the point at which the line of best fit crosses the y-axis. Not every point on the scatter plot will be on the line of best fit. The differences between the y-values of the points in the scatter plot and the corresponding y-values according to the equation of the line of best fit are the residuals. The line of best fit is also called the least-squares regression line because it is also the line that has the lowest sum of the squares of the residuals.

CORRELATION COEFFICIENT

The **correlation coefficient** is the numerical value that indicates how strong the relationship is between the two variables of a linear regression equation. A correlation coefficient of –1 is a perfect negative correlation. A correlation coefficient of +1 is a perfect positive correlation. Correlation coefficients close to –1 or +1 are very strong correlations. A correlation coefficient equal to zero indicates there is no correlation between the two variables. This test is a good indicator of whether or not the equation for the line of best fit is accurate. The formula for the correlation coefficient is

$$r = \frac{\sum_{i=1}^{n}(x_i - \bar{x})(y_i - \bar{y})}{\sqrt{\sum_{i=1}^{n}(x_i - \bar{x})^2}\sqrt{\sum_{i=1}^{n}(y_i - \bar{y})^2}}$$

where r is the correlation coefficient, n is the number of data values in the set, (x_i, y_i) is a point in the set, and \bar{x} and \bar{y} are the means.

Z-SCORE

A **z-score** is an indication of how many standard deviations a given value falls from the mean. To calculate a z-score, use the formula $\frac{x-\mu}{\sigma}$, where x is the data value, μ is the mean of the data set, and σ is the standard deviation of the population. If the z-score is positive, the data value lies above the mean. If the z-score is negative, the data value falls below the mean. These scores are useful in interpreting data such as standardized test scores, where every piece of data in the set has been counted, rather than just a small random sample. In cases where standard deviations are calculated from a random sample of the set, the z-scores will not be as accurate.

AREA UNDER A NORMAL CURVE

The area under a normal curve can be represented using one or two z-scores or a mean and a z-score. A z-score represents the number of standard deviations a score falls above, or below, the mean. A normal distribution table (z-table) shows the mean to z area, small portion area, and larger portion area, for any z-score from 0 to 4. The area between a mean and z-score is simply equal to the mean to z area. The area under the normal curve, between two z-scores, may be calculated by adding or subtracting the mean to z areas. An area above, or below, a z-score is equal to the smaller or larger portion area. The area may also be calculated by subtracting the mean to z area from 0.5, when looking at the smaller area, or adding the mean to z area to 0.5, when looking at the larger area.

CENTRAL LIMIT THEOREM

According to the **central limit theorem**, regardless of what the original distribution of a sample is, the distribution of the means tends to get closer and closer to a normal distribution as the sample size gets larger and larger (this is necessary because the sample is becoming more all-encompassing of the elements of the population). As the sample size gets larger, the distribution of the sample mean will approach a normal distribution with a mean of the population mean and a variance of the population variance divided by the sample size.

DISPLAYING INFORMATION

FREQUENCY TABLES

Frequency tables show how frequently each unique value appears in the set. A **relative frequency table** is one that shows the proportions of each unique value compared to the entire set. Relative frequencies are given as percentages; however, the total percent for a relative frequency table will not necessarily equal 100 percent due to rounding. An example of a frequency table with relative frequencies is below.

Favorite Color	Frequency	Relative Frequency
Blue	4	13%
Red	7	22%
Green		9%
Purple	6	19%
Cyan	12	38%

Review Video: Data Interpretation of Graphs
Visit mometrix.com/academy and enter code: 200439

A **two-way frequency table** quickly shows intersections and total frequencies. These values would have to be calculated from a manual list. The conditional probability, $P(B|A)$, read as "The probability of B, given A," is equal to $P(B \cap A)/A$. A two-way frequency table can quickly show these frequencies. Consider the table below:

	Cat	Dog	Bird	Total
Male	24	16	26	66
Female	32	12	20	64
Total	56	28	46	130

Find $P(Cat|Female)$. The two-way frequency table shows $C \cap F$ to be 32, while the total for female is 64. Thus, $P(Cat\,|\,Female) = 32/64 = 1/2$.

PICTOGRAPHS

A **pictograph** is a graph, generally in the horizontal orientation, that uses pictures or symbols to represent the data. Each pictograph must have a key that defines the picture or symbol and gives the quantity each picture or symbol represents. Pictures or symbols on a pictograph are not always shown as whole elements. In this case, the fraction of the picture or symbol shown represents the same fraction of the quantity a whole picture or symbol stands for. For example, a row with $3\frac{1}{2}$ ears of corn, where each ear of corn represents 100 stalks of corn in a field, would equal $3\frac{1}{2} \times 100 = 350$ stalks of corn in the field.

CIRCLE GRAPHS

Circle graphs, also known as *pie charts*, provide a visual depiction of the relationship of each type of data compared to the whole set of data. The circle graph is divided into sections by drawing radii to create central angles whose percentage of the circle is equal to the individual data's percentage of the whole set. Each 1% of data is equal to 3.6° in the circle graph. Therefore, data represented by a 90° section of the circle graph makes up 25% of the whole. When complete, a circle graph often looks like a pie cut into uneven wedges. The pie chart below shows the data from the frequency table referenced earlier where people were asked their favorite color.

Favorite Color

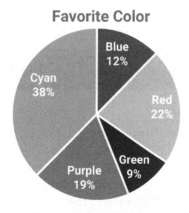

LINE GRAPHS

Line graphs have one or more lines of varying styles (solid or broken) to show the different values for a set of data. The individual data are represented as ordered pairs, much like on a Cartesian plane. In this case, the *x*- and *y*-axes are defined in terms of their units, such as dollars or time. The individual plotted points are joined by line segments to show whether the value of the data is increasing (line sloping upward), decreasing (line sloping downward) or staying the same (horizontal line). Multiple sets of data can be graphed on the same line graph to give an easy visual comparison. An example of this would be graphing achievement test scores for different groups of

students over the same time period to see which group had the greatest increase or decrease in performance from year-to-year (as shown below).

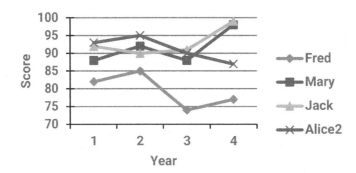

LINE PLOTS

A **line plot**, also known as a *dot plot*, has plotted points that are not connected by line segments. In this graph, the horizontal axis lists the different possible values for the data, and the vertical axis lists the number of times the individual value occurs. A single dot is graphed for each value to show the number of times it occurs. This graph is more closely related to a bar graph than a line graph. Do not connect the dots in a line plot or it will misrepresent the data.

STEM AND LEAF PLOTS

A **stem and leaf plot** is useful for depicting groups of data that fall into a range of values. Each piece of data is separated into two parts: the first, or left, part is called the stem; the second, or right, part is called the leaf. Each stem is listed in a column from smallest to largest. Each leaf that has the common stem is listed in that stem's row from smallest to largest. For example, in a set of two-digit numbers, the digit in the tens place is the stem, and the digit in the ones place is the leaf. With a stem and leaf plot, you can easily see which subset of numbers (10s, 20s, 30s, etc.) is the largest. This information is also readily available by looking at a histogram, but a stem and leaf plot also allows you to look closer and see exactly which values fall in that range. Using all of the test scores from above, we can assemble a stem and leaf plot like the one below.

Test Scores

7	4	8							
8	2	5	7	8	8				
9	0	0	1	2	2	3	5	8	9

BAR GRAPHS

A **bar graph** is one of the few graphs that can be drawn correctly in two different configurations – both horizontally and vertically. A bar graph is similar to a line plot in the way the data is organized on the graph. Both axes must have their categories defined for the graph to be useful. Rather than placing a single dot to mark the point of the data's value, a bar, or thick line, is drawn from zero to the exact value of the data, whether it is a number, percentage, or other numerical value. Longer bar

lengths correspond to greater data values. To read a bar graph, read the labels for the axes to find the units being reported. Then look where the bars end in relation to the scale given on the corresponding axis and determine the associated value.

The bar chart below represents the responses from our favorite color survey.

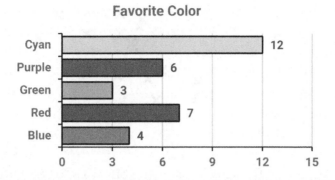

HISTOGRAMS

At first glance, a **histogram** looks like a vertical bar graph. The difference is that a bar graph has a separate bar for each piece of data and a histogram has one continuous bar for each *range* of data. For example, a histogram may have one bar for the range 0–9, one bar for 10–19, etc. While a bar graph has numerical values on one axis, a histogram has numerical values on both axes. Each range is of equal size, and they are ordered left to right from lowest to highest. The height of each column on a histogram represents the number of data values within that range. Like a stem and leaf plot, a histogram makes it easy to glance at the graph and quickly determine which range has the greatest quantity of values. A simple example of a histogram is below.

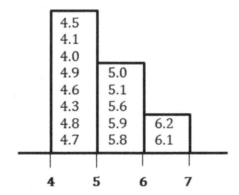

BIVARIATE DATA

Bivariate data is simply data from two different variables. (The prefix *bi-* means *two*.) In a *scatter plot*, each value in the set of data is plotted on a grid similar to a Cartesian plane, where each axis represents one of the two variables. By looking at the pattern formed by the points on the grid, you

can often determine whether or not there is a relationship between the two variables, and what that relationship is, if it exists. The variables may be directly proportionate, inversely proportionate, or show no proportion at all. It may also be possible to determine if the data is linear, and if so, to find an equation to relate the two variables. The following scatter plot shows the relationship between preference for brand "A" and the age of the consumers surveyed.

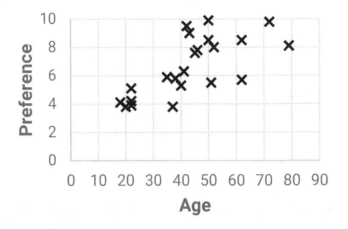

SCATTER PLOTS

Scatter plots are also useful in determining the type of function represented by the data and finding the simple regression. Linear scatter plots may be positive or negative. Nonlinear scatter plots are generally exponential or quadratic. Below are some common types of scatter plots:

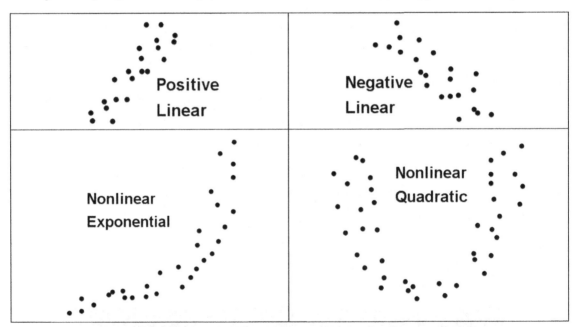

Review Video: Scatter Plot
Visit mometrix.com/academy and enter code: 596526

5-NUMBER SUMMARY

The **5-number summary** of a set of data gives a very informative picture of the set. The five numbers in the summary include the minimum value, maximum value, and the three quartiles. This information gives the reader the range and median of the set, as well as an indication of how the data is spread about the median.

BOX AND WHISKER PLOTS

A **box-and-whisker plot** is a graphical representation of the 5-number summary. To draw a box-and-whiskers plot, plot the points of the 5-number summary on a number line. Draw a box whose ends are through the points for the first and third quartiles. Draw a vertical line in the box through the median to divide the box in half. Draw a line segment from the first quartile point to the minimum value, and from the third quartile point to the maximum value.

68-95-99.7 RULE

The **68–95–99.7 rule** describes how a normal distribution of data should appear when compared to the mean. This is also a description of a normal bell curve. According to this rule, 68 percent of the data values in a normally distributed set should fall within one standard deviation of the mean (34 percent above and 34 percent below the mean), 95 percent of the data values should fall within two standard deviations of the mean (47.5 percent above and 47.5 percent below the mean), and 99.7 percent of the data values should fall within three standard deviations of the mean, again, equally distributed on either side of the mean. This means that only 0.3 percent of all data values should fall more than three standard deviations from the mean. On the graph below, the normal curve is centered on the y-axis. The x-axis labels are how many standard deviations away from the center you are. Therefore, it is easy to see how the 68-95-99.7 rule can apply.

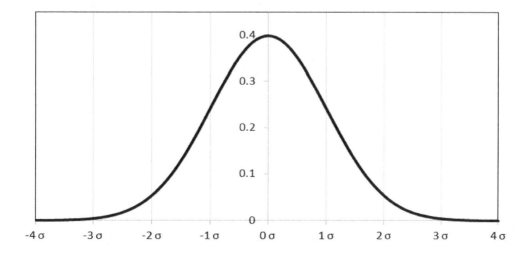

Practice

P1. Determine which of the following statements are TRUE or FALSE:

(a) Just because a sample is random, does not guarantee that it is representative.

(b) Qualitative data cannot be statistically analyzed, since the data is non-numeric.

(c) Sample statistics are a useful tool to estimate population parameters.

P2. Suppose the class average on a final exam is 87, with a standard deviation of 2 points. Find the z-score of a student that got an 82.

P3. Given the following graph, determine the range of patient ages:

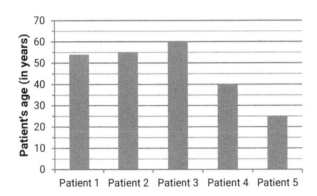

P4. Calculate the sample standard deviation for the dataset $\{10, 13, 11, 5, 8, 18\}$

P5. Today, there were two food options for lunch at a local college cafeteria. Given the following survey data, what is the probability that a junior selected at random from the sample had a sandwich?

	Freshman	Sophomore	Junior	Senior
Salad	15	12	27	36
Sandwich	24	40	43	35
Nothing	42	23	23	30

Practice Solutions

P1. (a). TRUE: A good representative sample will also be a random sample, but sampling 10 random people from a city of 4 million will not be a representative sample.

(b) FALSE: Even though qualitative data is often non-numeric, there are special methods designed to specifically tally and analyze qualitative data.

(c) TRUE: The entire field of statistics is built upon this, since it is almost always beyond the scope of researchers to survey or collect data on an entire population.

P2. Using the formula for z-score: $z = \frac{82-87}{2} = -2.5$

P3. Patient 1 is 54 years old; Patient 2 is 55 years old; Patient 3 is 60 years old; Patient 4 is 40 years old; and Patient 5 is 25 years old. The range of patient ages is the age of the oldest patient minus the age of the youngest patient. In other words, $60 - 25 = 35$. The range of ages is 35 years.

P4. To find the standard deviation, first find the mean:

$$\frac{10 + 13 + 12 + 5 + 8 + 18}{6} = \frac{66}{6} = 11$$

Now, apply the formula for sample standard deviation:

$$s = \sqrt{\frac{\sum_{i=1}^{n}(x_i - \bar{x})^2}{n-1}} = \sqrt{\frac{\sum_{i=1}^{6}(x_i - 11)^2}{6-1}}$$
$$= \frac{\sqrt{(10-11)^2 + (13-11)^2 + (12-11)^2 + (5-11)^2 + (8-11)^2 + (18-11)^2}}{5}$$
$$= \frac{\sqrt{(-1)^2 + 2^2 + 1^2 + (-6)^2 + (-3)^2 + 7^2}}{5}$$
$$= \frac{\sqrt{1 + 4 + 1 + 36 + 9 + 49}}{5}$$
$$= \frac{\sqrt{100}}{5} = \frac{10}{5} = 2$$

P5. With two-way tables it is often most helpful to start by totaling the rows and columns:

	Freshman	Sophomore	Junior	Senior	Total
Salad	15	12	27	36	90
Sandwich	24	40	43	35	142
Nothing	42	23	23	30	118
Total	81	75	93	101	350

Since the question is focused on juniors, we can focus on that column. There was a total of 93 juniors surveyed and 43 of them had a sandwich for lunch. Thus, the probability that a junior selected at random had a sandwich would be $\frac{43}{93} \cong 0.462 \cong 46.2\%$.

Discrete Mathematics

DISCRETE MATHEMATICS

Among mathematicians, there is not an agreed-upon definition of discrete math. What is agreed upon is the fact that discrete math deals with processes that use a finite, or countable, number of elements. In discrete math, the elements will be discontinuous, as this branch of mathematics does not involve the continuity that processes of calculus do. Generally, discrete math uses countable sets of rational numbers, although they do not use the set of all real numbers, as that would then make the math continuous and put it in the category of algebra or calculus. Discrete math has numerous applications in the fields of computer science and business.

ELEMENT OF A SET

A set is a mathematical collection of items, and an element is an item that is included in the set. These items are typically sets of numbers, or sets of geometrical points, or even sets of sets.

Whether an item is an **element of a set** is a binary property. In other words, a particular item either is or is not an element of a given set. There are not different degrees of belonging to a set, and one element of a set cannot be more an element than another. Additionally, the elements do not have any particular order, and there is no count of how many times an element appears in a set. for example, in the set $\{0, 2, 1, 2, 4\}$, the numbers 0, 1, 2, and 4 are elements of the set. Two is not more of an element than the others because it is listed twice. Any number other than these, such as 3, is not an element of the set.

The mathematical symbol \in means "is an element of." for instance, "$1 \in A$" means that "the number 1 is an element of set A". The symbol can be negated with a diagonal slash, so "$1 \notin A$" means "the number 1 is NOT an element of set A."

EMPTY SET

The empty set contains no elements. the symbol for the **empty set** is a circle with a line through it, \emptyset, or the empty set can be written in roster form as $\{\ \ \}$. Although it may seem trivial, the empty set is important for the same reason that zero is an important number—without the empty set, many set operations and definitions would be incomplete. For instance, the intersection of two non-overlapping sets is the empty set. the set of all prime numbers that are perfect squares is the empty set, because there are no such numbers. Other sets can be constructed using the empty set. for instance, a set *containing* the empty set, $\{\{\ \ \}\}$ or $\{\emptyset\}$, is different from the empty set itself, since it's not actually empty—it contains one element, the empty set.

The empty set is, by definition, a subset of every set, including itself. This is because every element that is an element of the empty set is also an element of any other set, since the empty set contains no elements that could make this statement false.

SUBSET, PROPER SUBSET, AND SUPERSET

Set A is a **subset** of set B if set A is contained entirely within set B. More formally, set A is a subset of set B if every element of set A is also in set B. We can write this as $\forall \in A\ x \in B$. the symbol for subset is \subseteq, so we can write "$A \subseteq B$" to mean "set A is a subset of set B," or "$A \nsubseteq B$" to mean "set A is NOT a subset of set B".

Any set is a subset of itself, since naturally any element in a set is in that set. A **proper subset** means a subset that it not equal to the other set. In other words, set A is a proper subset of set B if

170

set A is a subset of set B but they are not the same, so $A \subseteq B$ but $B \nsubseteq A$. for example, $\{0, 1, 2\}$ is a proper subset of $\{0, 1, 2, 3\}$ because every element in the first set is included in the second set but the two sets are not identical. the symbol for proper subset is \subset, so we write "$A \subset B$" to mean "set A is a proper subset of set B," and "$A \not\subset B$" to mean "set A is not a proper subset of set B."

The converse of a subset is a **superset**. If A is a subset of B, then B is a superset of A. In the example above, $\{0, 1, 2, 3\}$ is a superset of $\{0, 1, 2\}$ because the first set contains every element of the second plus more.

UNION OF TWO OR MORE SETS

The **union** of two or more sets includes all the elements that are included in all of the sets. An element is in the union of sets A and B if it is in set A or in set B, or in both. The union is written with the symbol \cup, so "$A \cup B$" (read "A union B") means the union of sets A and B.

For example, given the sets $A = \{1, 2, 3, 4\}$ and $B = \{2, 4, 6, 8\}$, then $A \cup B = \{1, 2, 3, 4, 6, 8\}$. 1 and 3 are in $A \cup B$ because they are in set A, and 6 and 8 are in $A \cup B$ because they are in set B. 2 and 4 appear in both A and B, so they are in $A \cup B$, but they only appear once.

The union operation on sets is both commutative and associative. That is, $A \cup B = B \cup A$, and $(A \cup B) \cup C = A \cup (B \cup C)$.

INTERSECTION OF TWO OR MORE SETS

The intersection of two or more sets is a set including every element that appears in *all* of the sets. An element is in the intersection of sets A and B if and only if the element appears in both set A and set B. For instance, if set $A = \{0, 1, 2, 3\}$ and set $B = \{2, 3, 4, 5\}$, the intersection of sets A and B includes the elements 2 and 3, because these are the only elements that appear in both sets. the intersection is written with the symbol \cap, so "$A \cap B$" (read "A intersection B") means the intersection of sets A and B.

The intersection operation on sets is both commutative and associative. That is, $A \cap B = B \cap A$, and $(A \cap B) \cap C = A \cap (B \cap C)$. The union and intersection operations also jointly have distributive properties: $A \cap (B \cup C) = (A \cap B) \cup (A \cap C)$ and $A \cup (B \cap C) = (A \cup B) \cap (A \cup C)$.

COMPLEMENT OF A SET

The complement of a set is a set containing all the elements that are *not* in the original set. To determine this, we must also define the **universe of discourse**—the set of all possible elements we're considering, abbreviated U. For mathematical applications, the universe of discourse is commonly the set of all integers (abbreviated \mathbb{Z}), or the set of all real numbers (abbreviated \mathbb{R}). If U is the set of all integers, for example, then the complement of the set $A = \{1, 2, 3\}$ would include elements such as -3, 0, or 6, but it would not include elements such as $\sqrt{7}$ or $\frac{1}{4}$, because these are not in the universe of discourse.

The **complement of a set** is often written either by drawing a line over the name of the original set, or by adding an apostrophe or a superscripted C. The complement of set A, for instance, could be written as \bar{A}, as A', or as A^C.

For example, given set $A = \{2, 4, 6, 8\}$ with a universe of discourse of $U = \{1, 2, 3, 4, 5, 6, 7, 8, 9, 10\}$, the complement of a would be $\{1, 3, 5, 7, 9, 10\}$—all the elements of U that are not in A.

DIFFERENCE OF TWO SETS

The difference of two sets is a set containing all the elements that are in the first set but not in the second. the difference of sets A and B is also referred to as the **relative complement** of set A with respect to set B, and is written $A \setminus B$ or $A - B$. the difference is always a subset of the first set: $A \setminus B \subseteq A$. However, it is *not* necessarily the case that $A \setminus B \subseteq B$. In fact, because any element of $A \setminus B$ is by definition not an element of B, the only time that $A \setminus B$ can be a subset of B is if $A \setminus B$ has no elements, i.e. if $A \setminus B = \emptyset$, which is true if and only if $A \subseteq B$.

Unlike the union and intersection, the operation of the difference between sets is neither commutative nor associative. In general, $A \setminus B \neq B \setminus A$, and $A \setminus (B \setminus C) \neq (A \setminus B) \setminus C$.

For example, consider the sets $A = \{1, 2, 3\}$, $B = \{2, 4\}$, and $C = \{1, 2\}$. Then $A \setminus B = \{1, 3\}$ since 1 and 3 are in set A but not in set B. Similarly, $B \setminus A = \{4\}$, $B \setminus C = \{4\}$, $C \setminus B = \{1\}$, and $A \setminus C = \{3\}$. However, $C \setminus A = \emptyset$, i.e., set C is a subset of set A, so there are no elements that appear in C but not in A, which means the difference between C and A is the empty set.

SYMBOLS FOR SETS COMMONLY USED IN MATHEMATICS

Certain sets are used frequently enough in mathematics to have their own symbols. the standard symbols for these sets resemble upper-case letters of the Latin alphabet, but in a typeface with double lines. Among the most commonly used **sets** are:

- \mathbb{R} – the set of all real numbers
- \mathbb{Z} – the set of all integers
- \mathbb{N} – the set of all natural numbers
- \mathbb{Q} – the set of all rational numbers (numbers that can be written as the ratio of two integers, $\frac{p}{q}$, where $q \neq 0$)
- \mathbb{C} – the set of all complex numbers (numbers of the form $a + bi$, where a and b are real numbers and $i = \sqrt{-1}$)

A superscripted plus or minus sign is used to restrict the set to positive or negative numbers. for instance, \mathbb{R}^+ would be the set of all positive real numbers, and \mathbb{Z}^- would be the set of all negative integers.

Some of these sets are, of course, subsets of others. Specifically, $\mathbb{N} \subset \mathbb{Z} \subset \mathbb{Q} \subset \mathbb{R} \subset \mathbb{C}$.

REPRESENTING SETS WITH RECURSIVE AND EXPLICIT FORMULAS

Sets of numbers can have a consistent relationship between the elements of the set. Some of these relationships can be represented with simple recursive or explicit formulas. For example, consider the set of all positive, even numbers (a) and the set of all positive, odd numbers (b):

POSITIVE, EVEN NUMBERS:

Recursive: $a_n = a_{n-1} + 2, n \geq 2, a_1 = 0$
Explicit: $a_n = 2n, n \geq 0$

POSITIVE, ODD NUMBERS:

Recursive: $b_n = b_{n-1} + 2, n \geq 2, b_1 = 1$
Explicit: $b_n = 2n + 1, n \geq 0$

Each set of numbers represents a linear function, with a constant rate of change of 2. The positive, even numbers represent a linear function that is proportional, whereas the positive, odd numbers

172

represent a linear function that is not proportional. The set of even, positive numbers is represented by a function with a y-intercept of 0. The set of odd, positive numbers is represented by a function with a y-intercept of 1.

SET OPERATIONS WITH VENN DIAGRAMS

A Venn diagram is a useful visual tool for representing two or three sets and their common elements. Each set is drawn as a **circle**, with the different circles overlapping. Elements are placed in the circle corresponding to the appropriate set or sets—or placed outside all the circles if they belong to the universe of discourse but not to any of the sets.

For example, suppose our universe of discourse is the integers from 1 to 9, and we have the three sets $A = \{1, 2, 3, 4, 5, 6\}$, $B = \{4, 5, 6, 7\}$, and $C = \{3, 6, 9\}$. This could be illustrated with the following **Venn diagram**:

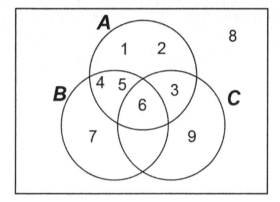

Note, for example, that 6 appears in the center of the diagram where all three circles overlap, because it is an element of all three sets. On the other hand, 8 is placed outside the three circles because it is not an element of any of the sets. Sometimes, instead of writing the elements themselves in the diagram, the total *number* of elements in each part of the Venn diagram is noted. This is especially useful for solving problems involving these numbers of elements.

USING VENN DIAGRAMS TO SOLVE PROBLEMS

Venn diagrams are useful for solving problems involving the numbers of elements in sets and in their intersections. By putting those numbers into a Venn diagram, it's simple to see how many must be in the "leftover" parts.

For example, suppose we're told that 200 voters were polled about two propositions, Proposition 1 and Proposition 2. Further,120 support Proposition 1, 85 support Proposition 2, and 50 support both propositions. To find how many of the voters support neither proposition, we can draw a Venn diagram with a circle representing the supporters of each proposition. We know 50 voters support both propositions, so we can write a 50 in the center of the diagram.

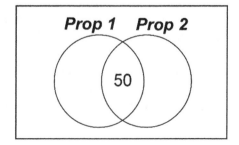

The Proposition 1 circle should contain 120 voters total, so subtracting the 50 voters in the overlap, the other section of the circle must contain $120 - 50 = 70$. Similarly, the nonoverlapping part of the Proposition 2 circle should contain $85 - 50 = 35$.

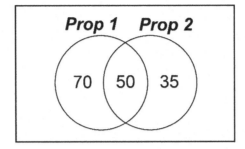

Adding all three sections, the total number of voters supporting either proposition is $70 + 50 + 35 = 155$, so there must be $200 - 155 = 45$ voters who support neither.

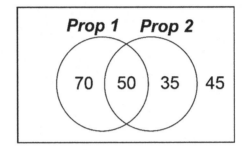

PROPERTIES OF INFINITE SETS

An infinite set has an infinite number of elements. a more technical definition is that a set is **infinite** if its elements can be put in one-to-one correspondence with the elements of one of its proper subsets. For instance, consider the set of all positive integers, \mathbb{Z}^+. If we remove the number 1, we can still match up every positive integer to an element of the remaining subset (by simply matching the number n to the number $n + 1$). \mathbb{Z}^+ is therefore an infinite set.

The union of an infinite set and any other set is always infinite. the intersection of two infinite sets may or may not be infinite. For instance, consider the set P of prime numbers, the set O of positive odd integers, and the set E of positive even integers—all infinite sets. $P \cap O$ is another infinite set, because there are infinitely many odd prime numbers. $P \cap E$ is finite, because there is only one even prime number. and $E \cap O$ is the empty set. Likewise, the complement of an infinite set may be infinite, finite, or the empty set (if the set equals the universe of discourse).

CARDINALITY

Although all infinite sets have infinitely many members, they may still have different sizes. Two sets are defined to have the same size—or more technically the same **cardinality**—if each element of one set can be matched up to a unique element of the other, with none left over. For example, the set of all integers, \mathbb{Z}, and the set of all *even* integers have the same cardinality, even though the latter is a proper subset of the former: every number n in \mathbb{Z} can be matched to a unique number $2n$ in the set of all *even* integers. Although it's more difficult to prove, the set of all rational numbers, \mathbb{Q}, also has the same cardinality as \mathbb{Z}. However, the set of all real numbers, \mathbb{R}, does *not* have the same cardinality—it is impossible to match each integer to a unique real number without any real numbers left over. The most famous proof of this fact was developed by Georg Cantor, and is called the *diagonal argument*.

Sets with the same cardinality as ℤ are said to be "countably infinite," or simply **countable**. Sets with a larger cardinality are said to be "uncountably infinite," or **uncountable**.

CARTESIAN PRODUCTS/RELATIONS

A Cartesian product is the product of two sets of data, X and Y, such that all elements x are a member of set X, and all elements y are a member of set Y. The product of the two sets, $X \times Y$ is the set of all ordered pairs (x, y). For example, given a standard deck of 52 playing cards, there are four possible suits (hearts, diamonds, clubs, and spades) and thirteen possible card values (the numbers 2 through 10, ace, jack, queen, and king). If the card suits are set X and the card values are set Y, then there are $4 \times 13 = 52$ possible different (x, y) combinations, as seen in the 52 cards of a standard deck.

A binary relation, also referred to as a relation, dyadic relation, or 2-place relation, is a subset of a Cartesian product. It shows the relation between one set of objects and a second set of objects, or between one set of objects and itself. The prefix *bi-* means *two*, so there are always two sets involved – either two different sets, or the same set used twice. The ordered pairs of the Cartesian product are used to indicate a binary relation. Relations are possible for situations involving more than two sets, but those are not called binary relations.

The five types of relations are reflexive, symmetric, transitive, antisymmetric, and equivalence. A reflexive relation has $x\Re x$ (x related to x) for all values of x in the set. A symmetric relation has $x\Re y \Rightarrow y\Re x$ for all values of x and y in the set. A transitive relation has $(x\Re y$ and $y\Re z) \Rightarrow x\Re z$ for all values of x, y, and z in the set. An antisymmetric relation has $(x\Re y$ and $y\Re x) \Rightarrow x = y$ for all values of x and y in the set. A relation that is reflexive, symmetric, and transitive is called an equivalence relation.

VERTEX-EDGE GRAPHS

A **vertex-edge graph** is a set of items or objects connected by pathways or links. As an example, consider the following set of nodes and a few graphs representing ways of connecting them with edges.

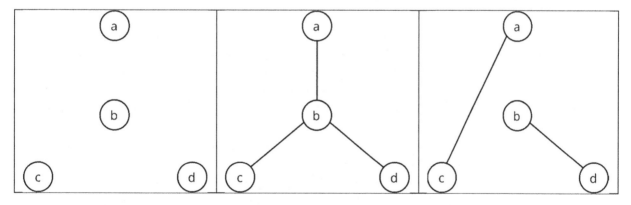

Vertex-edge graphs are useful for solving problems involving schedules, relationships, networks, or paths among a set number of objects. The number of objects may be large, but it will never be infinite. The **vertices** or points on the graph represent the objects and may also be referred to as **nodes**. The nodes are joined by line segments called **edges** or links that show the specific paths that connect the various elements represented by the nodes. The number of nodes does not have to equal the number of edges. There may be more or less, depending on the number of allowable paths.

175

An **endpoint** on a vertex-edge graph is a vertex on exactly one edge. In the case of a vertex that is an endpoint, the edge that the vertex is on is incident with the vertex. Two edges are considered to be adjacent if they share a vertex. Two vertices are considered to be adjacent if they share an edge.

In a vertex-edge graph, a **loop** is an edge that has the same vertex as both endpoints. To calculate the **degree of a vertex** in a vertex-edge graph, count the number of edges that are incident with the vertex, counting loops twice since they meet the vertex at both ends. The **degree sum formula** states that the sum of the degrees of all vertices on a vertex-edge graph is always equal to twice the number of edges on the graph. Thus, the sum of the degrees will never be odd, even if there are an odd number of vertices. Consider the following graph. Node d is an endpoint, there is a loop on node b, and the degree sum of the graph is $2 \times 5 = 10$.

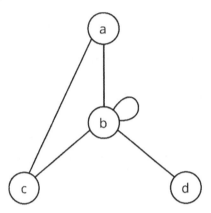

In a vertex-edge graph, a **path** is a given sequence of vertices that follows one or more edges to get from vertex to vertex. There is no jumping over spaces to get from one vertex to the next, although doubling back over an edge already traveled is allowed. A **simple path** is a path that does not repeat an edge in traveling from beginning to end. Think of the vertex-edge graph as a map, with the vertices as cities on the map, and the edges as roads between the cities. To get from one city to another, you must drive on the roads. A simple path allows you to complete your trip without driving on the same road twice.

In a vertex-edge graph, a **circuit** is a path that has the same starting and stopping point. Picturing the vertex-edge graph as a map with cities and roads, a circuit is like leaving home on vacation and then returning home after you have visited your intended destinations. You may go in one direction and then turn around, or you may go in a circle. A **simple circuit** on the graph completes the circuit without repeating an edge. This is like going on vacation and returning home without driving on the same road twice.

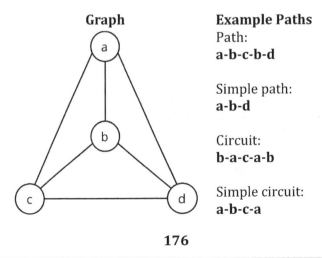

Graph

Example Paths
Path:
a-b-c-b-d

Simple path:
a-b-d

Circuit:
b-a-c-a-b

Simple circuit:
a-b-c-a

On a vertex-edge graph, any path that uses each edge exactly one time is called an **Euler path**. One simple way to rule out the possibility of an Euler path is to calculate the degree of each vertex. If more than two vertices have an odd degree, an Euler path is impossible. A path that uses each vertex exactly one time is called a **Hamiltonian path**.

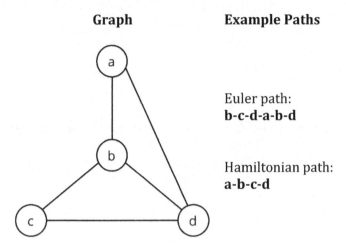

Graph

Example Paths

Euler path:
b-c-d-a-b-d

Hamiltonian path:
a-b-c-d

If every pair of vertices is joined by an edge, the vertex-edge graph is said to be **complete**. If the vertex-edge graph has no simple circuits in it, then the graph is said to be a **tree**. If every vertex is connected to every other vertex by some *path*, then the graph is said to be **connected**, otherwise it is **disconnected**.

Complete and Connected **Tree and Connected** **Disconnected**

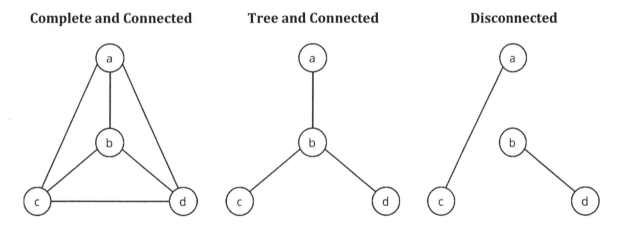

Practice

P1. Given the sets $X = \{1, 2, 3, 4, 5\}$, $Y = \{2, 4, 6, 8\}$, and $Z = \{1, 3, 7, 13, 21\}$ find the following:

 (a) $X \cup Y$

 (b) $X \cap Y$

 (c) $X \cup (Y \cap Z)$

 (d) $(X \cup Y) \cap Z$

P2. Give the most precise description of the following paths for the vertex-edge graph:

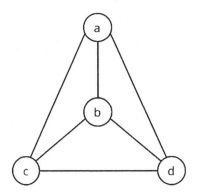

 (a) a-d-c

 (b) b-d-b-d-b

 (c) b-c-d-a-b-d

 (d) b-c-d-a

 (e) b-c-d-a-b

Practice Solutions

P1. (a) The union operation includes all elements of the sets being operated on. Thus:

$$X \cup Y = \{1, 2, 3, 4, 5, 6, 8\}$$

(b) The intersection operation includes only elements in both sets being operated on. Thus:

$$X \cap Y = \{2, 4\}$$

(c) First, find the intersection of Y and Z:

$$Y \cap Z = \{\emptyset\}$$

Then, since the intersection of Y and Z is the null set, the union with X is just the elements of X:

$$X \cup (Y \cap Z) = \{1, 2, 3, 4, 5\}$$

(d) First, find the union of X and Y:

$$X \cup Y = \{1, 2, 3, 4, 5, 6, 8\}$$

Then, the intersection of $X \cup Y$ with Z is:

$$(X \cup Y) \cap Z = \{1, 3\}$$

P2. Determine the start and end vertices, whether the path uses all vertices or edges, and whether the path repeats any vertices or edges:

	Same Start and End	Uses All Vertices	Uses All Edges	Repeats Vertices	Repeats Edges	Result
(a)	No	No	No	No	No	Simple Path
(b)	Yes	No	No	Yes	Yes	Circuit
(c)	No	Yes	No	Yes	No	Path
(d)	No	Yes	No	No	No	Hamiltonian Path
(e)	Yes	Yes	No	Yes	No	Simple Circuit

Mathematical Reasoning

PREMISE AND ARGUMENT

A premise is a statement that precedes a conclusion, in an argument. It is the proposition, or assumption, of an argument. An argument will have two or more premises.

Example:

> If it is hot, then I will go swimming. (Premise)
> It is hot. (Premise)
> _____
> Therefore, I will go swimming. (Conclusion)

SIMPLE AND COMPOUND STATEMENTS

A **statement** in propositional logic is any sentence or expression that has a truth value—that is, that may in principle be considered true or false. "Hello!", for example, is not a statement; there's no sense in which it could be considered true or false. On the other hand, "2 = 3" *is* a statement, albeit a clearly false one. A **compound statement** is a statement that contains one or more other statements, combined or modified in some way. A **simple statement**, or a **proposition**, is a statement that cannot be broken down further into smaller statements.

For example, consider the statement, "If it rains tomorrow, then the streets will be flooded and traffic will be slow." This is a compound statement, because two smaller statements are embedded within it: "it rains tomorrow" and "the streets will be flooded and traffic will be slow." the former cannot be broken down further, and is therefore a simple statement, but the latter is another compound statement, because it includes two simple statements: "the streets will be flooded" and "traffic will be slow."

Common operations used to combine and modify simple statements into compound statements include conjunction, disjunction, negation, and implication.

CONJUNCTION

Conjunction is an operation that combines two or more statements into a compound statement that is true if and only if all of the component statements are true. When the statements are written out, conjunction is marked by the word "and." For example, the statement "Roses are red and violets are blue" is a compound statement that is a conjunction of the two simple statements "roses are red" and "violets are blue."

Conjunction is represented by the operator ∧. In the previous example, if proposition P is "roses are red" and proposition Q is "violets are blue," then the compound statement "roses are red and violets are blue" would be written as "$P \land Q$."

DISJUNCTION

Disjunction is an operation that combines two or more statements into a compound statement that is true if and only if at least one of the component statements is true. When the statements are written out, conjunction is marked by the word "or." For example, the statement "I'll clean the closet today, or you'll clean it tomorrow" is a compound statement that is a disjunction of the simple statements "I'll clean the closet today" and "you'll clean the closet tomorrow."

180

Disjunction is represented by the operator ∨. In the previous example, if proposition P is "I'll clean the closet today" and proposition Q is "you'll clean the closet tomorrow," then the compound statement "I'll clean the closet today, or you'll clean it tomorrow" would be written as "$P \lor Q$."

Note that while in everyday language "or" implies exclusivity, as one or the other option but not both, in formal logic disjunction includes the possibility of both propositions being true. If I clean the closet today *and* you clean it tomorrow, then the sample statement "I'll clean the closet today, or you'll clean it tomorrow" is true.

CONDITIONAL AND BICONDITIONAL STATEMENTS

A conditional statement, or **implication**, is a compound statement of the form "if P, then Q." for instance, the statement "if a snake has rattles, then it's venomous" is a conditional statement. It can also be written "P implies Q" ("that a snake has rattles implies that it's venomous") or "P only if Q" ("a snake has rattles only if it's venomous"). the conditional statement is true when both P and Q are true, and even when P is false, regardless of Q. In other words, the conditional statement is false only when P is true and Q is false. the conditional statement is written as "$P \rightarrow Q$." P is called the **premise** of the statement, and Q the **conclusion**.

A **biconditional statement** is a combination of two conditional statements: both "if P, then Q" and "if Q, then P." To state it more concisely, "P if and only if Q." an example is "A number is even if and only if it is divisible by 2." the biconditional statement is true when P and Q are either both true or both false; it is false if P is true and Q is false or vice versa. the biconditional statement is written "$P \leftrightarrow Q$."

EXISTENTIAL AND UNIVERSAL QUANTIFIERS

A **quantifier** is a logical construct used in a compound statement to give information on the number of subjects for which a statement is true. The **existential quantifier** specifies that the statement is true for at least one subject. It is usually introduced as "there exists," such as "there exists a real number that is equal to its own square." The symbol ∃ is used to signify the existential quantifier. For example, the preceding statement could be written as "$\exists x \in \mathbb{R}\ x = x^2$." The **universal quantifier** specifies that the statement is true for *every* subject. It is usually said as "all" or "for all", such as "all real numbers are less than their own squares plus one." The symbol ∀ is used to signify the universal quantifier. For example, the preceding statement could be written as

$$\forall x \in \mathbb{R}\ x < x^2 + 1$$

Sometimes it is useful to specify that there exists *exactly* one subject that meets a given criterion. In other words, there exists a *unique* such subject. This can be signified by adding an exclamation mark after the existential quantifier: "$\exists!\ x \in \mathbb{R}\ |x| = 0$" means "there exists a unique real number that has an absolute value of zero."

TRUTH TABLES

A truth table shows the truth value of one or more compound statements for each possible combination of truth values of the propositions within it. The truth table contains one column for each **proposition**, and one column for each of the **compound statements** to be analyzed. It has one row for each combination of **truth values** of the propositions. Since each proposition has two possible truth values, the number of possible combinations for N propositions is 2^N, so the truth table will have 2^N rows.

The table below is a simple truth table for some common compound statements involving two propositions.

P	Q	$P \wedge Q$	$P \vee Q$	$\neg P$	$\neg Q$	$P \to Q$	$Q \to P$	$P \leftrightarrow Q$
T	T	T	T	F	F	T	T	T
T	F	F	T	F	T	F	T	F
F	T	F	T	T	F	T	F	F
F	F	F	F	T	T	T	T	T

Truth tables are useful for comparing two compound statements to see if they are equivalent. They are also useful for analyzing whether complicated compound statements are true or false. A table can have a column for each of the increasingly complex compound statements that combine to form the total statement.

TRUTH TABLE TO VALIDATE THE RULE OF DETACHMENT

The Rule of Detachment states that given the premises, $P \to Q$ and P, the valid conclusion is Q.

In other words, for every case where $(P \to Q) \wedge P$ is true, Q will also be true. The truth table below illustrates this fact:

P	Q	$P \to Q$	$(P \to Q) \wedge P$
T	T	T	T
T	F	F	F
F	T	T	F
F	F	T	F

Notice the first cell under $(P \to Q) \wedge P$ is true, while the first cell under Q is also true. Thus, for every case where $(P \to Q) \wedge P$ was true, Q was also true.

TRUTH TABLE TO VALIDATE THE CHAIN RULE

The Chain Rule states that given the premises, $P \to Q$ and $Q \to R$, the valid conclusion is $P \to R$.

In other words, for every case where $(P \to Q) \wedge (Q \to R)$ is true, $P \to R$ will also be true. The truth table below illustrates this fact:

P	Q	R	$P \to Q$	$Q \to R$	$(P \to Q) \wedge (Q \to R)$	$P \to R$
T	T	T	T	T	T	T
T	T	F	T	F	F	F
T	F	T	F	T	F	T
T	F	F	F	T	F	F
F	T	T	T	T	T	T
F	T	F	T	F	F	T
F	F	T	T	T	T	T
F	F	F	T	T	T	T

Notice that for every case where $(P \to Q) \wedge (Q \to R)$ was true, $P \to R$ was also true.

For example, consider the premises below:

If I hike a mountain, I will not eat a sandwich.
If I do not eat a sandwich, I will drink some water.
I will not drink some water.

Write a valid conclusive statement. Explain how you arrived at your answer. Be specific in your explanation.

Valid conclusive statement: I will not hike a mountain.

Application of the chain rule and rule of contraposition give the valid conclusion of $\neg P$. According to the chain rule, given $P \to \neg Q$ and $\neg Q \to R$, then $P \to R$. According to the rule of contraposition, $P \to R$ and $\neg R$ yields $\neg P$. On a truth table, for every place where $(P \to R) \land \neg R$ is true, $\neg P$ is also true. Thus, this is a valid conclusive statement.

NEGATION

In propositional logic, negation refers to the inversion of the truth value of a statement. The **negation** of a statement is true if the original statement is false, and false if the original statement is true. Negation can be signified by the word "not." For instance, the negation of the statement "Bob's cat is black" is "Bob's cat is not black." the symbol for negation is \neg. So, if the proposition P is "Bob's cat is black," then $\neg P$ would be "Bob's cat is not black." Two negations cancel each other out: $\neg\neg P = P$, or "not not P equals P."

It's important to be careful when combining negation with **quantifiers**. The negation of "there exists a cow that has a blue horn" is not "there exists a cow that does not have a blue horn." Rather, the negation is "there does not exist a cow that has a blue horn." the statements $\neg \exists x\, P(x)$ and $\exists x\, \neg P(x)$ are not equivalent. the same is true for the universal quantifier: $\neg \forall x\, P(x)$ and $\forall x\, \neg P(x)$ do not mean the same thing. There is, however, a connection between the negated quantifiers: $\neg \exists x\, P(x)$ is equivalent to $\forall x\, \neg P(x)$, and $\exists x\, \neg P(x)$ is equivalent to $\neg \forall x\, P(x)$.

DE MORGAN'S LAWS

De Morgan's Laws are a set of useful relations connecting negation, conjunction, and disjunction. They can be stated briefly as "the negation of a conjunction is the disjunction of the negations" and "the negation of a disjunction is the conjunction of the negations." This can be written as:

$$\neg(P \land Q) \leftrightarrow (\neg P) \lor (\neg Q) \text{ and } \neg(P \lor Q) \leftrightarrow (\neg P) \land (\neg Q)$$

For instance, if proposition P is "$x > 3$" and proposition Q is "$y > 3$", then De Morgan's Laws state that "it is not true that both x and y are greater than 3" is equivalent to "either x is not greater than 3, or y is not greater than 3."

The validity of **De Morgan's Laws** can be shown with truth tables. Note that the columns highlighted in the same color match:

P	Q	$\neg P$	$\neg Q$	$(\neg P) \land (\neg Q)$	$(\neg P) \lor (\neg Q)$	$P \land Q$	$P \lor Q$	$\neg(P \land Q)$	$\neg(P \lor Q)$
T	T	F	F	F	F	T	T	F	F
T	F	F	T	F	T	F	T	T	F
F	T	T	F	F	T	F	T	T	F
F	F	T	T	T	T	F	F	T	T

CONVERSE, INVERSE, AND CONTRAPOSITIVE OF A CONDITIONAL STATEMENT

The converse of a conditional statement is a conditional statement with the premise and conclusion interchanged. the converse of $P \rightarrow Q$ is $Q \rightarrow P$. The **inverse** has the premise and conclusion both negated. The inverse of $P \rightarrow Q$ is $\neg P \rightarrow \neg Q$. The **contrapositive** has the premise and conclusion both negated *and* interchanged. The contrapositive of $P \rightarrow Q$ is $\neg Q \rightarrow \neg P$.

For example, given the **conditional statement**, "If there is a key in the lock, then someone is home," the **converse** is "if someone is home, then there is a key in the lock," the **inverse** is "if there is not a key in the lock, then no one is home," and the **contrapositive** is "if no one is home, then there is not a key in the lock."

Note that the converse and inverse of a statement are *not* logically equivalent to the original statement. For instance, the statement "if $x = 4$, then $x > 2$" is true, but its converse "if $x > 2$, then $x = 4$" is not, because there are many numbers greater than 2, not just 4. A statement *is*, however, logically equivalent to its contrapositive—and the converse and inverse, while not equivalent to the original statement, are equivalent to each other. The following truth table summarizes the relationships:

P	Q	$\neg P$	$\neg Q$	$P \rightarrow Q$ (statement)	$Q \rightarrow P$ (converse)	$\neg P \rightarrow \neg Q$ (inverse)	$\neg Q \rightarrow \neg P$ (contrapositive)
T	T	F	F	T	T	T	T
T	F	F	T	F	T	T	F
F	T	T	F	T	F	F	T
F	F	T	T	T	T	T	T

INDUCTIVE REASONING

Inductive reasoning is a method used to make a conjecture, based on patterns and observations. The conclusion of an inductive argument may be true or false.

Mathematical Example:

A cube has 6 faces, 8 vertices, and 12 edges. A square pyramid has 5 faces, 5 vertices, and 8 edges. A triangular prism has 5 faces, 6 vertices, and 9 edges. Thus, the sum of the numbers of faces and vertices, minus the number of edges, will always equal 2, for any solid.

Non-Mathematical Example:

Almost all summer days in Tucson are hot. It is a summer day in Tucson. Therefore, it will probably be hot.

DEDUCTIVE REASONING

Deductive reasoning is a method that proves a hypothesis or set of premises. The conclusion of a valid deductive argument will be true, given that the premises are true. Deductive reasoning utilizes logic to determine a conclusion. For instance, consider the following application of the chain rule:

If a ding is a dong, then a ping is a pong.	$p \rightarrow q$
If a ping is a pong, then a ring is a ting.	$q \rightarrow r$
A ding is a dong.	p
Therefore, a ring is a ting.	$\therefore r$

FORMAL REASONING

Formal reasoning, in mathematics, involves justification using formal steps and processes to arrive at a conclusion. Formal reasoning is utilized when writing proofs and using logic. For example, when applying logic, validity of a conclusion is determined by truth tables. A set of premises will yield a given conclusion. This type of thinking is formal reasoning. Writing a geometric proof also employs formal reasoning. For example:

> If a quadrilateral has four congruent sides, it is a rhombus.
> If a shape is a rhombus, then the diagonals are perpendicular.
> A quadrilateral has four congruent sides.
> Therefore, the diagonals are perpendicular.

INFORMAL REASONING

Informal reasoning, in mathematics, uses patterns and observations to make conjectures. The conjecture may be true or false. Several, or even many, examples may show a certain pattern, shedding light on a possible conclusion. However, informal reasoning does not provide a justifiable conclusion. A conjecture may certainly be deemed as likely or probable. However, informal reasoning will not reveal a certain conclusion. Consider the following example:

Mathematical Idea – Given a sequence that starts with 1 and each term decreases by a factor of $\frac{1}{2}$, the limit of the sum of the sequence will be 2.

Informal Reasoning – The sum of 1 and $\frac{1}{2}$ is $1\frac{1}{2}$. The sum of 1, $\frac{1}{2}$, and $\frac{1}{4}$ is $1\frac{3}{4}$. The sum of 1, $\frac{1}{2}$, $\frac{1}{4}$, and $\frac{1}{8}$ is $1\frac{7}{8}$. Thus, it appears that as the sequence approaches infinity, the sum of the sequence approaches 2.

PROOFS

A **proof** serves to show the deductive or inductive process that relates the steps leading from a hypothesis to a conclusion. A proof may be direct ($p \rightarrow q$), meaning that a conclusion is shown to be true, given a hypothesis. There are also proofs by contradiction ($p \wedge \sim q$), whereby the hypothesis is assumed to be true, and the negation of the conclusion is assumed to be true. (In other words, the statement is assumed to be false.) Proofs by contraposition ($\sim q \rightarrow \sim p$) show that the negation of the conclusion leads to the negation of the hypothesis. (In other words, the negation of the conclusion is assumed to be true, and it must be shown that the negation of the hypothesis is also true.) A mathematical induction proof seeks to show that $P(1)$ is true and that $P(k + 1)$ is true, given that $P(k)$ is true. Direct proofs, proofs by contradiction, and proofs by contraposition use deductive methods, while a mathematical induction proof uses an inductive method.

Direct proofs are those that assume a statement to be true. The purpose of such a proof is to show that the conclusion is true, given that the hypothesis is true. A sample of a direct proof is shown below:

Prove "If m divides a and m divides b, then m divides $a + b$."

Proof:

- Assume m divides a and m divides b.
- Thus, a equals the product of m and some integer factor, p, by the definition of division, and b equals the product of m and some integer factor, q, by the definition of division. According to substitution, $a + b$ may be rewritten as $(m \times p) + (m \times q)$. Factoring out the m gives $m(p + q)$. Since m divides $p + q$, and $p + q$ is an integer, according to the closure property, we have shown that m divides $a + b$, by the definition of division.

Indirect proofs (or proofs by contradiction) are those that assume a statement to be false. The purpose of such a proof is to show that a hypothesis is false, given the negation of the conclusion, indicating that the conclusion must be true. A sample of an indirect proof is shown below:

Prove "If $3x + 7$ is odd, then x is even."

Proof:

- Assume $3x + 7$ is odd and x is odd.
- According to the definition of odd, $x = 2a + 1$, where a is an element of the integers.
- Thus, by substitution, $3x + 7 = 3(2a + 1) + 7$, which simplifies as $6a + 3 + 7$, or $6a + 10$, which may be rewritten as $2(3a + 5)$. Any even integer may be written as the product of 2 and some integer, k. Thus, we have shown the hypothesis to be false, meaning that the conditional statement must be true.

A **proof by contraposition** is one written in the form, $\sim Q \to \sim P$. In other words, a proof by contraposition seeks to show that the negation of Q will yield the negation of P. A sample of a proof by contraposition is shown below:

Prove "If $5x + 7$ is even, then x is odd."

Proof:

- Assume that if x is even, then $5x + 7$ is odd.
- Assume x is even.
- Thus, by the definition of an even integer, $x = 2a$.

By substitution, $5x + 7$ may be rewritten as $5(2a) + 7$, which simplifies as $10a + 7$. This expression cannot be written as the product of 2 and some factor, k. Thus, $5x + 7$ is odd, by definition of an odd integer. So, when $5x + 7$ is even, x is odd, according to contraposition.

A **proof by contradiction** is one written in the form, $p \wedge \sim q$. In other words, a proof by contradiction seeks to show the negation of q will result in a false hypothesis, indicating that the conclusion of the statement, as written, must be true. In other words, the conditional statement of $p \to q$ is true.

Mometrix

MATHEMATICAL INDUCTION PROOF UTILIZING INDUCTIVE REASONING

A mathematical induction proof utilizes inductive reasoning in its assumption that if $P(k)$ is true, then $P(k + 1)$ is also true. The induction hypothesis is $P(k)$. This step utilizes inductive reasoning because an observation is used to make the conjecture that $P(k + 1)$ is also true.

Example:

For all natural numbers, n, the sum is equal to $(n + 1)\left(\frac{n}{2}\right)$.

Show that $P(1)$ is true.

$1 = (1 + 1)\left(\frac{1}{2}\right)$.

Assume P(k) is true.

$1 + 2 + 3 + 4 + \cdots + k = (k + 1)\left(\frac{k}{2}\right)$.

This previous step is the inductive hypothesis. This hypothesis may be used to write the conjecture that $P(k + 1)$ is also true: $(1 + 2 + 3 + 4 + \cdots + k) + (k + 1) = [(k + 1) + 1]\left(\frac{k+1}{2}\right)$

$$(k + 1)\left(\frac{k}{2}\right) + (k + 1) = [(k + 1) + 1]\left(\frac{k}{2} + \frac{1}{2}\right)$$

$$(k + 1)\left(\frac{k}{2}\right) + (k + 1) = \left(\frac{k}{2}(k + 1) + \frac{k}{2}\right) + \left(\frac{1}{2}(k + 1) + \frac{1}{2}(1)\right)$$

$$(k + 1)\left(\frac{k}{2}\right) + (k + 1) = \frac{k}{2}(k + 1) + \frac{k}{2} + \frac{k + 1}{2} + \frac{1}{2}$$

$$(k + 1)\left(\frac{k}{2}\right) + (k + 1) = \frac{k}{2}(k + 1) + \frac{2k + 2}{2}$$

$$(k + 1)\left(\frac{k}{2}\right) + (k + 1) = \frac{k}{2}(k + 1) + (k + 1)$$

187

Practice

P1. Given the following statements:

> If I get a bonus, then I will go on vacation.
> If I go on vacation, then I will visit Egypt.
> I got a bonus.
> Therefore, I will visit Egypt.

(a) Rewrite the statements in logical notation.

(b) Make a truth table for the scenario.

(c) Determine if the argument is logical.

(d) TRUE or FALSE: It would contradict this argument to visit Egypt and not have received a bonus.

P2. Given the following statements:

> I will run a marathon in January if and only if the Cubs win the World Series.
> I will not run a marathon in January.
> Therefore, the Cubs did not win the World Series.

(a) Rewrite the statements in logical notation.

(b) Make a truth table for the scenario.

(c) Determine if the argument is logical.

(d) TRUE or FALSE: It is logically equivalent to the first premise above to say, "I will not run a marathon in January if and only if the Cubs do not win the World Series.

P3. Use proof by induction to demonstrate: "The sum of n odd natural numbers is equal to n^2."

P4. Use informal reasoning to justify the statement, "If n is a whole number, then $n^2 + n + 1$ is odd." Explain the reasoning steps used.

P5. Use formal reasoning to justify the statement, "If a divides b, a divides c, and a divides d, then a divides the sum of b, c, and d." Show the formal proof.

Practice Solutions

P1. (a) Let us say "getting a bonus" = B, "going on vacation" = V, and "visiting Egypt" = E:

If I get a bonus, then I will go on vacation.	$B \to V$
If I go on vacation, then I will visit Egypt.	$V \to E$
I got a bonus.	B
Therefore, I will visit Egypt.	$\therefore E$

(b) The truth table for the scenario:

B	V	E	$B \to V$	$V \to E$	$(B \to V) \land (V \to E)$	$B \to E$
T	T	T	T	T	T	T
T	T	F	T	F	F	F
T	F	T	F	T	F	T
T	F	F	F	T	F	F
F	T	T	T	T	T	T
F	T	F	T	F	F	T
F	F	T	T	T	T	T
F	F	F	T	T	T	T

(c) This is an instance of the chain rule and is logically sound.

(d) FALSE: It would NOT contradict this argument to visit Egypt and not have received a bonus. Look at the rows of the truth table where $B = $ F and $E = $ T, in these cases both statements hold:

B	V	E	$B \to V$	$V \to E$	$(B \to V) \land (V \to E)$	$B \to E$
F	T	T	T	T	T	T
F	F	T	T	T	T	T

P2. (a) Let us say "Cubs win" = C and "running a marathon" = M:

I will run a marathon in January if and only if the Cubs win the World Series.	$C \leftrightarrow M$
I will not run a marathon in January.	$\neg M$
Therefore, the Cubs did not win the World Series.	$\therefore \neg C$

(b) The truth table for the scenario:

C	M	$\neg C$	$\neg M$	$C \leftrightarrow M$	$C \leftrightarrow M \land \neg M$	$\neg M \to \neg C$
T	T	F	F	T	F	T
T	F	F	T	F	F	F
F	T	T	F	F	T	T
F	F	T	T	T	T	T

(c) Based on the truth table, it is clear that $C \leftrightarrow M \land \neg M$ is logically equivalent to $\neg C$.

(d) TRUE: The following truth table demonstrates the equivalence:

C	M	$\neg C$	$\neg M$	$C \leftrightarrow M$	$\neg M \leftrightarrow \neg C$
T	T	F	F	T	T
T	F	F	T	F	F
F	T	T	F	F	F
F	F	T	T	T	T

P3. Show that $P(1)$ is true.

$1 = 1^2$.

Assume $P(k)$ is true.

$1 + 3 + 5 + \cdots + (2k + 1) = k^2$.

We want to show that $1 + 3 + 5 + \cdots + (2(k + 1) + 1) = (k + 1)^2$.

$1 + 3 + 5 + \cdots + (2k + 1) + [2k + 1] = k^2 + [2k + 1]$.

We can distribute 2 to each of the k terms:

$(1 + 2) + (3 + 2) + (5 + 2) + \cdots + (2k + 1 + 2) + [1] = k^2 + [2k + 1]$.

$3 + 5 + 7 + \cdots + \big((2k + 2) + 1\big) + [1] = k^2 + 2k + 1$.

Rearrange and simplify:

$1 + 3 + 5 + 7 + \cdots + (2(k + 1) + 1) = (k + 1)^2$.

$P(k + 1)$ is true. Thus, according to mathematical induction,

$1 + 3 + 5 + \cdots + (2n + 1) = n^2$.

P4. Using the sequence, 0, 1, 2, 3, 4, 5, 6, ... for n, evaluation of the expression, $n^2 + n + 1$, gives $0^2 + 0 + 1, 1^2 + 1 + 1, 2^2 + 2 + 1, 3^2 + 3 + 1, 4^2 + 4 + 1, 5^2 + 5 + 1$, and $6^2 + 6 + 1$, or 1, 3, 7, 13, 21, 31, and 43, all of which are odd numbers. Thus, it appears that given any whole number, n, evaluation of the expression $n^2 + n + 1$ will yield an odd number.

P5. Direct Proof:

Assume a divides b, a divides c, and a divides d.

Given the definition of divides, a divides b indicates that there exists some integer, r, such that $b = a \times r$. Also, a divides c indicates that there exists some integer, s, such that $c = a \times s$. Finally, a divides d indicates that there exists some integer, t, such that $d = a \times t$. By substitution, the sum of b, c, and d may be written as $(a \times r) + (a \times s) + (a \times t)$. Factoring out an a gives $a(r + s + t)$. The factor $(r + s + t)$ is an integer, according to the closure property under addition. Thus, a divides the sum of b, c, and d.

Stopping here.

Practice Test #1

1. $6.42 - 3.7 =$

 a. 2.72

 b. 3.35

 c. 6.05

 d. 6.35

2. Which of the following fractions is equal to 0.375?

 a. $\frac{2}{5}$

 b. $\frac{2}{7}$

 c. $\frac{3}{8}$

 d. $\frac{4}{9}$

3. $5\frac{1}{6} - 2\frac{1}{2} =$

 a. $2\frac{1}{4}$

 b. $2\frac{2}{3}$

 c. $3\frac{1}{4}$

 d. $3\frac{1}{3}$

4. What is the proper ordering (from least to greatest) of the following numbers?

 I. 0.32

 II. 0.32%

 III. 3.2%

 IV. $\frac{32}{99}$

 a. II, III, I, IV

 b. II, III, IV, I

 c. III, II, I, IV

 d. IV, I, III, II

5. Which of the following is the best estimate for $23.97124 \div 8.023$?

 a. 2

 b. 3

 c. 16

 d. 20

6. The two legs of a right triangle have side lengths of 5 and 12. What is the length of the hypotenuse?

 a. 13

 b. 17

 c. $\sqrt{60}$

 d. $\sqrt{119}$

7. **Which of the following fractions cannot be converted to a terminating decimal?**

 a. $\frac{1}{2}$

 b. $\frac{1}{3}$

 c. $\frac{1}{4}$

 d. $\frac{1}{5}$

8. **A dress is marked as 20% off. With the discount, the current price is \$40.00. What is the price of the dress without the discount?**

 a. \$32

 b. \$45

 c. \$48

 d. \$50

9. **Which of the following inequalities is TRUE?**

 a. $\frac{4}{5} < \frac{5}{7}$

 b. $\frac{5}{7} > \frac{3}{5}$

 c. $\frac{2}{3} > \frac{4}{5}$

 d. $\frac{1}{2} < \frac{2}{5}$

10. $17.92 \div 3.2 =$

 a. 5.1

 b. 5.6

 c. 6.1

 d. 6.6

11. **Which of the following is *not* equal to the others?**

 a. $\frac{10}{3}$

 b. $\frac{30}{9}$

 c. $2\frac{4}{3}$

 d. $3\frac{2}{3}$

12. **If it takes Alice twelve minutes to make one ring, how many rings can she make in six hours?**

 a. 2

 b. 6

 c. 30

 d. 72

13. **Which of the following is closest to $\frac{111}{223} \times 5,940$?**

 a. 1,000

 b. 2,000

 c. 3,000

 d. 4,000

14. $2.22 + 0.1 + 0.623 =$

 a. 0.855

 b. 8.46

 c. 2.853

 d. 2.943

15. Three treasure hunters decide to split up their haul. The first treasure hunter gets $\frac{1}{3}$ of the treasure. The second treasure hunter gets $\frac{1}{4}$ of the treasure. What fraction of the treasure does the third treasure hunter get?

 a. $\frac{1}{2}$

 b. $\frac{1}{5}$

 c. $\frac{5}{7}$

 d. $\frac{5}{12}$

16. What percentage is equal to $\frac{3}{20}$?

 a. 6%

 b. 15%

 c. 30%

 d. 60%

17. Which of the following exponential expressions represents the smallest number?

 a. $8^{\frac{3}{2}}$

 b. 16

 c. $4^{\frac{5}{2}}$

 d. $2^{\frac{7}{2}}$

18. $1\frac{3}{4} \div \frac{7}{10} =$

 a. $2\frac{1}{2}$

 b. $2\frac{1}{14}$

 c. $1\frac{11}{14}$

 d. $\frac{4}{10}$

19. A rectangular lot is three yards wide and four yards long. What is the area of the lot in square feet?

 a. 4 ft²

 b. 12 ft²

 c. 36 ft²

 d. 108 ft²

20. $\frac{2}{3} + \frac{2}{5} =$

 a. $\frac{1}{4}$

 b. $\frac{1}{2}$

 c. $\frac{8}{15}$

 d. $1\frac{1}{15}$

21. What is $|x| + |x - 2|$ when $x = 1$?

 a. 0

 b. 1

 c. 2

 d. 3

22. Which of the following inequalities is correct?

 a. $\frac{1}{3} < \frac{2}{7} < \frac{5}{12}$

 b. $\frac{2}{7} < \frac{1}{3} < \frac{5}{12}$

 c. $\frac{5}{12} < \frac{2}{7} < \frac{1}{3}$

 d. $\frac{5}{12} < \frac{1}{3} < \frac{2}{7}$

23. There are five favorite parking spaces in the game, Shopping Extravaganza. You receive two tokens if you land on Parking Space #1, six tokens if you land on Parking Space #2, two tokens if you land on Parking Space #3, three tokens if you land on Parking Space #4, and seven tokens if you land on Parking Space #5. You have an equal chance of landing on each space. What is the expected value of the number of tokens during a play in the game?

 a. 2

 b. 3

 c. 4

 d. 7

24. $(2x^2 + 3x + 2) - (x^2 + 2x - 3) =$

 a. $x^2 + x + 5$

 b. $x^2 + x - 1$

 c. $x^2 + 5x + 5$

 d. $x^2 + 5x - 1$

25. A rectangle is twice as long as it is wide. If its area is 200 cm², what is its width?

 a. 10 cm

 b. 20 cm

 c. $10\sqrt{2}$ cm

 d. $20\sqrt{2}$ cm

26. Kyle bats third in the batting order for the Badgers baseball team. The table below shows the number of hits that Kyle had in each of 7 consecutive games played during one week in July.

Day	Monday	Tuesday	Wednesday	Thursday	Friday	Saturday	Sunday
Hits	1	2	3	1	1	4	2

What is the mode of the numbers in the distribution shown in the table?

 a. 1
 b. 2
 c. 3
 d. 4

27. $\frac{\sqrt{2}}{\sqrt{6}} =$

 a. $\sqrt{3}$
 b. $2\sqrt{3}$
 c. $\frac{\sqrt{3}}{2}$
 d. $\frac{\sqrt{3}}{3}$

28. $\frac{2}{3}(3-2) + \frac{1}{2}(2-4) =$

 a. $-\frac{1}{3}$
 b. $-\frac{1}{2}$
 c. $\frac{1}{2}$
 d. $\frac{1}{3}$

29. Which of the following is *not* a factor of $x^3 - 3x^2 - 4x + 12$?

 a. $x - 2$
 b. $x + 2$
 c. $x - 3$
 d. $x + 3$

30. Last year, Jenny tutored students in math, in chemistry, and for the ACT. She tutored ten students in math, eight students in chemistry, and seven students for the ACT. She tutored five students in both math and chemistry, and she tutored four students both in chemistry and for the ACT, and five students both in math and for the ACT. She tutored three students in all three subjects. How many students did Jenny tutor last year?

 a. 34
 b. 25
 c. 23
 d. 14

31. The probability that Alisha chooses a philosophy class is 0.30. The probability that she chooses a qualitative methods class, given that she chooses a philosophy class, is 0.40. Finally, the probability she chooses a philosophy class or a qualitative methods class is 0.62. What is the probability she chooses a qualitative methods class?

 a. 0.32
 b. 0.38
 c. 0.44
 d. 0.52

32. Which of these graphs is NOT representative of the data set shown below?

$$
\begin{array}{c|l}
3 & 6\,7\,9\,9 \\
4 & 2\,3\,8\,8\,9 \\
5 & 0\,1\,1\,1\,5\,7 \\
6 & 0\,0\,1\,2\,3 \\
\end{array}
$$

KEY

$2|123 = 21, 22, 23$

a.

b.

c.

d. All of these graphs represent the data set.

33. Simplify $\frac{x^6}{y^4} \times x^2 y^3$.

 a. $x^4 y$

 b. $\frac{x^4}{y}$

 c. $x^8 y$

 d. $\frac{x^8}{y}$

34. If $6q + 3 = 8q - 7$, what is q?

 a. $-\frac{5}{7}$

 b. $\frac{5}{7}$

 c. 5

 d. -7

35. Attending a summer camp are 12 six-year-olds, 15 seven-year-olds, 14 eight-year-olds, 12 nine-year-olds, and 10 ten-year-olds. If a camper is randomly selected to participate in a special event, what is the probability that he or she is at least eight years old?

 a. $\frac{2}{9}$

 b. $\frac{22}{63}$

 c. $\frac{4}{7}$

 d. $\frac{3}{7}$

36. A communications company charges $5.00 for the first ten minutes of a call and $1.20 for each minute thereafter. Which of the following equations correctly relates the price in dollars, d, to the number of minutes, m (when $m \geq 10$)?

 a. $d = 5 + 1.2m$

 b. $d = 5 + 1.2(m - 10)$

 c. $d = 5m + 1.2(m + 10)$

 d. $d = (m + 10)(5 + 1.2)$

37. Employees of a small company work in one of three departments and are distributed as shown. Two employees are chosen randomly and independently to attend a conference. What is the probability that the pair chosen includes a woman from Department 1 AND a man from Department 2?

	Dept. 1	Dept. 2	Dept. 3	Total
Women	11	27	16	54
Men	19	15	12	46
Total	30	42	28	100

 a. 1/30

 b. 1/40

 c. 1/50

 d. 1/60

38. Which of the following graphs represents the inequality $-2 < x \le 4$?

a.

-3 -2 -1 0 1 2 3 4 5

b.

-3 -2 -1 0 1 2 3 4 5

c.

-3 -2 -1 0 1 2 3 4 5

d.

-3 -2 -1 0 1 2 3 4 5

39. The numbers of volunteers in different states (Texas and New Mexico) for 15 different events are shown in the table below. Which of the following statements is true?

TX	8	17	18	19	20	21	21	21	22	28	29	31	41	45	52
NM	7	11	15	29	30	30	31	33	34	36	37	42	44	44	45

a. The Texas data have a larger median and larger standard deviation.
b. The Texas data have a larger median and smaller standard deviation.
c. The Texas data have a smaller median and larger standard deviation.
d. The Texas data have a smaller median and smaller standard deviation.

40. $(x + 2)(x - 3) = ?$

a. $x^2 - 1$
b. $x^2 - 6$
c. $x^2 - x - 6$
d. $x^2 - 5x - 1$

41. Which of the following completely describes the number of points in which two distinct quadratic functions can intersect?

a. 2
b. 0 or 1
c. 0 or 2
d. 1 or 2
e. 0, 1, or 2

42. $\log_5(5^3) =$

a. –2
b. 1
c. 3
d. 25
e. 243

43. Which of the following lines is perpendicular to the line $3x + 2y = 5$?

 a. $y = -\frac{1}{3}x + 2$

 b. $y = -\frac{2}{3}x + 5$

 c. $y = \frac{1}{3}x - 5$

 d. $y = \frac{2}{3}x - 7$

 e. $y = \frac{1}{3}x + 1$

44. If $\cos\theta + 1 = 0$, which of the following is a possible value of θ?

 a. $-180°$

 b. $-90°$

 c. $0°$

 d. $90°$

 e. $135°$

45. $(1 + i) \div (1 - i) =$

 a. i

 b. -1

 c. $-i$

 d. $-2i$

 e. $2i$

46. Suppose the area of the square in the diagram to the right is 64 in². (The square is not shown actual size.) What is the area of the circle?

 a. $16\pi \text{ in}^2$

 b. $64\pi \text{ in}^2$

 c. $\frac{64}{\pi} \text{ in}^2$

 d. $(64 + \pi) \text{ in}^2$

 e. $\frac{128}{\pi} \text{ in}^2$

47. How many solutions does the following system of equations have?

$$x^2 - y^2 = 2$$
$$x^2 + y^2 = 4$$

 a. 0

 b. 1

 c. 2

 d. 3

 e. 4

48. If $f(x) = x^3 + 2$, what is $f^{-1}(x)$?

 a. $x^{1/3} - 2$

 b. $x^{-3} - 2$

 c. $x^{-1/3} - 2$

 d. $(x - 2)^{1/3}$

 e. $(x - 2)^{-3}$

49. What is the period of the function $y = \tan(2x + 6)$?

 a. $\frac{\pi}{2}$

 b. π

 c. 2π

 d. 3π

 e. 6π

50. One root of a certain real polynomial is $3 - 2i$. Which of the following must also be a root of this polynomial?

 a. 0

 b. $-2i$

 c. $3 + 2i$

 d. $-3 + 2i$

 e. $2 - 3i$

51. What is the determinant of the matrix $\begin{bmatrix} 2 & 4 \\ 1 & 3 \end{bmatrix}$?

 a. -2

 b. -1

 c. 0

 d. 1

 e. 2

52. For one week, a hiker decides to walk two miles more each day than she walked the previous day. If she walks five miles on the first day, how many total miles has she walked by the end of the seventh day?

 a. 47

 b. 49

 c. 77

 d. 82

 e. 217

53. How many distinct ways are there to arrange the letters in the word PARABOLA?

 a. 1,680

 b. 6,720

 c. 13,440

 d. 20,160

 e. 40,320

54. Which of the following points is collinear with the points $(2, 3)$ and $(-1, 5)$?

 a. $(-6, 8)$
 b. $(0, 4)$
 c. $(3, 2)$
 d. $(5, 1)$
 e. $(7, 0)$

55. Which of the following is equivalent to $x^2 + 3 > 2x + 2$?

 a. $x < -1$
 b. $x \neq 1$
 c. $x > 1$
 d. $-1 < x < 1$
 e. $x < -1$ or $x > 1$

56. A gardener has 300 feet of fencing. He wants to use it to enclose six identically-sized gardens, arranged as in the diagram below (not necessarily to scale). What is the maximum total area he can enclose? (Round to the nearest square foot if necessary.)

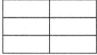

 a. $1600 \ \text{ft}^2$
 b. $1667 \ \text{ft}^2$
 c. $1869 \ \text{ft}^2$
 d. $1875 \ \text{ft}^2$
 e. $5625 \ \text{ft}^2$

57. The points $(1, 2)$ and $(2, 4)$ lie on the graph of $f(x)$. Which of the following points must lie on the graph of $f^{-1}(x)$?

 a. $(1, 4)$
 b. $(2, 1)$
 c. $(2, 4)$
 d. $(2, -4)$
 e. $(4, 1)$

58. Which of the following could be the graph of $y = ax^7 - bx^4 + cx^2 - d$ for some positive constants $a, b, c,$ and d? (Assume the graphs have no further maxima or minima beyond those shown.)

a. b. c.

d. e.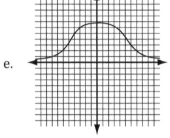

59. If $f(x) = x + 3$ and $f(g(x)) = g(f(x))$, which of the following could be $g(x)$?

a. $-x$
b. $x - 4$
c. $3x$
d. x^2
e. e^x

60. Which of the following expressions is equivalent to $\sin 2x \sec x$?

a. 1
b. $2 \sin x$
c. $2 \cos x$
d. $\sin^2 x$
e. $\tan 2x$

Answer Key and Explanations for Test #1

1. A: In order to subtract decimal numbers, write them one above the other with the decimal points aligned; then, carry out the subtraction normally, placing the decimal point in the same position in the result:

$$\begin{array}{r} 6.42 \\ -\ 3.70 \\ \hline 2.72 \end{array}$$

2. C: 0.375 is three hundred seventy-five thousandths, which, when written as a fraction, is $\frac{375}{1000}$. One way this fraction can be reduced by dividing both the numerator and denominator repeatedly by 5: $\frac{375}{1000} = \frac{75}{200} = \frac{15}{40} = \frac{3}{8}$.

3. B: One way to add or subtract mixed numbers is to first convert them to improper fractions. To get the numerator of the improper fraction, multiply the integer part of the mixed number by the denominator and add that product to the numerator; the denominator remains the same. So $5\frac{1}{6} = \frac{5\times 6 + 1}{6} = \frac{31}{6}$ and $2\frac{1}{2} = \frac{2\times 2 + 1}{2} = \frac{5}{2}$. Now convert the improper fractions to so that they have the lowest common denominator, which in this case is 6. $\frac{31}{6}$ already has a denominator of 6, but we need to convert $\frac{5}{2}$ to its equivalent fraction with a denominator of 6: $\frac{5}{2} = \frac{5\times 3}{2\times 3} = \frac{15}{6}$. We can now subtract. $\frac{31}{6} - \frac{15}{6} = \frac{16}{6}$, which we can reduce by dividing both sides by 2 to $\frac{16/2}{6/2} = \frac{8}{3}$. Finally, we convert back to a mixed number by dividing the numerator by the denominator; the quotient is the integer part, and the remainder is the new numerator. $8 \div 3 = 2$ with a remainder of 2, so $\frac{8}{3} = 2\frac{2}{3}$.

4. A: Recalling that percent just means "divided by 100," each of the given numbers can be represented as fractions:

$$\text{I. } 0.32 = \frac{32}{100}, \quad \text{II. } 0.32\% = \frac{0.32}{100} = \frac{32}{10000}, \quad \text{III. } 3.2\% = \frac{3.2}{100} = \frac{32}{1000}, \quad \text{IV. } \frac{32}{99}$$

All of the fractions share the same numerator. Among fractions with the same numerator, the largest fraction has the smallest denominator. We can order these fractions from least to greatest by ordering the denominators from greatest to least. The correct order is $\frac{32}{10,000} < \frac{32}{1,000} < \frac{32}{100} < \frac{32}{99}$, which corresponds to choice A.

5. B: 23.97124 is about 24, and 8.023 is about 8. So $23.97124 \div 8.023$ is about $24 \div 8 = 3$.

6. A: The legs and hypotenuse of a right triangle are related through the Pythagorean Theorem, $a^2 + b^2 = c^2$, where a and b are the lengths of the legs and c is the length of the hypotenuse. In this case, $a = 5$ and $b = 12$ (or vice-versa; it doesn't matter which leg we call a and which leg we call b), so $5^2 + 12^2 = c^2 \Rightarrow 25 + 144 = c^2 \Rightarrow 169 = c^2 \Rightarrow c = \sqrt{169} = 13$.

7. B: A terminating decimal is one that eventually stops; after a certain place all further digits are zeroes. To convert a fraction to a decimal, divide the numerator by the denominator. This quickly produces terminating decimals for $\frac{1}{2}, \frac{1}{4}$, and $\frac{1}{5}$: namely 0.5, 0.25, and 0.2, respectively. The decimal expansion of $\frac{1}{3}$, however, repeats indefinitely as 0.33333333…. Alternately, note that in order to

correspond to a terminating decimal, a fraction must have a denominator that is a factor of a power of ten; in other words, the only prime factors of the denominator must be 2 and 5. This is true of $\frac{1}{2}$, $\frac{1}{4}$, and $\frac{1}{5}$ but not of $\frac{1}{3}$. So, $\frac{1}{3}$ is the only one of the choices without a terminating decimal expansion.

8. D: If the dress's price is 20% off, it is $(100\% - 20\%) = 80\%$ of the regular price. So, the sales price of the dress, \$40, is 80% of what price? To find the answer, divide 40 by 80%, which is equivalent to the fraction $\frac{80}{100}$. Dividing by the fraction $\frac{80}{100}$ is the same as multiplying its reciprocal, $\frac{100}{80}$. $40 \times \frac{100}{80} = 40 \times \frac{5}{4} = \frac{200}{4} = 50$, so, the original price was \$50.00.

9. B: When comparing fractions, it is necessary to find common denominators.

a. $\frac{28}{35} = \frac{4}{5} < \frac{5}{7} = \frac{25}{35}$

b. $\frac{25}{35} = \frac{5}{7} > \frac{3}{5} = \frac{21}{35}$

c. $\frac{10}{15} = \frac{2}{3} > \frac{4}{5} = \frac{12}{25}$

d. $\frac{5}{10} = \frac{1}{2} < \frac{2}{5} = \frac{4}{10}$

Once all of the fractions have been represented using common denominators, it is easy to determine which of each pair is greater since the greater is the one with the larger numerator. Among the four choices, the only valid inequality is choice B.

10. B: To divide decimals, set up a long division problem, but then move the decimal point an equal number of places to the right in both the dividend and the divisor until it is at the right end of the divisor, making the divisor an integer. Then, put the decimal point in the quotient directly above the decimal point in the dividend. Add extra zeroes to the end of the dividend if needed.

$$
3.2\overline{)17.92} \quad = \quad 32\overline{)179.2} \\
\begin{array}{r}
5.6 \\
\hline
160 \\
\hline
19\,2 \\
19\,2 \\
\hline
0
\end{array}
$$

11. D: Multiplying both the numerator and denominator by the same constant does not change the value of a fraction; for instance, $\frac{10}{3} = \frac{10 \times 3}{3 \times 3} = \frac{30}{9}$, so choices A and B contain equivalent fractions. To convert a mixed number to a fraction, multiply the integer part by the denominator and add the product it to the numerator; this becomes the numerator of the improper fraction, while the denominator remains the same. So, $2\frac{4}{3} = \frac{2 \times 3 + 4}{3} = \frac{10}{3}$. (Note that $2\frac{4}{3}$ is a nonstandard mixed number because it has an improper fractional component; nevertheless, it is equivalent to $\frac{10}{3}$ and $\frac{30}{9}$.) Though choices A, B, and C are equal to each other, choice D contains a nonequivalent mixed number: $3\frac{2}{3} = \frac{3 \times 3 + 2}{3} = \frac{11}{3} \neq \frac{10}{3}$. (As a standard mixed number, $\frac{10}{3}$ would be equal to $3\frac{1}{3}$.)

12. C: Six hours is equal to $6 \times 60 = 360$ minutes. If Alice can create one ring in twelve minutes, then in 360 minutes she can create $\frac{360}{12} = 30$ rings.

Here is another way to solve the problem: A rate of one ring in twelve minutes is equivalent to a rate of $\frac{1 \text{ ring}}{12 \text{ minutes}} \times \frac{60 \text{ minutes}}{1 \text{ hour}} = \frac{5 \text{ rings}}{\text{hour}}$. Therefore, in six hours Alice can create $5 \times 6 = 30$ rings.

13. C: $\frac{111}{223}$ is very close to $\frac{1}{2}$. 5,940 is close to 6,000. So $\frac{111}{223} \times 5{,}940$ is about $\frac{1}{2} \times 6{,}000 = 3{,}000$.

14. D: In order to add decimal numbers, write them one above the other with the decimal points aligned, and then carry out the addition normally, placing the decimal point in the same position in the result:

$$
\begin{array}{r}
2.22 \\
0.1 \\
+0.623 \\
\hline
2.943
\end{array}
$$

15. D: The total must be 1, so the fraction that goes to the third treasure hunter is $1 - \frac{1}{3} - \frac{1}{4}$. To subtract these fractions, convert them all to fractions with the least common denominator, which is in this case 12. So $1 - \frac{1}{3} - \frac{1}{4} = \frac{1 \times 12}{1 \times 12} - \frac{1 \times 4}{3 \times 4} - \frac{1 \times 3}{4 \times 3} = \frac{12}{12} - \frac{4}{12} - \frac{3}{12} = \frac{12 - 4 - 3}{12} = \frac{5}{12}$.

16. B: A percentage is the numerator of a fraction with a denominator of 100. To convert a fraction to a percentage, set up a ratio: $\frac{3}{20} = \frac{x}{100}$. Since $20 \times 5 = 100$, we can multiply 3×5 to find that $\frac{3}{20}$ is 15%.

17. D: Each of the base numbers in these expressions is a power of 2. If we express each of them in terms of 2, it will be easier to compare them.

a. $8^{\frac{3}{2}} = (2^3)^{\frac{3}{2}} = 2^{\frac{9}{2}}$
b. $16 = 2^4 = 2^{\frac{8}{2}}$
c. $4^{\frac{5}{2}} = (2^2)^{\frac{5}{2}} = 2^{\frac{10}{2}}$
d. $2^{\frac{7}{2}}$

Once each of the choices has been expressed as a power of 2, we can see that choice D is the smallest.

18. A: To multiply or divide mixed numbers, first convert them to improper fractions. To get the numerator of the equivalent improper fraction, multiply the denominator of the mixed number's fractional component by the whole number component and add to the numerator of the fractional component; keep the denominator of the improper fraction the same as the denominator of the fractional component of the mixed number. So $1\frac{3}{4} = \frac{1 \times 4 + 3}{4} = \frac{7}{4}$. Dividing by a fraction is the same as multiplying by its reciprocal, so $\frac{7}{4} \div \frac{7}{10} = \frac{7}{4} \times \frac{10}{7} = \frac{70}{28}$, which reduces to $\frac{70 \div 7}{28 \div 7} = \frac{10}{4} = \frac{10 \div 2}{4 \div 2} = \frac{5}{2}$. Convert this back to a mixed number by dividing the numerator by the denominator: the quotient is the integer part of the mixed number, and the remainder is the numerator of the fractional part of the mixed number. $5 \div 2 = 2$ with a remainder of 1, so $\frac{5}{2} = 2\frac{1}{2}$.

19. D: There are three feet in a yard. In feet, the lot is $3 \times 3 = 9$ feet wide, and $4 \times 3 = 12$ feet long. So its area is 9 ft \times 12 ft = 108 square feet.

As an alternate way of solving the problem, first find the lot's area in square yards: 3 yards \times 4 yards = 12 square yards. Then, convert square yards to square feet: since there are 3 feet in a yard, there are $3^2 = 9$ square feet in a square yard. So the lot's area in square feet is $12 \times 9 = 108$ square feet.

20. D: To add or subtract fractions, first convert them to equivalent fractions which contain the lowest common denominator, which in this case is 15. So $\frac{2}{3} + \frac{2}{5} = \frac{2 \times 5}{3 \times 5} + \frac{2 \times 3}{5 \times 3} = \frac{10}{15} + \frac{6}{15} = \frac{16}{15}$. To convert this to a mixed number, divide the numerator by the denominator; the quotient is the integer part of the mixed number and the remainder is the numerator of the fractional part of the mixed number. $16 \div 15 = 1$ with a remainder of 1, so $\frac{16}{15} = 1\frac{1}{15}$.

21. C: $|x| + |x - 2| = |1| + |1 - 2| = |1| + |-1| = 1 + 1 = 2$.

22. B: One way to compare fractions is to convert them to equivalent fractions with common denominators. In this case the lowest common denominator of the three fractions is $7 \times 12 = 84$. Converting each of the fractions to this denominator, $\frac{1}{3} = \frac{1 \times 28}{3 \times 28} = \frac{28}{84}, \frac{2}{7} = \frac{2 \times 12}{7 \times 12} = \frac{24}{84}$, and $\frac{5}{12} = \frac{5 \times 7}{12 \times 7} = \frac{35}{84}$. Since $24 < 28 < 35$, it must be the case that $\frac{2}{7} < \frac{1}{3} < \frac{5}{12}$.

23. C: The expected value is equal to the sum of the products of the probability and tokens won for each space.

$$E(X) = \left(2 \times \frac{1}{5}\right) + \left(6 \times \frac{1}{5}\right) + \left(2 \times \frac{1}{5}\right) + \left(3 \times \frac{1}{5}\right) + \left(7 \times \frac{1}{5}\right) = \frac{2}{5} + \frac{6}{5} + \frac{2}{5} + \frac{3}{5} + \frac{7}{5} = \frac{20}{5} = 4$$

24. A: $(2x^2 + 3x + 2) - (x^2 + 2x - 3) = (2x^2 + 3x + 2) + (-1)(x^2 + 2x - 3)$. First, distribute the -1 to remove the parentheses: $2x^2 + 3x + 2 - x^2 - 2x + 3$. Next, combine like terms:

$$(2x^2 - x^2) + (3x - 2x) + (2 + 3) = x^2 + x + 5$$

25. A: The area A of a rectangle is equal to its length l times its width w: $A = l \times w$. The rectangle is twice as long as it is wide, so $l = 2w$. By replacing l with its equivalent $2w$, the area of this rectangle can be written as $A = 2w \times w = 2w^2$. So $2w^2 = 200 \text{ cm}^2 \Rightarrow w^2 = 100 \text{ cm}^2 \Rightarrow w = \sqrt{100 \text{ cm}^2} = 10$ cm.

26. A: The mode is the number that appears most often in a set of data. If no item appears most often, then the data set has no mode. In this case, Kyle achieved one hit a total of three times, two hits twice, three hits once, and four hits once. One hit occurred the most times, and therefore the mode of the data set is 1.

27. D: To rationalize the denominator of a ratio of radicals, multiply both sides of the fraction by the radical in the denominator and reduce if necessary: $\frac{\sqrt{2}}{\sqrt{6}} = \frac{\sqrt{2} \times \sqrt{6}}{\sqrt{6} \times \sqrt{6}} = \frac{\sqrt{12}}{6} = \frac{2\sqrt{3}}{6} = \frac{\sqrt{3}}{3}$.

28. A: $\frac{2}{3}(3 - 2) + \frac{1}{2}(2 - 4) = \frac{2}{3}(1) + \frac{1}{2}(-2) = \frac{2}{3} - \frac{2}{2} = \frac{2}{3} - 1 = \frac{2}{3} - \frac{3}{3} = -\frac{1}{3}$.

29. D: Note that the first two terms and the last two terms of $x^3 - 3x^2 - 4x + 12$ are each divisible by $x - 3$. Thus $x^3 - 3x^2 - 4x + 12 = x^2(x - 3) - 4(x - 3) = (x^2 - 4)(x - 3)$. $x^2 - 4$ is a

difference of squares, and since in general $x^2 - a^2 = (x + a)(x - a)$, we know $x^2 - 4 = (x + 2)(x - 2)$. The full factorization of $x^3 - 3x^2 - 4x + 12$ is therefore $(x + 2)(x - 2)(x - 3)$.

Alternatively, instead of factoring the polynomial, we could have divided the polynomial $x^3 - 3x^2 - 4x + 12$ by the expression contained in each answer choice. Of those listed, only the expression $x + 3$ yields a nonzero remainder when divided into $x^3 - 3x^2 - 4x + 12$, so it is not a factor.

30. D: Use a Venn diagram to help organize the given information. Start by filling in the space where the three circles intersect: Jenny tutored three students in all three areas. Use that information to fill in the spaces where two circles intersect: for example, she tutored four students in chemistry and for the ACT, and three of those were students she tutored in all three areas, so one student was tutored in chemistry and for the ACT but not for math. Once the diagram is completed, add the number of students who were tutored in all areas to the number of students tutored in only two of the three areas to the number of students tutored in only one area. The total number of students tutored was $3 + 2 + 2 + 1 + 3 + 2 + 1 = 14$.

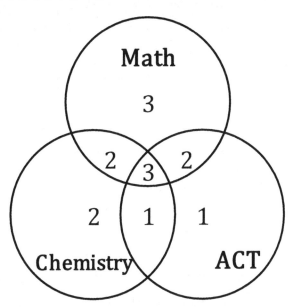

31. C: The problem may be solved by writing P(phil or qual) = P(phil) + P(qual) − P(phil and qual). The probability for philosophy or qualitative and the probability for philosophy may be substituted giving 0.62 = 0.30 + P(qual) − P(phil and qual). Next find the probability that she chooses both philosophy and qualitative by using the formula, P(phil and qual) = P(phil) × P(qual|phil). Substituting the probabilities of 0.30 and 0.40 gives P(phil and qual) = 0.30 × 0.40, or 0.12. Now, the probability of 0.12 may be substituted into the original equation, giving 0.62 = 0.30 + P(qual) − 0.12. Solving for P(qual) gives a probability of 0.44. Thus, there is a 0.44 probability that Alisha chooses a qualitative methods class.

32. D: To draw a box-and-whisker plot from the data, find the median, quartiles, and upper and lower limits.

```
3 | 6 7 9 9
4 | 2|3 8 8 9              Key
5 | 0|1 1 1 5|7         3 | 6 = 36
6 | 0 0 1 2 3
```

The median is $\frac{50+51}{2} = 50.5$, the lower quartile is $\frac{22+23}{2} = 22.5$, and the upper quartile is $\frac{57+60}{2} = 58.5$. The box of the box-and-whisker plot goes through the quartiles, and a line through the box represents the median of the data. The whiskers extend from the box to the lower and upper limits, unless there are any outliers in the set. In this case, there are no outliers, so the box-and-whisker plot in choice A correctly represents the data set.

To draw a pie chart, find the percentage of data contained in each of the ranges shown. There are four out of twenty numbers between 30 and 39, inclusive, so the percentage shown in the pie chart for that range of data is $\frac{4}{20} \cdot 100\% = 20\%$; there are five values between 40 to 49, inclusive, so the percentage of data for that sector is $\frac{5}{20} \cdot 100\% = 25\%$; $\frac{6}{20} \cdot 100\% = 30\%$ of the data is within the range of 50-59, and $\frac{5}{20} \cdot 100\% = 25\%$ is within the range of 60-69. The pie chart shows the correct percentage of data in each category.

To draw a cumulative frequency histogram, find the cumulative frequency of the data.

Range	Frequency	Cumulative frequency
30-39	4	4
40-49	5	9
50-59	6	15
60-69	5	20

The histogram shows the correct cumulative frequencies.

Therefore, all of the graphs represent the data set.

33. D: $\frac{x^6}{y^4} \times x^2 y^3 = x^6 y^{-4} \times x^2 y^3 = (x^6 x^2)(y^{-4} y^3) = x^{6+2} y^{-4+3} = x^8 y^{-1} = \frac{x^8}{y}$.

34. C: $6q + 3 = 8q - 7 \Rightarrow 6q + 3 + 7 = 8q \Rightarrow 6q + 10 = 8q \Rightarrow 10 = 8q - 6q \Rightarrow 10 = 2q \Rightarrow q = 5$.

35. C: The probability of an event is the number of possible occurrences of that event divided by the number of all possible outcomes. A camper who is at least eight years old can be eight, nine, or ten years old, so the probability of randomly selecting a camper at least eight years old is

$$\frac{\text{number of eight-, nine-, and ten - year - old campers}}{\text{total number of campers}} = \frac{14 + 12 + 10}{12 + 15 + 14 + 12 + 10} = \frac{36}{63} = \frac{4}{7}$$

36. B: The charge is $1.20 for each minute *past* the first ten minutes. The number of minutes after the first ten minutes is $m - 10$, so this amount charged for the part of the phone call exceeding 10

minutes is $1.2(m - 10)$. Adding this to the \$5.00 charge for the first ten minutes gives $d = 5 + 1.2(m - 10)$.

37. D: The probability of a woman from Department 1 being chosen is $11/100$ and the probability of a man from Department 2 is $15/99$, since there are only 99 employees left to choose from after the first employee has been selected. The probability of that pair being chosen is equal to the product of the two probabilities, since the picks are independent of one another. So, the product of the probabilities is $\frac{11}{100} \times \frac{15}{99} = \frac{165}{9900}$, which simplifies to $1/60$.

38. A: When graphing an inequality, a solid circle at an endpoint means that the number at that endpoint is included in the range, while a hollow circle means it is not. Since the inequality says that x is strictly greater than 2, the circle at 2 should therefore be hollow; since the inequality says that x is less than *or equal to* 4, the circle at 4 should be solid. $2 < x \leq 4$ indicates that x is between 2 and 4, so the area between the circles should be shaded; the two end rays in choice D would instead represent the pair of inequalities "$x < 2$ or $x \geq 4$".

39. C: The median number of volunteers in Texas is 21 and the median in New Mexico is 33. The standard deviation is a measure of variability or spread. Though standard deviation is not an easy measure of spread to quickly calculate, range is. The range of the values for Texas is slightly greater, hinting that the standard deviation should also be slightly larger for Texas. That is, in fact, the case. The correct answer is C.

40. C: A method commonly taught to multiply binomials is the "FOIL" method, an acronym for First, Outer, Inner, Last: multiply the first terms of each factor, then the outer terms, and so forth. Applied to $(x + 2)(x - 3)$, this yields:

$$(x)(x) + (x)(-3) + (2)(x) + (2)(-3) = x^2 - 3x + 2x - 6$$
$$= x^2 - x - 6$$

41. E: It is certainly possible for two distinct quadratic functions to intersect at no points; one simple example is provided by the quadratic functions $y = x^2$ and $y = x^2 + 1$. For these to have an intersection would require a solution to the equation $x^2 = x^2 + 1$, which implies $0 = 1$, which is clearly impossible. It is also possible for two quadratic functions to intersect in exactly one point, if that point is the vertex of both quadratic functions; take for instance the quadratic functions $y = x^2$ and $y = -x^2$, which intersect only at the origin, $(0, 0)$. Two distinct quadratic functions intersecting at a point other than a mutual vertex will intersect at two points; an example is the quadratic functions $y = x^2$ and $y = -x^2 + 2$, which will intersect at the points $(1,1)$ and $(-1,1)$.

42. C: For any base b, $\log_b x$ and b^x are inverse functions, so $\log_b(b^x) = b^{\log_b x} = x$. In particular, then, $\log_5(5^3) = 3$.

43. D: Perpendicular lines have opposite inverse slopes. The four answer choices are all in slope-intercept form, in which the slope is simply the coefficient of x; the slopes of the lines in the choices are, respectively, $-\frac{1}{3}, -\frac{2}{3}, \frac{1}{3}, \frac{2}{3}$, and $\frac{1}{3}$. The given line, $3x + 2y = 5$, is not in slope-intercept form but in standard form. To find its slope, we can convert the equation to slope-intercept form and determine the coefficient of x: $3x + 2y = 5 \Rightarrow 2y = -3x + 5 \Rightarrow y = -\frac{3}{2}x + \frac{5}{2}$. The slope of this line is $-\frac{3}{2}$. Its negative reciprocal is $-\left(-\frac{3}{2}\right)^{-1} = -\left(-\frac{2}{3}\right) = \frac{2}{3}$. This matches the slope of the line in choice D, which is therefore perpendicular to the given line.

44. A: If $\cos\theta + 1 = 0$, then $\cos\theta = -1$. This has only one solution in the interval $0° \leq \theta < 360°$, namely $\theta = 180°$. This is not one of the answer choices; however, the cosine function has a period of $360°$, which means that adding or subtracting any multiple of $360°$ to the argument does not change the result. Since $180° - 360° = -180°$, $\cos(-180°) = \cos(180°) = -1$, so $-180°$ is also a solution to the equation.

45. A: To divide complex numbers, write the quotient as a fraction, and then simplify it by multiplying both the numerator and denominator by the complex conjugate of the denominator. (The complex conjugate of $a + bi$ is defined as $a - bi$.) This guarantees that the new denominator will be a positive real number. So, $(1 + i) \div (1 - i) = \frac{(1+i)(1+i)}{(1-i)(1+i)} = \frac{1+i+i+i^2}{1+i-i-i^2} = \frac{1+2i+i^2}{1-i^2}$. Since $i^2 = -1$, this becomes $\frac{1+2i+(-1)}{1-(-1)} = \frac{2i}{2} = i$.

46. A: The area of a square is equal to the square of the length of one side. If the area is 64 in², the side length must therefore be $\sqrt{64\text{in}^2} = 8$ in. The circle is inscribed in the square, so the side length of the square is the same as the circle's diameter. If the circle's diameter is 8 in, then the circle's radius must be half of that, or 4 in. The area of a circle is equal to $A = \pi r^2 = \pi(4 \text{ in})^2 = 16\pi \text{ in}^2$.

47. E: The given pair of equations can be solved as a linear system of two variables, x^2 and y^2. This system can be solved by a number of methods; for instance, we can solve the first equation for x^2 to get $x^2 = y^2 + 2$ and then substitute that in to the second equation to get $(y^2 + 2) + y^2 = 4$, which simplifies to $2y^2 = 2$, or $y^2 = 1$. Substituting 1 for y^2 into $x^2 = y^2 + 2$ gives $x^2 = 1 + 2 = 3$. This gives a unique solution for x^2 and y^2, but not for x and y, since each of these can be positive or negative: if $x^2 = 3$, then $x = \pm\sqrt{3}$, and if $y^2 = 1$, then $y = \pm 1$. There are therefore four solutions in all: $x = \sqrt{3}, y = 1$; $x = -\sqrt{3}, y = 1$; $x = \sqrt{3}, y = -1$; or $x = -\sqrt{3}, y = -1$. (Note that it would have been possible to come to this conclusion about the number of solutions without actually finding the solutions.)

As an alternate method of solving the problem, note that the first equation describes a hyperbola and the second a circle, both centered at the origin. A graph of both functions shows that they intersect in four points, once in each quadrant.

48. D: $f^{-1}(x)$ signifies the *inverse function* of $f(x)$, the function such that $f(f^{-1}(x)) = f^{-1}(f(x)) = x$. Though we could try compositing each function given in the answer choices with the original $f(x)$ to see which composition simplified to x, there are more straightforward ways of finding inverse functions. Replace $f(x)$ in the original equation with x, and replace x in the original equation with x $f^{-1}(x)$. Thus, $x = \left(f^{-1}(x)\right)^3 + 2$. Now, simply solve for $f^{-1}(x)$. We can first subtract 2 from both sides to yield $x - 2 = \left(f^{-1}(x)\right)^3$, and then take the cube root of both sides (i.e. raise both sides to the power of $\frac{1}{3}$) to get $(x - 2)^{\frac{1}{3}} = f^{-1}(x)$.

49. A: The period of the unmodified tangent function $y = \tan(x)$ is simply π. However, when the x is multiplied by a coefficient $b \neq 1$, the function is compressed or stretched horizontally, changing its period to $\frac{\pi}{|b|}$. Here, $b = 2$, so the new period is $\frac{\pi}{2}$. (The "+6" in the given equation shifts the function horizontally but has no effect on the period.)

50. C: A real polynomial is a polynomial in which all of the coefficients are real numbers. ($3x^2 + 2x - 5$ is a real polynomial; $2x^2 + ix - 3$ is not since one of the coefficients, i, is imaginary.) It is possible for a real polynomial to have complex roots; however, if a complex number is a root of a

real polynomial, then its complex conjugate must also be a root of that polynomial. (The complex conjugate of $a + bi$ is defined as $a - bi$.) Therefore, if $3 - 2i$ is a root of a real polynomial, so must be its complex conjugate, $3 + 2i$.

51. E: The determinant of a 2×2 matrix $\begin{bmatrix} a & b \\ c & d \end{bmatrix}$ is $\begin{vmatrix} a & b \\ c & d \end{vmatrix} = ad - bc$. Plugging in the values of the given matrix gives $2 \times 3 - 4 \times 1 = 6 - 4 = 2$.

52. C: If the hiker walks two miles more each day than she walked the previous day, then the distances she walks on successive days make up an arithmetic sequence, with a common difference of 2. (The definition of an arithmetic sequence is that the difference between two adjacent terms is constant. Since the difference between the distances the hiker walks on any two consecutive days is 2, this condition is satisfied.) The formula for the nth term of an arithmetic sequence is $a_n = a_1 + (n - 1)d$, where a_1 is the first term and d is the common difference, and the sum of the first n terms of an arithmetic series is $S_n = \frac{n}{2}(a_1 + a_n)$. Here the distance the hiker walks on the seventh day is $a_7 = a_1 + (7 - 1)d = 5 + (6)(2) = 17$, and so the total distance she walks in all seven days is $S_7 = \frac{7}{2}(a_1 + a_7) = \frac{7}{2}(5 + 17) = \frac{7}{2}(22) = 77$.

53. B: In general, the number of ways to arrange 8 items is simply $8! = 40{,}320$. However, PARABOLA has three As; two arrangements of the letters of PARABOLA that differ only in changing the As around are not distinct words. Since the As can be ordered in $3! = 6$ ways, the general calculation of 8! counts each distinct arrangement of letters 6 times. So, to find the number of distinct arrangements of the letters in PARABOLA, it is necessary to divide: $\frac{8!}{3!} = \frac{40{,}320}{6} = 6{,}720$ (or, using the properties of factorials to simplify the calculation, $\frac{8!}{3!} = 8 \times 7 \times 6 \times 5 \times 4 = 6{,}720$).

54. D: "Collinear" means the points lie along the same line. There are several ways to solve this problem; one is to find the equation of the line that passes through the two given points and see which of the points in the answer choices fits the equation. The slope of the line passing through the points $(2, 3)$ and $(-1, 5)$ is $= \frac{y_2 - y_1}{x_2 - x_1} = \frac{5-3}{-1-2} = -\frac{2}{3}$. The equation of the line is therefore $y = -\frac{2}{3}x + b$ for some constant b. To find b, substitute either of the original points as x and y; using $(2, 3)$, we get $3 = -\frac{2}{3}(2) + b \Rightarrow 3 = -\frac{4}{3} + b \Rightarrow b = 3 + \frac{4}{3} = \frac{9}{3} + \frac{4}{3} = \frac{13}{3}$. So, the equation of the line is $y = -\frac{2}{3}x + \frac{13}{3}$. If we put in the coordinates of the four given points, the only one that satisfies the equation is $(5,1)$: $-\frac{2}{3}(5) + \frac{13}{3} = -\frac{10}{3} + \frac{13}{3} = \frac{3}{3} = 1$.

55. B: To simplify the given inequality, first move all the terms to one side:

$$x^2 + 3 > 2x + 2$$
$$x^2 + 3 - 2x - 2 > 0$$
$$x^2 - 2x + 1 > 0$$

Now, factor the left-hand side:

$$x^2 - 2x + 1 = (x - 1)(x - 1) = (x - 1)^2$$

The original inequality is equivalent to $(x - 1)^2 > 0$. Since the square of a negative number is positive, $(x - 1)^2 > 0$ everywhere except where $x - 1 = 0$, i.e. at $x = 1$.

56. D: Call the total width of the enclosed plot x and the length y. Then the area enclosed is $A = xy$. We can reduce this to a function of one variable by using other information. Note from the diagram that there are four stretches of fencing spanning the full width and three spanning the length, so the total amount of fencing used is $4x + 3y$. Since the gardener has 300 feet of fencing, $4x + 3y = 300$. Solving for y yields $y = -\frac{4}{3}x + 100$. Substitute $-\frac{4}{3}x + 100$ into the area equation: $A = x\left(-\frac{4}{3}x + 100\right) = -\frac{4}{3}x^2 + 100x$. This is the equation of a parabola opening downward, so the maximum value of the area occurs at the parabola's vertex. We can find the coordinates of the vertex of the parabola, (h, k), by completing the square to put the area equation in standard form, $A = (x - h)^2 + k$, but a faster method is to simply use the equation for the x-coordinate of the vertex, $h = -\frac{b}{2a}$ (where a and b are respectively the coefficients of x^2 and of x). Consequently:

$$h = -\frac{100}{2\left(\frac{4}{3}\right)} = -\frac{100}{\frac{8}{3}} = -\frac{300}{8} = -37.5$$

So, the area is at a maximum when $x = 37.5$. Putting this into the area equation $A = x\left(-\frac{4}{3}x + 100\right)$ yields $A = 37.5\left(-\frac{4}{3}(37.5) + 100\right) = 37.5(-50 + 100) = (37.5)(50) = 1,875$ square feet.

57. B: If the point (a, b) lies on the graph of $f(x)$, then $f(a) = b$. If $f(a) = b$, then $f^{-1}(b) = a$. Therefore, if the point (a, b) lies on the graph of $f(x)$, the point (b, a) must lie on the graph of $f^{-1}(x)$. So since $(1,2)$ lies on the graph of $f(x)$, $(2,1)$ must lie on the graph of $f^{-1}(x)$.

58. A: Consider the end behavior of the polynomial, which is entirely determined by its highest-order term, the term with the largest exponent. If the exponent is odd and the coefficient positive, then the graph goes down on the left and up on the right; if the exponent is odd and the coefficient is negative, the graph goes up on the left and down on the. If the exponent is even and the coefficient is positive, then the graph goes up on both sides; if the exponent is even and the coefficient is negative, the graph goes down on both sides. Here the highest-order term is ax^7; we are told that all the coefficients are positive, so the term has an odd exponent and a positive coefficient. This means it must go down on the left and up on the right, and the only graph among the answer choices that does this is A. (Choice E doesn't go down on either side, but instead tends toward a horizontal asymptote; this cannot occur for a polynomial, though it's possible for a rational function.)

59. B: If $f(x) = x + 3$, then $f\big(g(x)\big) = g(x) + 3$ and $g\big(f(x)\big) = g(x + 3)$. We are asked for which of these possibilities of $g(x)$ is it true that $g(x) + 3 = g(x + 3)$. The only one for which this is true is $g(x) = x - 4$: $g(x) + 3 = (x - 4) + 3 = x - 1$, and $g(x + 3) = (x + 3) - 4 = x - 1$. Since $x - 1 = x - 1$, the condition is satisfied. In contrast if we try, for example, choice A, $g(x) = -x$, we get $g(x) + 3 = (-x) + 3 = -x + 3$, and $g(x + 3) = -(x + 3) = -x - 3$; $-x + 3 \neq -x - 3$, so this does not satisfy the condition of the problem.

60. B: The most straightforward way of solving this problem is to take advantage of the double-angle formula, $\sin 2x = 2 \sin x \cos x$.

$$\sin 2x \sec x = 2 \sin x \cos x \sec x$$
$$= 2 \sin x \cos x \left(\frac{1}{\cos x}\right)$$
$$= 2 \sin x$$

Practice Test #2

1. Which of the following is equivalent to $\frac{27}{8}$?

 a. $2\frac{7}{8}$

 b. $3\frac{3}{8}$

 c. $4\frac{5}{8}$

 d. $9\frac{3}{8}$

2. $6.32 - 3.5 =$

 a. 2.82

 b. 3.18

 c. 3.27

 d. 5.97

3. A box is 30 cm long, 20 cm wide, and 15 cm high. What is the volume of the box?

 a. 65 cm^3

 b. 260 cm^3

 c. $1,125 \text{ cm}^3$

 d. $9,000 \text{ cm}^3$

4. What is the proper ordering (from greatest to least) of the following numbers?

 I. 0.071%

 II. 0.71

 III. 7.1%

 IV. $\frac{71}{101}$

 a. II, III, I, IV

 b. II, IV, III, I

 c. III, II, I, IV

 d. IV, I, III, II

5. 9.5% of the people in a town voted for a certain proposition in a municipal election. If the town's population is 51,623, about how many people in the town voted for the proposition?

 a. $3,000$

 b. $5,000$

 c. $7,000$

 d. $10,000$

6. What is $\frac{5}{6}$ of $\frac{3}{4}$?

 a. $\frac{2}{3}$

 b. $\frac{3}{5}$

 c. $\frac{4}{5}$

 d. $\frac{5}{8}$

213

7. There are twelve inches in a foot, and three feet in a yard. How many inches are in five yards?

 a. 20

 b. 41

 c. 75

 d. 180

8. $2.2 \times 31.3 =$

 a. 6.886

 b. 68.86

 c. 688.6

 d. 6886.00

9. What is the average of $\frac{1}{3}, \frac{2}{3}$, and $\frac{1}{4}$?

 a. $\frac{1}{2}$

 b. $\frac{2}{5}$

 c. $\frac{3}{8}$

 d. $\frac{5}{12}$

10. Which of the following inequalities is TRUE?

 a. $\frac{7}{8} < \frac{6}{7}$

 b. $\frac{9}{10} > \frac{11}{12}$

 c. $\frac{2}{3} > \frac{9}{13}$

 d. $\frac{1}{4} < \frac{2}{7}$

11. Which of the following is equal to 0.0023?

 a. 2.3×10^{-3}

 b. 2.3×10^{-2}

 c. 2.3×10^{2}

 d. 2.3×10^{3}

12. A reporter for a school newspaper surveys the students at the school to ask if they prefer chocolate, vanilla, or strawberry ice cream. Of the students who answer her question, 35% prefer vanilla, and 40% prefer chocolate. What percent of the students she surveyed prefer strawberry?

 a. 15%

 b. 25%

 c. 45%

 d. There is not enough information to say.

13. A cookie recipe calls for $2\frac{1}{4}$ cups of milk. Brian has $1\frac{1}{2}$ cups available. How much more milk does he need in order to make cookies according to the recipe?

 a. $1\frac{1}{2}$ cups

 b. $1\frac{1}{4}$ cups

 c. $\frac{3}{4}$ cup

 d. $\frac{1}{4}$ cup

14. Which of the following fractions is closest to $\frac{15,012}{19,938}$?

 a. $\frac{1}{4}$

 b. $\frac{3}{4}$

 c. $\frac{4}{5}$

 d. $\frac{5}{9}$

15. $\frac{2}{5} \times 2.5 =$

 a. 1

 b. 2

 c. 4

 d. 6

16. Which of the following represents the largest number?

 a. $\left(\frac{1}{3}\right)^{-4}$

 b. $9^{\frac{3}{2}}$

 c. $27^{\frac{2}{3}}$

 d. $3^{-\frac{25}{3}}$

17. Sam runs for fifteen minutes at eight miles per hour, and then jogs for forty-five minutes at four miles per hour. What is his average speed during this time?

 a. 5 miles per hour

 b. 5.5 miles per hour

 c. 6 miles per hour

 d. 7 miles per hour

18. In the diagram to the right, all five angles are equal. What is the measure of each angle?

 a. 20°

 b. 36°

 c. 60°

 d. 72°

19. What percent of 800 is 40?

 a. 2%
 b. 5%
 c. 20%
 d. 32%

20. $\frac{3}{16} =$

 a. 0.025
 b. 0.533
 c. 0.1875
 d. 0.2025

21. Which of the following is equivalent to $3 - 2x < 5$?

 a. $x < 1$
 b. $x > 1$
 c. $x < -1$
 d. $x > -1$

22. $6\left(-\frac{2}{3}\right) - 2\left(-\frac{7}{2}\right) =$

 a. -9
 b. -4
 c. 3
 d. 4

23. A game is played with an eight-component spinner with labeled with the numbers 1 through 8. A player receives two marbles each time the arrow lands on a 2 or 3, four marbles each time the arrow lands on the 6, eight marbles each time the arrow lands on a 7 or 8, and no marbles when the arrow lands on any of the other options. What is the expected value for the number of marbles that a player will receive on one spin?

 a. 3
 b. 5
 c. 15
 d. 24

24. Which of the following is equivalent to $\left(\sqrt[3]{x^4}\right)^5$?

 a. $x^{\frac{12}{5}}$
 b. $x^{\frac{15}{4}}$
 c. $x^{\frac{20}{3}}$
 d. x^{60}

25. If $x > 2$, then $\left(\frac{x^2-5x+6}{x+1}\right) \times \left(\frac{x+1}{x-2}\right) =$

 a. $x + 1$
 b. $x - 3$
 c. $\frac{x^2+2x+1}{x-2}$
 d. $\frac{x^2-2x-3}{x+1}$

26. Kyle bats third in the batting order for the Badgers baseball team. The table below shows the number of hits that Kyle had in each of 7 consecutive games played during one week in July.

Day	Monday	Tuesday	Wednesday	Thursday	Friday	Saturday	Sunday
Hits	1	2	3	1	1	4	2

What is the mean of the numbers in the distribution shown in the table?

 a. 1
 b. 2
 c. 3
 d. 4

27. $|x| > x$ for what values of x?

 a. $x < 0$
 b. $x > 0$
 c. $|x| > x$ for all real values of x.
 d. There is no real number x such that $|x| > x$.

28. Consider the following graphic showing demographics of a high school with 1219 total students:

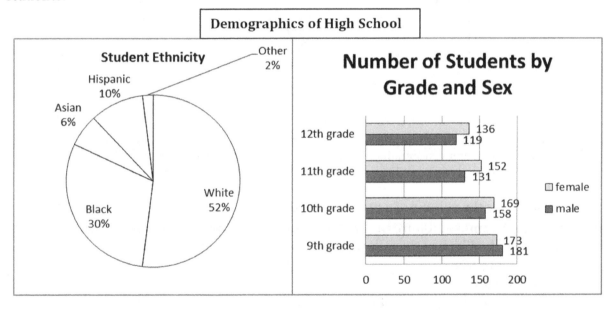

Which of these is the least quantity?

 a. The average number of Black students in the 9th and 10th grades
 b. The number of Asian female students at the school
 c. The difference in the number of male and female students at the school
 d. The difference in the number of 10th and 12th grade students at the school

29. $\left(\sqrt{2} + \sqrt{3}\right) \times \left(2 + \sqrt{6}\right) = ?$

 a. $2\sqrt{6} + 4$
 b. $3\sqrt{2} + 2\sqrt{3}$
 c. $5\sqrt{2} + 4\sqrt{3}$
 d. $2\sqrt{5} + \sqrt{30}$

30. A random sample of 90 students at an elementary school were asked these three questions:

Do you like carrots?
Do you like broccoli?
Do you like cauliflower?

The results of the survey are shown below. If these data are representative of the population of students at the school, which of these is most probable?

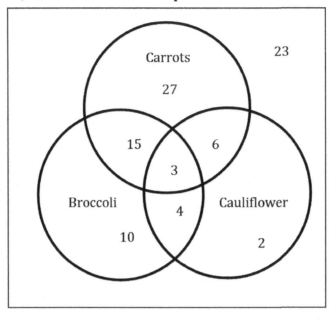

a. A student chosen at random likes broccoli.
b. If a student chosen at random likes carrots, they will also like at least one other vegetable.
c. If a student chosen at random likes cauliflower and broccoli, they will also like carrots.
d. A student chosen at random does not like carrots, broccoli, or cauliflower.

31. The formula for the volume of a pyramid is $\frac{1}{3}Bh$, where *B* is the area of the base and *h* is the height. The Pyramid of Khafre in Giza has a square base about 700 feet on a side and is about 450 feet high. Which of the following is closest to its volume?

a. 18 million cubic feet
b. 55 million cubic feet
c. 75 million cubic feet
d. 220 million cubic feet

32. In an election in Kimball County, Candidate A obtained 36,800 votes. His opponent, Candidate B, obtained 32,100 votes. 2,100 votes went to write-in candidates. What percentage of the vote went to Candidate A?

a. 51.8%
b. 53.4%
c. 52.6%
d. 46.8%

33. What is $\frac{x^3+2x}{x+3}$ when $= -1$?

 a. $-\frac{3}{2}$

 b. $-\frac{2}{3}$

 c. $\frac{1}{2}$

 d. $\frac{3}{4}$

34. A reporter for a school newspaper surveys the students at the school to ask if they prefer chocolate, vanilla, or strawberry ice cream. Of the students who answer her question, 35% prefer vanilla, and 40% prefer chocolate. What percent of the students she surveyed prefer strawberry?

 a. 15%

 b. 25%

 c. 45%

 d. There is not enough information to say.

35. A certain exam has 30 questions. A student gets 1 point for each question he gets right and loses half a point for a question he answers incorrectly; he neither gains nor loses any points for a question left blank. If C is the number of questions a student gets right and B is the number of questions he leaves blank, which of the following represents his score on the exam?

 a. $C - \frac{1}{2}B$

 b. $C - \frac{1}{2}(30 - B)$

 c. $C - \frac{1}{2}(30 - B - C)$

 d. $(30 - C) - \frac{1}{2}(30 - B)$

36. Freshmen and sophomore students at a high school were asked which caffeinated beverage they prefer. Given the two-way frequency table shown below with a summary of their responses, what is the probability that a student is a sophomore OR prefers lattes?

	Cappuccino	Latte	Frappuccino	Total
Freshman	20	29	22	71
Sophomore	19	26	22	67
Total	39	55	44	138

 a. $\frac{48}{59}$

 b. $\frac{37}{51}$

 c. $\frac{48}{69}$

 d. $\frac{39}{50}$

37. $\frac{|2|+|-2|}{|3|-|-1|} =$

 a. 0

 b. 1

 c. 2

 d. 4

38. $\dfrac{x^2}{y^2} + \dfrac{x}{y^3} =$

 a. $\dfrac{x^3 + x}{y^3}$

 b. $\dfrac{x^2 + xy}{y^3}$

 c. $\dfrac{x^2y + xy}{y^3}$

 d. $\dfrac{x^2y + x}{y^3}$

39. The numbers of volunteers in different states (Texas and New Mexico) for 15 different events are shown in the table below. If the following data are representative of the volunteering patterns of both states, which of the following statistics would be least helpful in determining the number of lunches that might be needed to feed the volunteers at the next event?

TX	8	17	18	19	20	21	21	21	22	28	29	31	41	45	52
NM	7	11	15	28	29	30	31	33	34	36	37	42	44	44	45

 a. Mode

 b. Mean

 c. Median

 d. Standard Deviation

40. Every person attending a certain meeting hands out a business card to every other person at the meeting. If there are a total of 30 cards handed out, how many people are at the meeting?

 a. 5

 b. 6

 c. 10

 d. 15

41. What is the area of a parallelogram with vertices $(0, 0)$, $(4, 5)$, $(10, 7)$, and $(6, 2)$?

 a. 20

 b. 22

 c. 24

 d. 26

 e. 28

42. If $3^x = 2$, then $x =$

 a. 9

 b. $\sqrt{3}$

 c. $\sqrt[3]{2}$

 d. $\log_3 2$

 e. $\log_2 3$

43. Which of these is described by the equation $9x^2 + 6xy + y^2 - 5x + y = 13$?

a. An ellipse
b. A parabola
c. A hyperbola
d. A spiral
e. Two parallel lines

44. If $f(x) = \tan(2x + 4)$, then $f^{-1}(x) =$

a. $\tan^{-1}(2x + 4)$
b. $\sec(2x + 4)$
c. $\tan^{-1}\left(\frac{1}{2}x - 2\right)$
d. $2\tan^{-1}(x) - 4$
e. $\frac{1}{2}\tan^{-1}(x) - 2$

45. $\sqrt[5]{\left(\sqrt[8]{9^{10}}\right)^6} =$

a. 1
b. 3
c. $3\sqrt{3}$
d. 27
e. 81

46. $|6 + 2i| =$

a. $2\sqrt{3}$
b. $2\sqrt{10}$
c. 6
d. 8
e. 12

47. A certain rectangular room is twice as wide as it is tall, and three times as long as it is wide. If the room has a volume of 12,000 ft³, what is its width?

a. 10 ft.
b. 12 ft.
c. 20 ft.
d. 30 ft.
e. $10\sqrt[3]{12}$ ft.

48. When $(a + 2b)^5$ is expanded into a polynomial, which of the following terms does *not* appear?

a. a^5
b. $10a^4b$
c. $32b^5$
d. $40ab^4$
e. $80a^2b^3$

49. Which of the following is equivalent to $\ln 7 + \ln 5 - \ln 3$?

　a. $\ln 4$

　b. $\ln 9$

　c. $\ln \frac{35}{3}$

　d. $\log_3 12$

　e. $\log_7 2$

50. If $\sec \theta = 2$, then which of the following is a possible value for $\sin \theta$?

　a. $-\frac{\sqrt{3}}{2}$

　b. $-\frac{1}{2}$

　c. 0

　d. 1

　e. $\frac{\sqrt{2}}{2}$

51. Which of the following is the correct graph of the system of inequalities below?

$$x - y > 1$$
$$2x + y > 2$$

a. 　　b.

c. 　　d.

e.

52. If $f(x) = 2x - 3$, $g(x) = x + \frac{3}{2}$, and $f\big(g(z)\big) = 6$, then $z =$

　a. -3

　b. -1

　c. 0

　d. 1

　e. 3

53. $1 + \frac{2}{3} + \frac{4}{9} + \frac{8}{27} + \cdots =$
- a. 3
- b. π
- c. 3π
- d. 9
- e. ∞

54. Which of the following matrices is *not* invertible?
- a. $\begin{bmatrix} 1 & 2 \\ 3 & 6 \end{bmatrix}$
- b. $\begin{bmatrix} 1 & 2 \\ 3 & 0 \end{bmatrix}$
- c. $\begin{bmatrix} 1 & 3 \\ 6 & 2 \end{bmatrix}$
- d. $\begin{bmatrix} 1 & 2 \\ 6 & 3 \end{bmatrix}$
- e. $\begin{bmatrix} 2 & 3 \\ 1 & 6 \end{bmatrix}$

55. A drawer contains eight pairs of socks. If Susan chooses four socks at random from the drawer, what are the chances that she will get two left socks and two right socks?
- a. 1/2
- b. 2/5
- c. 1/64
- d. 28/65
- e. 56/143

56. $(2 + \sqrt{3}) \div (2 - \sqrt{3}) =$
- a. 2
- b. $\sqrt{3}$
- c. 7
- d. $1 + 4\sqrt{3}$
- e. $7 + 4\sqrt{3}$

57. The half-life of the isotope ²²⁶Ra is about 1,600 years. A certain sample of rock contains two grams of radioactive ²²⁶Ra. How much did it contain 8,000 years ago?
- a. 0.4 g
- b. 5 g
- c. 10 g
- d. 20 g
- e. 64 g

58. Which of the following lines includes a diameter of the circle $(x-1)^2 + (y-2)^2 = 4$?
- a. $y = x - \frac{1}{2}$
- b. $y = 2x + 2$
- c. $y = 2x + 4$
- d. $y = 3x - 1$
- e. $y = 4x + 2$

223

59. Sylvia, who is just over five feet tall, stands 195 feet away from the base of a tower and looks toward the top of the tower with a 45° angle of inclination. Approximately how tall is the tower?

 a. 100 ft.
 b. 200 ft.
 c. 400 ft.
 d. $200\sqrt{3}$ ft.
 e. $400\sqrt{3}$ ft.

60. If $p^q = r$, then which of the following is equivalent to q?

 a. $p \ln r$
 b. $r \ln p$
 c. $\dfrac{\ln r}{\ln p}$
 d. $\dfrac{\ln p}{\ln r}$
 e. $\log_r p$

Answer Key and Explanations for Test #2

1. B: To convert an improper fraction to a mixed number, divide the numerator by the denominator: the quotient is the integer part of the mixed number, and the remainder is the numerator. $27 \div 8 = 3$ with a remainder of 3, so $\frac{27}{8} = 3\frac{3}{8}$.

2. A: In order to subtract decimal numbers, write them one above the other with the decimal points aligned, filling in zeroes as necessary, and then carry out the subtraction normally, placing the decimal point in the same position in the result:

$$\begin{array}{r} 6.32 \\ -\,3.50 \\ \hline 2.82 \end{array}$$

3. D: The volume of a right rectangular prism—that is, a box shape—is equal to the product of its length, width, and height. So the volume of the given box is equal to $(20 \text{ cm})(30 \text{ cm})(15 \text{ cm}) = 9{,}000 \text{ cm}^3$.

4. B: Recalling that percent just means "divided by 100," each of the given numbers can be represented as fractions:

I. $0.071\% = \frac{0.071}{100} = \frac{71}{100{,}000}$, II. $0.71 = \frac{71}{100}$, III. $7.1\% = \frac{7.1}{100} = \frac{71}{1{,}000}$, IV. $\frac{71}{101}$

All of the fractions share the same numerator. Among fractions with the same numerator, the largest fraction has the smallest denominator. We can order these fractions from greatest to least by ordering the denominators from least to greatest. The correct order is $\frac{71}{100} > \frac{71}{101} > \frac{71}{1{,}000} > \frac{71}{100{,}000}$ which corresponds to choice B.

5. B: The number of people who voted for the proposition is 9.5% of 51,623. If we only require an approximation, we can round 9.5% to 10%, and 51,623 to 50,000. Then 9.5% of 51,623 is about 10% of 50,000, or $(0.1)(50{,}000) = 5{,}000$.

6. D: In mathematics, the word "of" indicates multiplication. So $\frac{5}{6}$ of $\frac{3}{4}$ is just $\frac{5}{6} \times \frac{3}{4} = \frac{5 \times 3}{6 \times 4} = \frac{15}{24}$, which reduces to $\frac{15 \div 3}{24 \div 3} = \frac{5}{8}$.

7. D: If there are three feet in a yard, then to convert yards to feet we just multiply by 3. So five yards is equal to $5 \times 3 = 15$ feet. Likewise, since there are twelve inches in a foot, to convert feet to inches, we just multiply by 12. So 15 feet is equal to $15 \times 12 = 180$ inches.

8. B: To multiply decimals, first multiply the numbers normally ignoring the decimal point; then, position the decimal point in the answer so that the number of digits after the decimal point in the product is equal to the *sum* of the number of digits after the decimal point in both factors. Performing the multiplication without regard to the decimal point first, we get $22 \times 313 = 6886$. Since there is one digit after the decimal point in 2.2 and one digit after the decimal point in 31.3, there should be two digits after the decimal point in the product, which is therefore 68.86.

9. D: To find the average of a set of numbers, add the numbers together and divide by how many there are (in this case, three). So, to find the average of $\frac{1}{3}, \frac{2}{3},$ and $\frac{1}{4}$, we first add them together. To

225

add fractions, we can convert them all to fractions which have the least common denominator, which is in this case 12: $\frac{1}{3} + \frac{2}{3} + \frac{1}{4} = \frac{1 \times 4}{3 \times 4} + \frac{2 \times 4}{3 \times 4} + \frac{1 \times 3}{4 \times 3} = \frac{4}{12} + \frac{8}{12} + \frac{3}{12} = \frac{4+8+3}{12} = \frac{15}{12}$, which reduces to $\frac{15 \div 3}{12 \div 3} = \frac{5}{4}$. To get the average, we now divide this sum by three: $\frac{5}{4} \div 3 = \frac{5}{4} \times \frac{1}{3} = \frac{5 \times 1}{4 \times 3} = \frac{5}{12}$.

10. D: When comparing fractions it is necessary to find common denominators.

A. $\frac{49}{56} = \frac{7}{8} < \frac{6}{7} = \frac{48}{56}$

B. $\frac{108}{120} = \frac{9}{10} > \frac{11}{12} = \frac{110}{120}$

C. $\frac{26}{39} = \frac{2}{3} > \frac{9}{13} = \frac{27}{39}$

D. $\frac{7}{28} = \frac{1}{4} < \frac{2}{7} = \frac{8}{28}$ <Correct>

Once all of the fractions have been represented using common denominators, it is easy to determine which of each pair is greater since the greater is the one with the larger numerator. Among the four choices, the only valid inequality is choice D.

11. A: To convert a number to scientific notation, move the decimal point until there is just one digit before it (not counting leading zeroes), and rewrite the number as the result times a power of ten. The exponent of the power of ten is equal to the number of places the decimal point was moved—positive if the decimal was moved left, and negative if the decimal was moved right. Starting with 0.0023, to put only one digit before the decimal point, we have to move the decimal point three places to the right. Therefore, $0.0023 = 2.3 \times 10^{-3}$.

12. B: Since all students who answered her survey said they prefer one of the three flavors, the percentages must add up to 100%. Therefore the percentage of students who prefer strawberry must be $100\% - (35\% + 40\%) = 100\% - 75\% = 25\%$.

13. C: To find out how much more milk he needs, subtract the amount he has from the amount he needs: $2\frac{1}{4} - 1\frac{1}{2}$. To add or subtract mixed numbers, first convert them to improper fractions. We can do this by multiplying the integer part by the denominator and adding that to the numerator. So, $2\frac{1}{4} = \frac{2 \times 4 + 1}{4} = \frac{9}{4}$, and $1\frac{1}{2} = \frac{1 \times 2 + 1}{2} = \frac{3}{2}$. Now convert both fractions so that they share the lowest common denominator, which in this case is 4. $\frac{9}{4}$ already has a denominator of 4, so we need to convert $\frac{3}{2}$: $\frac{3}{2} = \frac{3 \times 2}{2 \times 2} = \frac{6}{4}$. We can now subtract: $\frac{9}{4} - \frac{6}{4} = \frac{3}{4}$.

14. B: 15,012 is close to 15,000, and 19,938 is close to 20,000. We would therefore expect $\frac{15,012}{19,938}$ to be close to $\frac{15,000}{20,000} = \frac{15}{20} = \frac{15 \div 5}{20 \div 5} = \frac{3}{4}$.

15. A: To multiply a fraction by a decimal, it is helpful to either convert both numbers to decimals or both to fractions. If we convert $\frac{2}{5}$ to a fraction, we divide 2 by 5, putting a decimal point after the 2 and keeping track of where the digits of the quotient are relative to the decimal point:

$$
\begin{array}{r}
.4 \\
5\overline{)2.0} \\
\underline{2\ 0} \\
0
\end{array}
$$

So $\frac{2}{5} = 0.4$, and $\frac{2}{5} \times 2.5 = 0.4 \times 2.5$. $4 \times 25 = 100$, and since 0.4 and 2.5 each have one digit after the decimal point, the product should have two digits after the decimal point, so the answer is 1.00, or simply 1.

Alternately, if we convert 2.5 to a fraction, we can write $2.5 = 2 + 0.5 = 2 + \frac{5}{10} = 2 + \frac{1}{2} = \frac{5}{2}$. Then, $\frac{2}{5} \times \frac{5}{2} = \frac{2 \times 5}{5 \times 2} = \frac{10}{10} = 1$.

16. A: It is helpful to put the expressions in similar terms. In this case, all of the options can be expressed in terms of 3.

A. $\left(\frac{1}{3}\right)^{-4} = 3^4$

B. $9^{\frac{3}{2}} = 3^3$

C. $27^{\frac{2}{3}} = (3^3)^{\frac{2}{3}} = 3^2$

D. $3^{-\frac{25}{3}} = \left(\frac{1}{3}\right)^{\frac{25}{3}} < 1$

The first three options are powers of 3 of which choice A is the highest (positive) power and hence represents the largest number. Choice C is a negative power that indicates the positive power is associated with the reciprocal of the base value. In this case, 3 to a negative power is equivalent to 1/3 to the corresponding positive power. Any number less than one to a positive power greater than 1 is a number less than 1.

17. A: To find Sam's average speed, we have to divide the total distance he travelled by the total travel time. Note that fifteen minutes is a quarter hour, and forty-five minutes is $\frac{3}{4}$ hours. During the first fifteen minutes, therefore, the distance Sam runs is 8 mph $\times \frac{1}{4}$ hour = 2 miles. During the next forty-five minutes, he jogs 4 mph $\times \frac{3}{4}$ hours = 3 miles. So, the total distance he runs is $2 + 3 = 5$ miles. The time he runs is $\frac{1}{4}$ hour $+ \frac{3}{4}$ hours = 1 hour, so his average speed is 5 miles / 1 hour = 5 miles per hour.

18. D: Since the five angles together go all the way around the central point, they must add up to a complete rotation of 360°. Therefore, if the angles are all equal, each angle must have a measure of $\frac{360°}{5} = 72°$.

19. B: Translate "What percent of 800 is 40?" into the mathematical equation $x\% \cdot 800 = 40$. To solve, divide 40 by 800 and convert the answer to a percent. To divide a smaller number by a larger, add a decimal point after the smaller number and add zeroes as necessary, putting the decimal point in the same position in the quotient as it appears in the dividend:

$$\begin{array}{r} .05 \\ 800\overline{)40.00} \\ 40\,00 \\ \hline 0 \end{array}$$

So $40 \div 800 = 0.05$. To express this as a percent, just multiply by 100, which moves the decimal point two places to the left: $0.05 = 5\%$.

20. C: To convert a fraction into a decimal, divide the numerator by the denominator. To divide a smaller number by a larger, add a decimal point after the smaller number and add zeroes as necessary, putting the decimal point in the same position in the quotient as it appears in the dividend:

$$
\begin{array}{r}
0.1875 \\
16\overline{)3.0000} \\
1\ 6 \\
\overline{1\ 40} \\
1\ 28 \\
\overline{120} \\
112 \\
\overline{80} \\
80 \\
\overline{0}
\end{array}
$$

21. D: To simplify the inequality $3 - 2x < 5$, we can first subtract 3 from both sides: $3 - 2x - 3 < 5 - 3 \Rightarrow -2x < 2$. Now, we can divide both sides of the inequality by -2. When an inequality is multiplied or divided by a negative number, its direction changes ($<$ becomes $>$, \leq becomes \geq, and vice versa). So $-2x < 2$ becomes $\frac{-2x}{-2} > \frac{2}{-2}$, or $x > -1$.

22. C: $6\left(-\frac{2}{3}\right) - 2\left(-\frac{7}{2}\right) = \left(\frac{6}{1}\right)\left(-\frac{2}{3}\right) - \left(\frac{2}{1}\right)\left(-\frac{7}{2}\right) = -\left(\frac{6}{1}\right)\left(\frac{2}{3}\right) - \left(-\left(\frac{2}{1}\right)\left(\frac{7}{2}\right)\right) = -\frac{6 \times 2}{1 \times 3} + \frac{2 \times 7}{1 \times 2} = -\frac{12}{3} + \frac{14}{2} = -4 + 7 = 3$.

23. A: The expected value is equal to the sum of the products of the probability and marbles won for each value of the spinner.

$$E(X) = \left(2 \cdot \frac{1}{8}\right) + \left(2 \cdot \frac{1}{8}\right) + \left(4 \cdot \frac{1}{8}\right) + \left(8 \cdot \frac{1}{8}\right) + \left(8 \cdot \frac{1}{8}\right) + \left(0 \cdot \frac{1}{8}\right) + \left(0 \cdot \frac{1}{8}\right) + \left(0 \cdot \frac{1}{8}\right)$$

$$= \frac{2}{8} + \frac{2}{8} + \frac{4}{8} + \frac{8}{8} + \frac{8}{8} + 0 + 0 + 0 = \frac{24}{8} = 3$$

24. C: The nth root of x is equivalent to x to the power of $\frac{1}{n}$, i.e. $\sqrt[n]{x} = x^{\frac{1}{n}}$. This means in particular that $\sqrt[3]{x} = x^{\frac{1}{3}}$, and so $\left(\sqrt[3]{(x^4)}\right)^5 = \left((x^4)^{\frac{1}{3}}\right)^5$. Raising a power to another power is equivalent to multiplying the exponents together, so this equals $x^{4 \times \frac{1}{3} \times 5} = x^{\frac{20}{3}}$.

25. B: $\left(\frac{x^2 - 5x + 6}{x+1}\right) \times \left(\frac{x+1}{x-2}\right) = \frac{(x^2 - 5x + 6) \times (x+1)}{(x+1) \times (x-2)}$. Before carrying out the multiplication of the polynomials, notice that there is a factor of $x + 1$ in both the numerator and denominator, so the

expression reduces to $\frac{x^2-5x+6}{x-2}$. We can simplify further by factoring the numerator. One way to factor a quadratic expression with a leading coefficient of 1 is to look for two numbers that add to the coefficient of x (in this case -5) and multiply to the constant term (in this case 6). Two such numbers are -2 and -3: $(-2) + (-3) = -5$ and $(-2) \times (-3) = 6$. So $x^2 - 5x + 6 = (x - 2)(x - 3)$. That means $\frac{x^2-5x+6}{x-2} = \frac{(x-2)(x-3)}{x-2}$. The $x - 2$ in the numerator and denominator can cancel, so we are left with just $x - 3$. (Note that if $x = -1$ or $x = 2$, the obtained simplified expression would not be true: either value of x would result in a denominator of zero in the original expression, so the whole expression would be undefined. Therefore, it is necessary to state that these values of x are excluded from the domain. For a domain of $x > 2$, both -1 and 2 are excluded as possible values of x.)

26. G: The mean, or average, is the sum of the numbers in a data set, divided by the total number of items. This data set contains seven items, one for each day of the week. The total number of hits that Kyle had during the week is the sum of the numbers in the right-hand column, or 14. This gives

$$Mean = \frac{14}{7} = 2.$$

27. A: When $x \geq 0$, $|x| = x$, so it is not true that $|x| > x$. However, when < 0, $|x| = -x$. This means x is negative and $|x|$ is positive, and since any positive number is greater than any negative number, $|x| > x$ when $x < 0$.

28. B: The difference in the number of male and female students at the school is $630 - 589 = 41$, and the difference in the number of 9th and 12th grade students at the school is 327 - 255 = 72. There are approximately 38 Asian females at the school (0.06 * 630). The average number of black students is more than 90 (30% of 300) because there are more than 90 in the 10th grade and the class is smaller than the 9th grade group.

29. C: A method commonly taught to multiply two binomials is the "FOIL" method, an acronym for First, Outer, Inner, Last: multiply the first terms of each factor, then the outer terms, and so forth. Applied to $\left(\sqrt{2} + \sqrt{3}\right) \times (2 + \sqrt{6})$, this yields $\left(\sqrt{2}\right)(2) + \left(\sqrt{2}\right)\left(\sqrt{6}\right) + \left(\sqrt{3}\right)(2) + \left(\sqrt{3}\right)\left(\sqrt{6}\right) = 2\sqrt{2} + \sqrt{12} + 2\sqrt{3} + \sqrt{18}$. Two of these terms can be simplified: $12 = 4 \times 3$, so $\sqrt{12} = \sqrt{4} \times \sqrt{3} = 2\sqrt{3}$, and $18 = 9 \times 2$, so $\sqrt{18} = \sqrt{9} \times \sqrt{2} = 3\sqrt{2}$. Therefore, the produce can be written as $2\sqrt{2} + 2\sqrt{3} + 2\sqrt{3} + 3\sqrt{2}$, which simplifies to $5\sqrt{2} + 4\sqrt{3}$ after like terms are combined.

30. B: The results are displayed in a Venn diagram, so to get the number of students who like any particular vegetable, sum all of the numbers that appear within the circle for that vegetable. 32 of the 90 students like broccoli, so the probability of A is $\frac{32}{90} \approx 0.356$. There are 51 students who like carrots, and of those 51, 24 also like another vegetable, so the probability of B is $\frac{24}{51} \approx 0.471$. There are 7 students who like broccoli and cauliflower, and of those 7, 3 also like carrots, so the probability of C is $\frac{3}{7} \approx 0.429$. 23 of the 90 students did not like any of the vegetables, so the probability of D is $\frac{23}{90} \approx 0.256$. B has the highest probability of these choices.

31. C: The area of the square base is just the square of the side length: $(700 \text{ ft})^2 = 490,000 \text{ ft}^2$. Since we only need an approximation, we can round that to $500,000 \text{ ft}^2$, or half a million square feet. The volume is therefore $\frac{1}{3}Bh \approx \frac{1}{3}\left(\frac{1}{2} \text{ million ft}^2\right)(450 \text{ ft}) = \frac{450}{6}\text{ million ft}^3 = 75 \text{ million ft}^3$.

32. A: Candidate A's vote percentage is determined by the number of votes that he obtained, divided by the total number of votes cast, and then multiplied by 100 to convert the decimal into a percentage. Therefore,

$$\text{Candidate A's vote percentage} = \frac{36{,}800}{36{,}800+32{,}100+2{,}100} = \frac{36{,}800}{71{,}000} = 51.8\%.$$

33. A: To evaluate $\frac{x^3+2x}{x+3}$ at $=-1$, substitute in -1 for x in the expression: $\frac{(-1)^3+2(-1)}{(-1)+3} = \frac{(-1)+(-2)}{2} = \frac{-3}{2} = -\frac{3}{2}$.

34. B: Since all students who answered her survey said they prefer one of the three flavors, the percentages must add up to 100%. Therefore the percentage of students who prefer strawberry must be $100\% - (35\% + 40\%) = 100\% - 75\% = 25\%$.

35. C: If the exam has 30 questions, and the student answered C questions correctly and left B questions blank, then the number of questions the student answered incorrectly must be $30 - B - C$. He gets one point for each correct question, or $1 \times C = C$ points, and loses $\frac{1}{2}$ point for each incorrect question, or $\frac{1}{2}(30 - B - C)$ points. Therefore, one way to express his total score is $C - \frac{1}{2}(30 - B - C)$

36. C: We can find the probability by adding the distinct probabilities that a given student is a sophomore and that a given student prefers lattes. However, we must also remember to subtract off the probabilities that a student is a Sophomore AND prefers lattes. Our previous calculation double counted these students. The probability may be written as: $P(S \text{ or } L) = \frac{67}{138} + \frac{55}{138} - \frac{26}{138}$. Thus, the probability a student is a Sophomore or prefers Lattes is $\frac{48}{69}$.

37. C: $|-2| = |2| = 2$, $|3| = 3$, and $|-1| = 1$. So $\frac{|2|+|-2|}{|3|-|-1|} = \frac{2+2}{3-1} = \frac{4}{2} = 2$.

38. D: To add the two fractions, first rewrite them with the least common denominator, which is in this case y^3. $\frac{x}{y^3}$ already has this denominator, and we can rewrite $\frac{x^2}{y^2}$ as $\frac{x^2 \times y}{y^2 \times y} = \frac{x^2 y}{y^3}$. Thus, $\frac{x^2}{y^2} + \frac{x}{y^3} = \frac{x^2 y}{y^3} + \frac{x}{y^3} = \frac{x^2 y + x}{y^3}$.

39. A: The Mean and Median both offer insight into how many volunteers to expect. The standard deviation would give an idea as to how much that number may vary. The mode is the least helpful. For example in this case, although the Texas mode (21) reasonably represents its data, the New Mexico mode (44) is not a good representation of the data set.

40. B: Call the number of people present at the meeting x. If each person hands out a card to every *other* person (that is, every person besides himself), then each person hands out $x - 1$ cards. The total number of cards handed out is therefore $(x - 1)$. Since we are told there are a total of 30 cards handed out, we have the equation $(x - 1) = 30$, which we can rewrite as the quadratic equation $x^2 - x - 30 = 0$. We can solve this equation by factoring the quadratic expression. One way to do this is to find two numbers that add to the coefficient of x (in this case -1) and that multiply to the constant term (in this case -30). Those two numbers are 5 and -6. Our factored equation is therefore $(x + 5)(x - 6) = 0$. To make the equation true, one or both of the factors must be zero: either $+5 = 0$, in which case $x = -5$, or $x - 6 = 0$, in which case $x = 6$. Obviously the number of people at the meeting cannot be negative, so the second solution, $x = 6$, must be correct.

Mometrix

41. B: The area of the parallelogram can be determined in several ways. Recall that the area of a parallelogram is equal to the magnitude of the cross product of the vectors representing two adjacent sides. We can express the side connecting the points $(0,0)$ and $(4,5)$ as the vector $(4-0,5-0) = (4,5)$ and the side connecting the points $(0,0)$ and $(6,2)$ as the vector $(6-0,2-0) = (6,2)$. For two vectors in the xy plane (u_1, v_1) and (u_2, v_2), the magnitude of the cross product is $|u_1 v_2 - u_2 v_1|$, which in this case would be $|4 \times 2 - 6 \times 5| = |-22| = 22$.

42. D: To solve the equation $3^x = 2$, we need to take the logarithm base three of both sides of the equation. (b^x and $\log_b x$ are inverse functions and cancel each other out for any positive base b.) Then we have $\log_3(3^x) = \log_3 2$, or simply $x = \log_3 2$. Alternatively, just keep in mind that $a^b = c$ is equivalent to $\log_a c = b$ for any positive a and c, so $3^x = 2$ is equivalent to $\log_3 2 = x$.

43. B: In general, any equation of the form $Ax^2 + Bxy + Cy^2 + Dx + Ey + F = 0$ describes a (possibly degenerate) conic section. (In the given equation, the constant term is on the right-hand side of the equation, but that's unimportant; we can easily convert it to the above form by simply subtracting 13 from both sides.) To determine which kind of conic section the equation corresponds to, we can look at the discriminant, $B^2 - 4AC$. If the discriminant is positive, the equation represents a hyperbola, if the discriminant is negative, the equation represents an ellipse or circle; and if the discriminant is zero, the equation represents a parabola. Here the discriminant is $6^2 - 4(9)(1) = 36 - 36 = 0$, so the equation represents a parabola.

44. E: One way to find an inverse function is to take the original equation describing the function, replace $f(x)$ with x and x with $f^{-1}(x)$, and then solve for $f^{-1}(x)$. In this case, $f(x) = \tan(2x + 4)$ becomes $x = \tan(2f^{-1}(x) + 4)$. To solve for $f^{-1}(x)$, first take the inverse tangent of both sides: $\tan^{-1} x = \tan^{-1}(\tan(2f^{-1}(x) + 4)) = 2f^{-1}(x) + 4$. Now subtract four from both sides: $\tan^{-1} x - 4 = 2f^{-1}(x)$. Finally, divide both sides by 2: $\frac{1}{2}(\tan^{-1} x - 4) = f^{-1}(x)$, or $f^{-1}(x) = \frac{1}{2}\tan^{-1} x - 2$.

45. D: $\sqrt[n]{x}$ is equivalent to $x^{\frac{1}{n}}$, so $\sqrt[5]{\left(\sqrt[8]{9^{10}}\right)^6}$ can be rewritten as $\left(\left((9^{10})^{\frac{1}{8}}\right)^6\right)^{\frac{1}{5}}$. When raising a power to another power, the exponents multiply, so this is equivalent to $9^{10 \times \frac{1}{8} \times 6 \times \frac{1}{5}}$. $10 \times \frac{1}{8} \times 6 \times \frac{1}{5} = \frac{10}{1} \times \frac{1}{8} \times \frac{6}{1} \times \frac{1}{5} = \frac{10 \times 1 \times 6 \times 1}{5 \times 1 \times 8 \times 1} = \frac{60}{40}$, which reduces to $\frac{3}{2}$. The original expression therefore reduces to $9^{\frac{3}{2}}$, which is equal to $\left(\sqrt{9}\right)^3 = 3^3 = 27$.

46. B: The absolute value of a complex number $a + bi$ is equal to $\sqrt{a^2 + b^2}$. $|6 + 2i|$ is therefore $\sqrt{6^2 + 2^2} = \sqrt{36 + 4} = \sqrt{40} = \sqrt{4} \times \sqrt{10} = 2\sqrt{10}$.

47. C: The volume of a rectangular solid is the product of its length, width, and height, $= l \times w \times h$. In this case, we're told the room is twice as wide as it is tall, and three times as long as it is wide, so we can write $w = 2h$ — or, equivalently, $h = \frac{w}{2}$ —and $l = 3w$. Our volume equation then becomes $V = 3w \times w \times \frac{w}{2} = \frac{3}{2}w^3$. Setting that equal to the given volume of 12,000 ft³, we have $\frac{3}{2}w^3 = 12{,}000$, so $w^3 = \frac{2}{3} \times 12{,}000 = 8{,}000$, and $w = \sqrt[3]{8{,}000} = 20$ ft.

48. D: A power of a binomial can be expanded by the binomial theorem, $(x + y)^n = \sum_{i=0}^{n} \binom{n}{i} x^{n-i} y^i$, where $\binom{n}{i}$ is the binomial coefficient, which can be derived either from Pascal's

triangle or from the equation $\binom{n}{i} = \frac{n!}{i!(n-i)!}$. That is, $(x+y)^n = \binom{n}{0}x^n + \binom{n}{1}x^{n-1}y + \binom{n}{2}x^{n-2}y^2 + \binom{n}{n}y^n$. In this case, where $n=5$, $x=a$, and $y=2b$, we have:

$$
\begin{aligned}
(a+2b)^5 &= \binom{5}{0}a^5 + \binom{5}{1}a^4(2b) + \binom{5}{2}a^3(2b)^2 + \binom{5}{3}a^2(2b)^3 + \binom{5}{4}a(2b)^4 + \binom{5}{5}(2b)^5 \\
&= (1)a^5 + (5)a^4(2b) + (10)a^3(4b^2) + (10)a^2(8b^3) + (5)a(16b^4) + (1)(32b^5) \\
&= a^5 + 10a^4b + 40\,a^3b^2 + 80\,a^2b^3 + 80ab^4 + 32b^5
\end{aligned}
$$

The only one of the answer choices that does not appear as a term of this polynomial is D, $40ab^4$.

49. C: The sum of two logarithms of the same base is equal to the logarithm of the product, and the difference of two logarithms of the same base is equal to the logarithm of the quotient. That is, $\log_b x + \log_b y = \log_b(xy)$, and $\log_b x - \log_b y = \log_b \frac{x}{y}$. Therefore, $\ln 7 + \ln 5 - \ln 3 = \ln(7 \times 5) - \ln 3 = \ln 35 - \ln 3 = \ln\frac{35}{3}$.

50. A: $\sec\theta = \frac{1}{\cos\theta}$, or, equivalently, $\cos\theta = \frac{1}{\sec\theta}$. Therefore, if $\sec\theta = 2$, then $\cos\theta = \frac{1}{2}$. $\cos\theta = \frac{1}{2}$ when $\theta = 60°$ or $300°$; $\sin 60° = \frac{\sqrt{3}}{2}$ and $\sin 300° = -\frac{\sqrt{3}}{2}$. Alternatively, use the Pythagorean identity $\sin^2\theta + \cos^2\theta = 1$ to find $\sin\theta$, so $\sin^2\theta = 1 - \cos^2\theta$, and $\sin\theta = \pm\sqrt{1-\cos^2\theta} = \pm\sqrt{1-\left(\frac{1}{2}\right)^2} = \pm\sqrt{1-\frac{1}{4}} = \pm\sqrt{\frac{3}{4}} = \pm\frac{\sqrt{3}}{2}$. (Whether the sine is positive or negative depends on what quadrant the angle is in; there is not enough information given in the problem to determine that, which is why the problem only asks which of the answer choices is a *possible* value for $\sin\theta$.)

51. C: The five choices all have the two lines that mark the boundaries of the inequalities plotted identically; the only difference is which sides are shaded. It's therefore not necessary to check that the lines are correct; simply determine which of the areas bounded by the lines pertain to the system of inequalities. One way to do that is to pick a point in each region and check whether it satisfies the inequalities. For instance, in the region on the left, we can pick the origin, $(0,0)$. Since $0 - 0 \not> 1$ and $2(0) + 0 \not> 2$, this does not satisfy either inequality. From the top region we can choose, for example, the point $(0,3)$. $0 - 3 \not> 1$, so this fails to satisfy the first inequality. From the bottom region we can choose, for instance, $(0,-2)$. $0 - (-2) > 1$, so the first inequality is satisfied, but $2(0) + (-2) \not> 2$, so the second is not. Finally, from the rightmost region we can choose, for example, the point $(2,0)$. $2 - 0 > 1$ and $2(2) + 0 > 2$, so both inequalities are satisfied; this is the only region that should be shaded in.

52. E: $f\big(g(x)\big) = f\left(x + \frac{3}{2}\right) = 2\left(x + \frac{3}{2}\right) - 3 = 2x + 2 \times \frac{3}{2} - 3 = 2x + 3 - 3 = 2x$. So the statement that $f\big(g(z)\big) = 6$ is equivalent to $2z = 6$. Dividing both sides of this equation by 2, we find $z = 3$.

53. A: The numbers $1, \frac{2}{3}, \frac{4}{9}, \frac{8}{27}, \ldots$ form a geometric sequence, since the ratio of any two consecutive terms is the same, namely $\frac{2}{3}$. What the problem is asking for, then, is the sum of an infinite geometric sequence. This sum exists (and is finite) whenever the absolute value of the common ratio r is less than one; since $\left|\frac{2}{3}\right| < 1$, that condition is satisfied. The formula for the sum of an infinite geometric series is $S_\infty = \frac{a_1}{1-r}$, where a_1 is the first term of the series and r is the common ratio; putting in the appropriate values of $a_1 = 1$ and $r = \frac{2}{3}$, we get $S_\infty = \frac{1}{1-\frac{2}{3}} = \frac{1}{\frac{1}{3}} = 3$.

54. A: A square matrix A is invertible—that is, there exists another matrix A^{-1} such that $A\,A^{-1} = A^{-1}A = I$, where I is the identity matrix, $\begin{bmatrix} 1 & 0 \\ 0 & 1 \end{bmatrix}$ (or its higher-order version)—if and only if its *determinant* is nonzero. For a 2×2 matrix $\begin{bmatrix} a & b \\ c & d \end{bmatrix}$ like the ones given in the answer choices, the determinant is $ad - bc$. The determinant of the matrix in choice A is $1 \times 6 - 2 \times 3 = 6 - 6 = 0$, so that matrix is not invertible. The determinants of the matrices in the other four choices are -6, -16, -9, and 9, respectively: since these determinants are all nonzero, the four matrices in choices B, C, D, and E are all invertible.

55. D: To determine the probability of Susan's drawing two left and two right socks from the drawer, we can determine the total number of possible sets of two left socks and two right socks, and divide by the total number of possible sets of four socks. If there are eight pairs of socks in the drawer, then there are eight left socks, so the total number of possible sets of two left socks that can be drawn is $_8C_2 = \binom{8}{2} = \frac{8!}{2!(8-2)!} = \frac{8 \times 7 \times 6!}{2! \times 6!} = \frac{56}{2} = 28$. By the same logic, there are also 28 possible sets of two right socks that can be drawn. Since there are 16 socks in the drawer in all, the total number of possible sets of four socks that can be drawn is $_{16}C_4 = \binom{16}{4} = \frac{16!}{4!(16-4)!} =$

$$\frac{16 \times 15 \times 14 \times 13 \times 12!}{4! \times 12!} = \frac{16 \times 15 \times 14 \times 13}{4 \times 3 \times 2 \times 1}$$

$= 4 \times 5 \times 7 \times 13 = 1820$. The probability of her drawing two left socks and two right socks is therefore $\frac{28 \times 28}{1820} = \frac{28}{65}$.

56. E: We can write the quotient as a fraction: $\frac{2+\sqrt{3}}{2-\sqrt{3}}$. Now, we need to *rationalize the denominator* -- that is, to convert this fraction to a form without any radicals in the denominator. To do this, we multiply both sides of the fraction by the conjugate of the denominator: $\frac{(2+\sqrt{3}) \times (2+\sqrt{3})}{(2-\sqrt{3}) \times (2+\sqrt{3})}$. We can simplify both the numerator and the denominator by using the FOIL method, for First, Inner, Outer, Last:

$$\left(2 + \sqrt{3}\right) \times \left(2 + \sqrt{3}\right) = 2 \times 2 + 2 \times \sqrt{3} + \sqrt{3} \times 2 + \sqrt{3} \times \sqrt{3} = 4 + 2\sqrt{3} + 2\sqrt{3} + 3 = 7 + 4\sqrt{3}$$
$$\left(2 - \sqrt{3}\right) \times \left(2 + \sqrt{3}\right) = 2 \times 2 + 2 \times \sqrt{3} + \left(-\sqrt{3}\right) \times 2 + \left(-\sqrt{3}\right) \times \sqrt{3} = 4 + 2\sqrt{3} - 2\sqrt{3} - 3 = 1$$

The fraction then becomes $\frac{7+4\sqrt{3}}{1}$, or simply $7 + 4\sqrt{3}$.

57. E: The half-life of an isotope is the amount of time it takes for it to decay to half its former amount. 8,000 years is five times the half-life of 1,600 years, so the amount of ^{226}Ra would have been halved five times. That is, the original amount would have been multiplied by $\left(\frac{1}{2}\right)^5 = \frac{1}{32}$. So if we call the original amount of ^{226}Ra x, then we know $\frac{1}{32}x = 2$ g, so $x = 2$ g $\times 32 = 64$ g.

58. D: Any diameter of a circle must pass through its center, and, conversely, any line through the center of a circle includes a diameter of the circle. The question, then, is equivalent to asking which of the given lines passes through the center of the circle. The standard form of the equation of a circle is $(x - h)^2 + (y - k)^2 = r^2$, where r is the circle's radius and (h, k) is its center. In the case of the given equation, $(x - 1)^2 + (y - 2)^2 = 4$, $h = 1$ and $k = 2$, so the center of the circle is the point $(1, 2)$. The simplest way to check which line passes through the point $(1, 2)$ is just to substitute $x = 1$ and $y = 2$ into the equation of each line and see which equation remains true. Since $2 \neq 1 - \frac{1}{2}$,

$2 \neq 2 \times 1 + 2$, $2 \neq 2 \times 1 + 4$, and $2 \neq 4 \times 1 + 2$, the lines in choices A, B, C, and E do not pass through the point $(1, 2)$. However, $2 = 3 \times 1 - 1$, so the equation of line D is satisfied.

59. B: From the given information, we can sketch the following figure (not to scale):

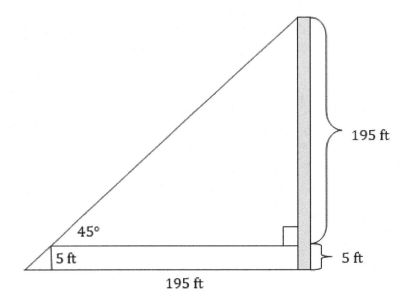

The legs of a 45°-45°-90° triangle are congruent; therefore, the vertical distance from the top of the tower to Sylvia's horizontal line of sight is the same as the distance Sylvia stands from the tower, 195 feet. Since Sylvia is approximately 5 feet tall, the height of the tower is approximately 195 ft + 5 ft = 200 ft.

60. C: By the relation of logarithms to exponents, if $p^q = r$ then $q = \log_p r$. This, however, is not one of the answer choices. (Choice E is $\log_r p$, but this reverses the p and the r and is not the same thing.) However, we can use the change of base formula, $\log_x y = \frac{\log_b y}{\log_b x}$ for any positive base B. In particular, we can choose $b = e$, the base of the natural logarithm, so $\log_p r = \frac{\log_e r}{\log_e p} = \frac{\ln r}{\ln p}$.

Practice Test #3

1. $4\frac{1}{5} - 2\frac{1}{3} =$

 a. $1\frac{13}{15}$

 b. $2\frac{1}{4}$

 c. $2\frac{2}{15}$

 d. $4\frac{1}{2}$

2. $(2.2 \times 10^3) \times (3.5 \times 10^{-2}) =$

 a. 7.7×10^{-6}

 b. 7.7×10^1

 c. 7.7×10^5

 d. 7.7×10^6

3. **What is the proper ordering (from least to greatest) of the following numbers?**

 I. $\frac{58}{67}$

 II. 0.58

 III. 58%

 IV. 5.8%

 a. I, III, II, IV

 b. III, IV, II, I

 c. I, III, IV, II

 d. IV, I, III, II

4. **In the diagram to the right (not to scale), $x = 91°$ and $y = 42°$. What is z?**

 a. $47°$

 b. $49°$

 c. $66\frac{1}{2}°$

 d. $133°$

5. **Doug drives without backtracking from his apartment to a campsite in another state. After two hours, he is halfway to his destination. After four hours, he is two-thirds of the way there. Which of the following could represent the fraction of his travel distance he has covered after three hours?**

 a. $\frac{2}{5}$

 b. $\frac{3}{5}$

 c. $\frac{3}{4}$

 d. $\frac{4}{5}$

235

6. What is 10% of 40%?

a. 4%
b. 30%
c. 50%
d. 400%

7. $2.62 \times 7.1 =$

a. 1.462
b. 14.62
c. 16.062
d. 18.602

8. Alan has a large number of cubical building blocks 4 cm on a side. He wants to use them to make a larger solid cube 20 cm on a side. How many building blocks will he need for this?

a. 25
b. 94
c. 125
d. 150

9. Which of the following inequalities is NOT TRUE?

a. $\frac{1}{2} > \frac{1}{3} > \frac{1}{4}$
b. $\frac{1}{5} < \frac{3}{10} < \frac{7}{20}$
c. $\frac{7}{9} > \frac{2}{3} > \frac{6}{7}$
d. $\frac{1}{5} < \frac{2}{7} < \frac{3}{10}$

10. Which of the following is closest to $\frac{149}{1502}$?

a. 0.012
b. 0.77
c. 0.103
d. 0.151

11. Water drains from a bathtub at a rate of one gallon every fifteen seconds. If the bathtub initially has twelve gallons of water in it, how long will it take to drain completely?

a. 48 seconds
b. 1 minute 15 seconds
c. 3 minutes
d. 4 minutes

12. $\frac{7}{8} \times \frac{2}{3} \times \frac{4}{5} \times \frac{3}{7} =$

a. $\frac{1}{7}$
b. $\frac{1}{5}$
c. $\frac{3}{8}$
d. 1

236

13. What is the average of 2.02, 0.275, and 1.98?

a. 1.1375
b. 1.375
c. 1.425
d. 2.25

14. The following numbers are constants (shown with their three digit approximations) from mathematics and science:

$$\gamma \approx 0.577$$
$$\phi \approx 1.618$$
$$\pi \approx 3.142$$

Which of the following represents the smallest number?

a. $\gamma + \phi + \pi$
b. $(\pi - \phi)^\gamma$
c. ϕ^γ
d. π^γ

15. What is 60% of $\frac{5}{6}$?

a. $\frac{1}{2}$
b. $\frac{3}{4}$
c. $\frac{5}{12}$
d. $\frac{25}{36}$

16. A particular map has a scale of 1 inch = 5 miles. On the map, Lost Canyon Road is one foot long. How long is the actual road?

a. 2.4 miles
b. 6 miles
c. 24 miles
d. 60 miles

17. $3\frac{1}{4} + 2\frac{5}{6} =$

a. $5\frac{1}{2}$
b. $5\frac{3}{5}$
c. $6\frac{1}{12}$
d. $6\frac{1}{2}$

18. 50 is what percent of 40?

a. 80
b. 90
c. 120
d. 125

19. Which of the following is largest?

 a. 0.55
 b. 0.500
 c. 0.505
 d. 0.0555

20. All of the following represent the same number EXCEPT

 a. 0.05
 b. $\frac{1}{50}$
 c. 5×10^{-2}
 d. 5%

21. What is the value of $\frac{2x-2}{x+3}$ when $x = -1$?

 a. 0
 b. 1
 c. 2
 d. −2

22. Suppose Olivia rolls a regular six-sided die 10 times. What is the expected value for the number of fours that she would have gotten after 10 rolls of the die?

 a. $\frac{3}{4}$
 b. $\frac{5}{2}$
 c. $\frac{5}{3}$
 d. $\frac{8}{9}$

23. Which of the following correctly represents the solution to the inequality $x^2 + 2x \geq x + 6$?

 a.

 b.

 c.

 d.

24. If $\frac{1}{2x} + \frac{1}{x} = \frac{1}{6}$, then $x =$

 a. 2
 b. 4
 c. 9
 d. 12

25. Kyle bats third in the batting order for the Badgers baseball team. The table below shows the number of hits that Kyle had in each of 7 consecutive games played during one week in July.

Day	Monday	Tuesday	Wednesday	Thursday	Friday	Saturday	Sunday
Hits	1	2	3	1	1	4	2

What is the median of the numbers in the distribution shown in the table?

 a. 1
 b. 2
 c. 3
 d. 4

26. A building has a number of floors of equal height, as well as a thirty-foot spire above them all. If the height of each floor in feet is h, and there are n floors in the building, which of the following represents the building's total height in feet?

 a. $n + h + 30$
 b. $nh + 30$
 c. $30n + h$
 d. $30h + n$

27. $x(y - 2) + y(3 - x) =$

 a. $xy + y$
 b. $-2x + 3y$
 c. $2xy - 2x + 3y$
 d. $xy + 3y - x - 2$

28. Which of the following lists of numbers is ordered from least to greatest?

 a. $1, \frac{1}{3}, -\frac{1}{4}, \frac{1}{5}$
 b. $\frac{1}{5}, -\frac{1}{4}, \frac{1}{3}, 1$
 c. $-\frac{1}{4}, 1, \frac{1}{3}, \frac{1}{5}$
 d. $-\frac{1}{4}, \frac{1}{5}, \frac{1}{3}, 1$

29. Consider the following graphic showing demographics of a high school with 1219 total students:

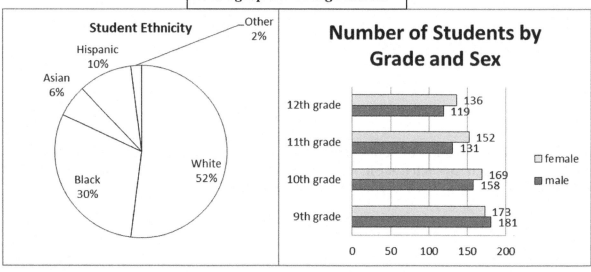

Which of these is the greatest quantity?

a. The average number of male students in the 11th and 12th grades
b. The number of Hispanic students at the school
c. The difference in the number of male and female students at the school
d. The difference in the number of 9th and 12th grade students at the school

30. In the figure shown, the height of the triangle is three times the height of the square on which it is resting. If the square's width is s, what is the total area taken up by the figure?

a. $\frac{5}{2}s^2$
b. $s^2 + \frac{3}{2}s$
c. $\frac{5}{3}s^2$
d. $s^2 + 3s$

31. Students at Sunnyside High School participate in football and band. 35% of students play football and play in the band. 42% of students play football. Approximately what percentage of students who play football also march in the band?

 a. 7%
 b. 15%
 c. 23%
 d. 83%

32. $(x + 6)(x - 6) =$

 a. $x^2 - 12x - 36$
 b. $x^2 + 12x - 36$
 c. $x^2 + 12x + 36$
 d. $x^2 - 36$

33. Prizes are to be awarded to the best pupils in each class of an elementary school. The number of students in each grade is shown in the table, and the school principal wants the number of prizes awarded in each grade to be proportional to the number of students. If there are twenty prizes, how many should go to fifth-grade students?

Grade	1	2	3	4	5
Students	35	38	38	33	36

 a. 5
 b. 4
 c. 6
 d. 3

34. If $x + 2y = 3$ and $-x - 3y = 4$, then $x =$

 a. 1
 b. 5
 c. 7
 d. 17

35. Joanie is playing songs on her MP3 player from a 15-song playlist in which every song is equally likely to be played next. Three of the 15 songs are by Beyonce . What is the probability that the next two songs will both be by an artist who is not Beyonce?

 a. 1 in 25
 b. 9 in 25
 c. 16 in 25
 d. 24 in 25

36. At a school carnival, three students spend an average of $10. Six other students spend an average of $4. What is the average amount of money spent by all nine students?

 a. $5
 b. $6
 c. $7
 d. $8

37. Students at Elm and Oak High Schools were surveyed on their favorite type of movies. Given the table below summarizing the responses, which of the following best represents the probability that a student is enrolled at Elm OR prefers Comedies.

	Comedy	Drama	Action	Total
Elm High School	350	225	175	750
Oak High School	325	300	275	900
Total	675	525	450	1650

 a. 45%
 b. 55%
 c. 65%
 d. 75%

38. $-\dfrac{3}{2}\left(\dfrac{1}{2}+\dfrac{1}{3}\right)-\dfrac{2}{3}\left(\dfrac{1}{2}-\dfrac{3}{4}\right)=$

 a. $-1\dfrac{5}{12}$
 b. $-1\dfrac{1}{12}$
 c. $-1\dfrac{1}{2}$
 d. $1\dfrac{5}{12}$

39. The numbers of volunteers in different states (Texas and New Mexico) for 15 different events are shown in the table below. Which of the following statements best describes the number of volunteers that should be expected at the next event?

TX	12	17	18	19	20	21	21	21	22	28	29	31	41	45	52
NM	7	11	15	28	29	30	31	33	34	36	37	42	44	44	45

 a. More volunteers would be expected in New Mexico because it has had more volunteers on 10 of 15 occasions.
 b. More volunteers would be expected in Texas because it had the larger maximum number of volunteers.
 c. More volunteers would be expected in New Mexico because both the two distributions are reasonably symmetric and New Mexico has a larger median.
 d. More volunteers would be expected in Texas because it had a larger mean number of volunteers.

40. How many solutions are there to the equation $\left|x^2-2\right|=x$?

 a. 0
 b. 1
 c. 2
 d. 4

41. If $\sqrt{2}^{2} \cdot 2^{\sqrt{2}} = \left(\sqrt{2}^{\sqrt{2}}\right)^{x}$, then $x =$

 a. 2
 b. $\sqrt{2}$
 c. $2\sqrt{2}$
 d. $2^{\sqrt{2}}$
 e. $2 + \sqrt{2}$

42. The interior of what shape is described by the following two inequalities?

$$x^2 + y^2 < 4$$
$$x + y > 3$$

 a. A circle
 b. A semicircle
 c. A circular segment smaller than a semicircle
 d. A circular segment larger than a semicircle
 e. None; this system of inequalities has no solution.

43. $\dfrac{\ln 81}{\ln 3} =$

 a. 3
 b. $3\sqrt{3}$
 c. 4
 d. $\ln 3$
 e. $\ln 27$

44. Which of the following is a root of $x^2 - 4x + 5$?

 a. 4
 b. $10i$
 c. $1 - i$
 d. $2 + i$
 e. $4 - i$

45. In the triangle, which of the following is equal to $\sin \theta$?

 a. $\dfrac{a}{2b}$
 b. $\dfrac{2b}{a}$
 c. $\dfrac{a}{2c}$
 d. $\dfrac{2a}{c}$
 e. $\dfrac{b}{ac}$

46. If the lines $y = ax + b$ and $y = bx + 2a$ intersect at the point $(2, 3)$, then $a =$

 a. 0

 b. $\dfrac{2}{3}$

 c. 1

 d. $\dfrac{3}{2}$

 e. 3

47. What is the product of three consecutive odd integers, if the one in the middle is x?

 a. $x^2 - 3x$

 b. $x^2 - 5x$

 c. $x^3 - x$

 d. $x^3 - 4x$

 e. $x^3 + x - 4$

48. $f(x) = ax^b + cx + d$, where $a, b, c,$ and d are all integers. The equation $f(x) = 0$ has exactly one solution, which does *not* occur at a maximum or minimum of $f(x)$. Which of the following *must* be true?

 a. a is positive.

 b. a is negative.

 c. b is odd.

 d. b is even.

 e. c is zero.

49. Six people sit around a circular table at a party. If two of these people are the party's hosts and must sit next to each other, how many different possibilities are there for the order of the six people around the table? (Rotations are not counted as different orders.)

 a. 24

 b. 48

 c. 120

 d. 240

 e. 288

50. Which of the following graphs corresponds to the equation $y = 2\sin(\pi x - \pi)$?

a. b.

c. d.

e.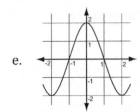

51. If $f(x) = e^{2x}$ and f^{-1} is the inverse of f, then $f\left(f^{-1}(f(x))\right) =$

 a. e^{2x}
 b. $e^{2\ln x}$
 c. $e^{2x}\ln x$
 d. $\ln\left(\frac{1}{2}e^{2x}\right)$
 e. $e^{2\ln\left(\frac{1}{2}e^{2x}\right)}$

52. What geometric shape is defined by the equation $ax + by + cz + d = 0$, where $a, b, c, d \neq 0$?

 a. A point
 b. A line
 c. A plane
 d. A sphere
 e. A hyperboloid

53. $\frac{x^7 + 2x^6 + x^5}{x^4 - x^2} =$

 a. $x^3 + 2z$
 b. $x^3 + x + 1$
 c. $\frac{x^5 + x^3}{x^2}$
 d. $\frac{x^4 + x^3}{x - 1}$
 e. $\frac{x^5 + x^3}{x^2 - 1}$

54. A chest is filled with large gold and silver coins, weighing a total of thirty pounds. If each gold coin weighs 12 ounces, each silver coin weighs 8 ounces, and there are fifty coins in all, how many gold coins does the chest contain? (There are sixteen ounces in a pound.)

 a. 10
 b. 15
 c. 20
 d. 25
 e. 30

55. An ellipse is described by the equation $3x^2 + 4y^2 = 48$. What is the length of its major axis?

 a. $2\sqrt{3}$
 b. 4
 c. $4\sqrt{3}$
 d. 8
 e. 12

56. The first three terms of a geometric sequence are 80, 120, and 180. Which of the following is equal to the tenth term of the sequence?

a. $\dfrac{5\times3^9}{2^5}$

b. $\dfrac{5\times3^{10}}{2^7}$

c. $\dfrac{5\times2^4}{3^{10}}$

d. $\dfrac{5\times2^{13}}{3^9}$

e. $\dfrac{5\times2^{14}}{3^{10}}$

57. If $f(x) = e^{x-3}$, $g(x) = 2x - 1$, and $h(x) = f(x) + g(x)$, then $h(3) =$

a. 2

b. 3

c. 4

d. 5

e. 6

58. If $2\sec\theta = \tan^2\theta$, which of the following is a possible value for $\sec\theta$?

a. 2

b. $\sqrt{2}$

c. $\sqrt{2} - 1$

d. $2 - \sqrt{2}$

e. $1 + \sqrt{2}$

59. The population of the town of Wrassleton has tripled every ten years since 1950. If P_0 is the town's population in 1950 and t is the number of years since 1950, which of the following describes the town's growth during this time?

a. $P(t) = 10\,P_0^{3t}$

b. $P(t) = P_0^{\frac{3}{10}t}$

c. $P(t) = P_0 \times 3^{\frac{t}{10}}$

d. $P(t) = P_0 \times \left(\dfrac{3}{10}\right)^t$

e. $P(t) = \left(\dfrac{3}{10}P_0\right)^t$

60. If $f(1) = 2$, $g(2) = 3$, $f^{-1}(3) = 4$, and $g^{-1}(4) = 1$, which of the following is *not* necessarily true?

a. $f\big(g(1)\big) = 3$

b. $f\big(g(3)\big) = 1$

c. $g\big(f^{-1}(2)\big) = 4$

d. $g^{-1}\big(f^{-1}(3)\big) = 1$

e. $g(2) = f(4)$

Answer Key and Explanations for Test #3

1. A: One way to add or subtract mixed numbers is to first convert them to improper fractions. We can do this by multiplying the integer part of the mixed number by the denominator and adding that product to the numerator; this sum is the numerator of the improper fraction, and its denominator is the same as the denominator in the fractional part of the mixed number. So $4\frac{1}{5} = \frac{4\times5+1}{5} = \frac{21}{5}$ and $2\frac{1}{3} = \frac{2\times3+1}{3} = \frac{7}{3}$. Convert each fraction so that they contain the lowest common denominator, which in this case is 15. $\frac{21}{5} = \frac{21\times3}{5\times3} = \frac{63}{15}$ and $\frac{7}{3} = \frac{7\times5}{3\times5} = \frac{35}{15}$. We can now subtract: $\frac{63}{15} - \frac{35}{15} = \frac{28}{15}$. Finally, we convert back to a mixed number by dividing the numerator by the denominator. The quotient is the integer part, and the remainder is the new numerator; the denominator remains the same. $28 \div 15 = 1$ with a remainder of 13, so $\frac{28}{15} = 1\frac{13}{15}$.

2. B: To multiply numbers in scientific notation, first multiply the significands (the part before the power of ten), then multiply the powers of ten; when multiplying two numbers with the same base, add the exponents and keeping that base. So, to multiply 2.2×10^3 and 3.5×10^{-2}, we first multiply 2.2 by 3.5. To multiply decimals, first multiply the numbers normally ignoring the decimal point; then, position the decimal point in the answer so that the number of digits after the decimal point in the product is equal to the *sum* of the number of digits after the decimal point in both factors. $22 \times 35 = 770$, and since there is one digit after the decimal point in 2.2 and one digit after the decimal point in 3.5, there should be two digits after the decimal point in the product, which therefore becomes 7.70, or 7.7. Now, multiply the powers of 10: $10^3 \times 10^{-2} = 10^{3+(-2)} = 10^1$. The final answer is 7.7×10^1.

3. C: Recalling that percent just means "divided by 100," each of the given numbers can be represented as fractions:

I. $\frac{58}{67}$

II. $0.58 = \frac{.58}{100} = \frac{58}{10,000}$

III. $58\% = \frac{58}{100}$

IV. $5.8\% = \frac{5.8}{100} = \frac{58}{1,000}$

All of the fractions share the same numerator. Among fractions with the same numerator, the largest fraction has the smallest denominator. We can order these fractions from greatest to least by ordering the denominators from least to greatest. The correct order is $\frac{58}{67} > \frac{58}{100} > \frac{58}{1,000} > \frac{58}{10,000}$ which corresponds to choice C.

4. A: Together, these three angles form a straight angle, or 180°. So, $x + y + z = 180°$, which means $z = 180° - x - y = 180° - 91° - 42° = 47°$.

5. B: If he has covered $\frac{1}{2}$ the distance after two hours, and $\frac{2}{3}$ the distance after four hours, and he does not backtrack, then the fraction of the distance he has covered after three hours must be between $\frac{1}{2}$ and $\frac{2}{3}$. To compare fractions, we can convert them to equivalent fractions with the least common denominator. The least common denominator of $\frac{2}{3}$ and $\frac{3}{4}$ is 12; $\frac{2}{3} = \frac{2\times4}{3\times4} = \frac{8}{12}$ and $\frac{3}{4} = \frac{3\times3}{4\times3} =$

247

$\frac{9}{12}$. Since $\frac{9}{12} > \frac{8}{12}, \frac{3}{4}$ is not between $\frac{1}{2}$ and $\frac{2}{3}$. The least common denominator of $\frac{1}{2}$ and $\frac{2}{5}$ is 10; $\frac{1}{2} = \frac{1 \times 5}{2 \times 5} = \frac{5}{10}$ and $\frac{2}{5} = \frac{2 \times 2}{5 \times 2} = \frac{4}{10}$. Since $\frac{4}{10} < \frac{5}{10}, \frac{2}{5}$ is not between $\frac{1}{2}$ and $\frac{2}{3}$. Similarly, $\frac{4}{5} = \frac{4 \times 4}{5 \times 4} = \frac{16}{20}$ and $\frac{3}{4} = \frac{3 \times 5}{4 \times 5} = \frac{15}{20}$; since $\frac{16}{20} > \frac{15}{20}, \frac{2}{5}$ is not between $\frac{1}{2}$ and $\frac{2}{3}$. However, $\frac{3}{5} = \frac{3 \times 2}{5 \times 2} = \frac{6}{10} = \frac{3 \times 4}{5 \times 4} = \frac{12}{20}; \frac{6}{10} > \frac{5}{10}$ and $\frac{12}{20} < \frac{15}{20}$, so $\frac{1}{2} < \frac{3}{5} < \frac{3}{4}$.

6. A: x percent is the same thing as $\frac{x}{100}$, and finding x percent of a number is the same as multiplying that number by x percent. This is true even when the number is itself a percent. So, 10% of 40% is $40\% \times 10\% = 40\% \times \frac{10}{100} = 40\% \times \frac{1}{10} = 4\%$.

7. D: To multiply decimals, first multiply the numbers normally ignoring the decimal point; then, position the decimal point in the answer so that the number of digits after the decimal point in the product is equal to the *sum* of the number of digits after the decimal point in both factors. $262 \times 71 = 18,602$; there are two digits after the decimal point in 2.62 and one digit after the decimal point in 7.1, so there should be three digits after the decimal point in the product, which is therefore 18.602.

8. C: The ratio of volumes on two objects of the same shape is equal to the *cube* of the ratio of their lengths. Therefore, if the ratio of the length of the large cube to that of a building block is $\frac{20 \text{ cm}}{4 \text{ cm}} = 5$, the ratio of the *volume* of the large cube to that of a building block is 5^3, or 125— so that is how many building blocks it will take to make the large cube.

9. C: When comparing fractions it is necessary to find common denominators.

A. $\frac{1}{2} = \frac{6}{12} > \frac{1}{3} = \frac{4}{12} > \frac{1}{4} = \frac{3}{12}$

B. $\frac{1}{5} = \frac{4}{20} < \frac{3}{10} = \frac{6}{20} < \frac{7}{20}$

C. $\frac{7}{9} = \frac{49}{63} > \frac{2}{3} = \frac{42}{63} > \frac{6}{7} = \frac{54}{63}$ <Correct>

D. $\frac{1}{5} = \frac{70}{350} < \frac{2}{7} = \frac{100}{350} < \frac{3}{10} = \frac{105}{350}$

Once all of the fractions have been represented using common denominators, it is easy to determine which line of inequalities is not valid. Among the four choices, the only invalid inequality is choice C.

10. C: 149 is close to 150, and 1502 is close to 1500. Therefore, we would expect $\frac{149}{1502}$ to be close to $\frac{150}{1500}$, which reduces to $\frac{1}{10}$. As a decimal, $\frac{1}{10} = 0.1$. Choice C is the closest to this number.

11. C: We can start by rewriting the rate of drainage in gallons per minute. $\frac{1 \text{ gallon}}{15 \text{ seconds}} \times \frac{60 \text{ seconds}}{1 \text{ minute}} = \frac{60 \text{ gallons}}{15 \text{ minutes}} = 4$ gallons/minute. This means that in t minutes, the tub will have drained $4t$ gallons. We are asked to find how long the tub will take to drain 12 gallons, so $4t = 12$; dividing both sides by 4, we find $t = 3$.

12. B: While we *could* multiply together all the numbers in the numerator and all the numbers in the denominator and then simplify, it would be easier to cancel what we can first. There is a factor of 7 in both the numerator and the denominator; we can cancel those. The same goes for a factor of

3. That leaves us with $\frac{1}{8} \times \frac{2}{1} \times \frac{4}{5} \times \frac{1}{1}$. We can go further, though; since $2 \times 4 = 8$, the 2 and the 4 in the numerator cancel the 8 in the denominator, leaving us with just $\frac{1}{1} \times \frac{1}{1} \times \frac{1}{5} \times \frac{1}{1}$, or simply $\frac{1}{5}$.

13. C: To find the average, add together all the numbers and then divide by how many there are (in this case three). In order to add decimal numbers, write them one above the other with the decimal points aligned and carry out the addition normally, placing the decimal point in the same position in the result:

$$
\begin{array}{r}
2.02 \\
+\ 0.275 \\
+\ 1.98 \\
\hline
4.275
\end{array}
$$

Now, to divide, just carry out the division normally but put the decimal point in the same position in the quotient as ti appears in the dividend:

$$
\begin{array}{r}
1.425 \\
3\overline{)4.275} \\
\underline{3} \\
12 \\
\underline{12} \\
07 \\
\underline{6} \\
15 \\
\underline{15} \\
0
\end{array}
$$

14. B: The three constants given are gamma, phi, and pi, respectively. The sum of the three is greater than 5. The next three choices are each raised to the gamma power. Gamma is equal to about ½. Because all three are raised to the same power and because all three are positive, we know that the one with the smallest base is the smallest number. The difference of pi and phi is less than phi so choice B is the least of those three. Because choices B, C, and D all have positive bases less than 5 raised to a power less than 1, all three must be less than 5. Hence, choice B is the smallest number.

15. A: When dealing with percents or fractions, "of" generally means multiply; 60% of $\frac{5}{6}$ means $60\% \times \frac{5}{6}$. We can write $x\%$ as $\frac{x}{100}$; 60% is therefore $\frac{60}{100}$, which reduces to $\frac{6}{10} = \frac{3 \times 2}{5 \times 2} = \frac{3}{5}$. So 60% of $\frac{5}{6} = \frac{3}{5} \times \frac{5}{6} = \frac{3 \times 5}{5 \times 6} = \frac{3}{6} = \frac{1}{2}$.

16. D: One foot is equal to twelve inches, so the road is twelve inches long on the map. If the map's scale is 1 inch = 5 miles, then we can find the road's actual length by solving the proportion

$\frac{12 \text{ inches}}{x \text{ miles}} = \frac{1 \text{ inch}}{5 \text{ miles}}$, or simply $\frac{12}{x} = \frac{1}{5}$. One way to solve this is by cross-multiplying: $12 \times 5 = x \times 1$, so $x = 60$.

17. C: We can do this by multiplying the integer part of the mixed number by the denominator and adding that product to the numerator; this sum is the numerator of the improper fraction, and its denominator is the same as the denominator in the fractional part of the mixed number. So, $3\frac{1}{4} = \frac{3 \times 4 + 1}{4} = \frac{13}{4}$ and $2\frac{5}{6} = \frac{2 \times 6 + 5}{6} = \frac{17}{6}$. Convert each fraction to its equivalent so that both fractions contain the lowest common denominator, which in this case is 12. $\frac{13}{4} = \frac{13 \times 3}{4 \times 3} = \frac{39}{12}$ and $\frac{17}{6} = \frac{17 \times 2}{6 \times 2} = \frac{34}{12}$. We can now add: $\frac{39}{12} + \frac{34}{12} = \frac{73}{12}$. Finally, we convert back to a mixed number by dividing the numerator by the denominator. The quotient is the integer part, and the remainder is the new numerator; the denominator remains the same. $73 \div 12 = 6$ with a remainder of 1, so $\frac{73}{12} = 6\frac{1}{12}$.

18. D: Taking a percent of a number means multiplying by that percent: if 50 is $P\%$ of 40, then $50 = 40 \times P\%$. That means $P\%$ is just $\frac{50}{40}$. We can write that as a decimal by dividing, putting a decimal point after the dividend and adding zeroes as necessary:

$$
\begin{array}{r}
1.25 \\
40\overline{)50.00} \\
\underline{40} \\
10\ 0 \\
\underline{8\ 0} \\
2\ 00 \\
\underline{2\ 00} \\
0
\end{array}
$$

So $\frac{50}{40} = 1.25$. To convert to a percent, we can multiply by 100, which is equivalent to moving the decimal point two places to the right: $1.25 = 125\%$.

19. A: When comparing decimals, compare them one decimal place at a time. First compare the part before the decimal point; whichever has the largest whole part is largest. If the whole parts are equal, compare the tenths place, the place just after the decimal point; if they differ in that place, then whichever has the larger digit in that place is larger. If the digits in the tenths place are the same, compare the hundredths place, the second place after the decimal point, and so on. In this case, all the decimals have a zero before the decimal point, so we'll start by comparing the tenths place. 0.55, 0.500, and 0.505 all have a 5 in the tenths place, while 0.0555 has a zero in the tenths place. So, 0.55, 0.500, and 0.505 are larger than 0.0555. Now, compare the hundredths place of the remaining choices, discarding the 0.0555 that we now know is smallest. 0.55 has a 5 in the hundredths place, while 0.500 and 0.505 both have zeroes. So, 0.55 is the largest of the choices.

20. B: To convert a number to scientific notation, move the decimal point until there is just one digit before it (not counting leading zeroes), and rewrite the number as the result times a power of ten. The exponent of the power of ten is equal to the number of places the decimal point was moved—positive if the decimal was moved left, and negative if the decimal was moved right. Starting with 0.05, to put only one digit before the decimal point, we have to move the decimal

point two places to the left. Therefore, $0.05 = 5 \times 10^{-2}$, and choices A and C are equal. To convert a percent to a decimal, divide it by 100, which is equivalent to moving the decimal point two places to the left: so $5\% = 0.05$, and choices A and D are equal. However, expressed as a fraction, $0.05 = \frac{5}{100} = \frac{5 \times 1}{5 \times 20} = \frac{1}{20} \neq \frac{1}{50}$. So choices A, C, and D are equal, but B is not equal to the other three.

21. D: To solve this problem, all we need to do is substitute -1 for every x in the expression and then simplify: $\frac{2(-1)-2}{(-1)+3} = \frac{-2-2}{2} = \frac{-4}{2} = -2.$

22. C: The expected value is equal to the product of the theoretical probability of getting a 4 after one roll, and the number of rolls, 10. Thus, the expected value is $\frac{1}{6} \cdot 10$, or $\frac{5}{3}$.

23. B: To simplify the inequality $x^2 + 2x \geq x + 6$, we can first move all the terms to the left-hand side: $x^2 + 2x - x - 6 \geq 0$, which, after combining like terms, becomes $x^2 + x - 6 \geq 0$. We can now factor the left-hand side; since the leading coefficient is 1, one way to do this is to look for two numbers that add to the coefficient of x (here 1) and multiply to the constant term (here -6). The two numbers that qualify are -2 and 3, so $x^2 + x - 6 = (x - 2)(x + 3)$. This makes the inequality $(x - 2)(x + 3) \geq 0$. We know the dividing points for the regions that do and do not satisfy the inequality are then at $x - 2 = 0$ and at $x + 3 = 0$, that is at $x = 2$ and at $x = -3$. Consider the sign in each region: when $x < -3$, then $x - 2$ and $x + 3$ are both negative, and their product is positive. When $-3 < x < 2$, then $x - 2$ is negative and $x + 3$ is positive, so their product is negative. When $x > 2$, then then $x - 2$ and $x + 3$ are both positive, and their product is again positive.

$(x - 2)(x + 3) \geq 0$ when $x \leq -3$ or $x \geq 2$. This is correctly represented by choice B.

24. C: Probably the simplest way to solve this equation is to first get rid of the fractions by multiplying each term by their lowest common denominator, which is $6x$: then we have $\frac{6x}{2x} + \frac{6x}{x} = \frac{6x}{6}$, which reduces to $3 + 6 = x$. So, $x = 3 + 6 = 9$.

25. B: The median of a data set is the middle element of the set after it is sorted in numerical order. In this example the median is 2.

26. B: If there are n floors, and each floor has a height of h feet, then to find the total height of the floors, we just multiply the number of floors by the height of each floor: nh. To find the total height of the building, we must also add the height of the spire, 30 feet. So, the building's total height in feet is $nh + 30$.

27. B: First, let's distribute the x and y that are outside the parentheses and then combine like terms: $(y - 2) + y(3 - x) = (xy - 2x) + (3y - xy) = -2x + 3y + xy - xy = -2x + 3y.$

28. D: Any negative number is less than any positive number, so $-\frac{1}{4}$ must be the first in the list. For numbers with equal numerators, the number with the greater denominator is smaller. So $\frac{1}{5} < \frac{1}{3}$, and $\frac{1}{3} < \frac{1}{1} = 1$. The correct ordering for the given numbers is, therefore, $-\frac{1}{4}, \frac{1}{5}, \frac{1}{3}, 1.$

29. A: The average number of male students in the 11th and 12th grades is 125 $\left(\text{calculated as } \frac{131 + 119}{2}\right)$. The number of Hispanic students at the school is 10% of 1219, which is 122 students (rounded up from 121.9). The difference in the number of male and female students at the school is $630 - 589 = 41$, and the difference in the number of 9th and 12th grade students at the school is $354 - 255 = 99$.

30. C: Since the triangle is covering part of the square, the total area of the figure is the area of the triangle plus the area of the square that is not covered. The area of the triangle is calculated as $A = \frac{1}{2}bh$. The base is equal to the side length of the square, s, and the height is given to be $3s$. Thus the area of the triangle is $\frac{3s^2}{2}$. The area of the square not covered by the triangle is a pair of smaller triangles, each with a height of s. While we are not given enough information to find the exact base of either of these triangles individually, we can determine that the sum of their bases is $\frac{s}{3}$. This means that the total exposed area of the square is $\frac{1}{2} \times \frac{s}{3} \times s = \frac{s^2}{6}$. The total area of the figure then is $\frac{3s^2}{2} + \frac{s^2}{6} = \frac{9s^2 + s^2}{6} = \frac{10}{6}s^2 = \frac{5}{3}s^2$.

31. D: A basic definition for probability is success over total. In this case, the total is football players and the success is band members who also play football. The ratio 0.35/0.42 is equal to about 83%.

32. D: Use the rule that $(a + b)(a - b) = a^2 - b^2$ or multiply the binomials using the FOIL method: multiply together the First term of each factor, then the Outer, then the Inner, then the Last, and add the products together.

$$(x + 6)(x - 6) = x \times x + x \times (-6) + 6 \times x + 6 \times (-6) = x^2 - 6x + 6x - 36 = x^2 - 36.$$

33. B: First, determine the proportion of students in the fifth grade. Since the total number of students is 180, this proportion is $\frac{36}{180} = 0.2$, or 20%. Next, determine the same proportion of the total prizes, which is 20% of 20, or $0.2(20) = 4$.

34. D: There are several ways to solve a system of equations like this. One is by substitution. If $x + 2y = 3$, then $x = -2y + 3$. Substituting that into the other equation, $-x - 3y = 4$, we get $-(-2y + 3) - 3y = 4 \Rightarrow 2y - 3 - 3y = 4 \Rightarrow -y - 3 = 4 \Rightarrow -y = 7 \Rightarrow y = -7$. Now, putting that value for y back into one of the original equations, we get $x + 2(-7) = 3 \Rightarrow x - 14 = 3 \Rightarrow x = 17$.

35. C: Since 3 of the 15 songs are by Beyonce, the probability that any one song will be by Beyonce is $\frac{3}{15} = \frac{1}{5}$. The probability that the next song is NOT by Beyonce is $\frac{4}{5}$. Therefore, the probability that the next two songs are both not by Beyonce is $\frac{4}{5} * \frac{4}{5} = \frac{16}{25}$.

36. B: The average is the total amount spent divided by the number of students. The first three students spend an average of $10, so the total amount they spend is $3 \times \$10 = \30. The other six students spend an average of $4, so the total amount they spend is $6 \times \$4 = \24. The total amount spent by all nine students is $\$30 + \$24 = \$54$, and the average amount they spend is $\$54 \div 9 = \6.

37. C: We can find the probability we need by adding the distinct probabilities that a student attends Elm OR likes comedies. However, we must also remember to subtract off the probabilities that a student attends Elm AND likes comedies. Our previous calculation double counted these students. The probability may be written as $P(\text{Elm or Comedy}) = \frac{750}{1650} + \frac{675}{1650} - \frac{350}{1650}$, which simplifies to $P(A \text{ or } B) = \frac{1075}{1650}$ or approximately 65%.

38. B: $-\frac{3}{2}\left(\frac{1}{2} + \frac{1}{3}\right) - \frac{2}{3}\left(\frac{1}{2} - \frac{3}{4}\right) = -\frac{3}{2}\left(\frac{3}{6} + \frac{2}{6}\right) - \frac{2}{3}\left(\frac{2}{4} - \frac{3}{4}\right) = -\frac{3}{2}\left(\frac{5}{6}\right) - \frac{2}{3}\left(-\frac{1}{4}\right) = -\frac{3 \times 5}{2 \times 6} + \frac{2 \times 1}{3 \times 4} = -\frac{15}{12} + \frac{2}{12} = -\frac{13}{12}$. Finally, to convert this to a mixed number, divide the numerator by the denominator; the

quotient is the integer part, and the remainder is the new numerator, while the denominator remains the same. $13 \div 12 = 1$ with a remainder of 1, so $-\frac{13}{12} = -1\frac{1}{12}$.

39. C: Neither Texas' maximum nor the fact that New Mexico has had more volunteers on 10 occasions is indicative of the number of volunteers that should be expected in the future. In fact, Texas has a smaller mean and median than New Mexico and similar spreads. Mean is most closely related to expected value and closely related to median in symmetric distributions. Choice C is the best answer.

40. C: To solve an equation with an absolute value like $|x^2 - 2| = x$, we can treat it as two separate cases. If $x^2 - 2$ is positive, $|x^2 - 2| = x^2 - 2$, and the equation becomes simply $x^2 - 2 = x$, which can be rewritten as the quadratic equation $x^2 - x - 2 = 0$. Since the leading coefficient is 1, we can factor this quadratic equation by finding two numbers that add to the coefficient of x (−1) and multiply to the constant term (−2); the two qualifying numbers are 1 and −2, and the equation factors to $(x + 1)(x - 2) = 0$, yielding the solutions $x = -1$ and $x = 2$. If $x^2 - 2$ is negative, then $|x^2 - 2| = -(x^2 - 2)$, and the equation becomes $-(x^2 - 2) = x$, which we can rewrite as $x^2 + x - 2 = 0$. Again, this can be factored, as $(x - 1)(x + 2) = 0$, yielding the two additional solutions $x = 1$ and $x = -2$. However, this method of solving equations with an absolute value may result in spurious solutions, so we should check all these solutions in the original equation to make sure that they are genuine. A shortcut for this step is to see that x is equal to an absolute value, so it must be positive. You can then verify that 1 and 2 are both valid in the original equation, and determine that the equation has two valid solutions.

41. E: To combine a number of exponential terms, it is generally a good start to convert them to equivalent terms containing the same base. In this case, since two of the terms already have a base of $\sqrt{2}$, it may be easiest to convert them all to that base, using the fact that when an exponential is raised to a power, the exponents are multiplied: $\left(a^b\right)^c = a^{bc}$. So, $2^{\sqrt{2}} = \left(\sqrt{2}^2\right)^{\sqrt{2}} = \sqrt{2}^{2\sqrt{2}}$. The equation then becomes $\sqrt{2}^2 \times \sqrt{2}^{2\sqrt{2}} = \left(\sqrt{2}^{\sqrt{2}}\right)^x$, the right-hand side of which simplifies to $\sqrt{2}^{\sqrt{2}x}$. As for the left-hand side, we can simplify it using the fact that when terms of the same base are multiplied, the exponents are added: $a^b \times a^c = a^{b+c}$. So $\sqrt{2}^2 \times \sqrt{2}^{2\sqrt{2}} = \sqrt{2}^{2+2\sqrt{2}}$, and we have $\sqrt{2}^{2+2\sqrt{2}} = \sqrt{2}^{\sqrt{2}x}$, which implies $2 + 2\sqrt{2} = \sqrt{2}x$. Dividing both sides of the equation by $\sqrt{2}$, we obtain $\sqrt{2} + 2 = x$.

42. E: One way to solve a system of inequalities is to plot both inequalities and see where they overlap. In this case, the first inequality describes the interior of a circle, and the second a half-plane; plotting them both on the same graph produces this:

There is no overlap between the shaded areas representing the two inequalities. Therefore, this system of inequalities has no solution.

43. C: The change of base formula for logarithms states that $\log_a x = \frac{\log_b x}{\log_b a}$ for any positive base b. Since $\ln x$ is equivalent to $\log_e x$, we can apply to change of base formula to get $\frac{\ln 81}{\ln 3} = \log_3 81$. $\log_3 81$ can be written as $\log_3 81 = x$, which, by the definition of a logarithm, can be written in standard notation as $3^x = 81$. Since $81 = 3^4$, $\log_3 81 = 4$.

44. D: The quadratic expression $x^2 - 4x + 5$ is not easily factorable, so its roots are best found using the quadratic formula, $x = \frac{-b \pm \sqrt{b^2 - 4ac}}{2a}$. Putting in $a = 1$, $b = -4$, and $c = 5$, this yields $x = \frac{-(-4) \pm \sqrt{(-4)^2 - 4 \times 1 \times 5}}{2 \times 1} = \frac{4 \pm \sqrt{16 - 20}}{2} = \frac{4 \pm \sqrt{-4}}{2} = \frac{4 \pm 2i}{2} = 2 \pm i$.

45. A: This problem is most easily solved using the *law of sines*, which states that the ratio of the sine of each angle in a triangle to the length of the opposite side is equal: $\frac{\sin A}{a} = \frac{\sin B}{b} = \frac{\sin C}{c}$. In this case, angle θ is opposite side a, and the angle with a measure of $30°$ is opposite side b, so we can write $\frac{\sin \theta}{a} = \frac{\sin 30°}{b}$. Since $\sin 30° = \frac{1}{2}$, this becomes $\frac{\sin \theta}{a} = \frac{1/2}{b}$, or $\sin \theta = \frac{a}{2b}$.

46. D: If the two lines intersect at the point $(2, 3)$, that means $x = 2, y = 3$ is a solution to both equations, and we can substitute in those values for x and y to yield $3 = 2a + b$ and $3 = 2b + 2a$. We now have two equations and two unknowns. There are many ways to solve this system of equations, including the substitution method. We can solve the first equation for $2a$ and substitute the result into the second equation, which also contains the term $2a$: the first equation solved for $2a$ is $2a = 3 - b$, and when this value for 2a is substituted into the second equation, we can solve for b: $3 = 2b + (3 - b) \Rightarrow 3 = b + 3 \Rightarrow b = 0$. Since we already know $2a = 3 - b$, this means $2a = 3 - 0 = 3$, so $a = \frac{3}{2}$.

47. D: The difference between any two consecutive odd integers is 2. If there are three consecutive odd integers, therefore, and the middle number is x, the other two integers must be $x - 2$ and $x + 2$. So their product is $x(x - 2)(x + 2) = x(x^2 - 4)$ (since $(a - b)(a + b) = a^2 - b^2) = x^3 - 4x$.

48. C: Consider the end behavior of the function. If b were even, then the function would either go to ∞ on both ends or to $-\infty$ on both ends; either way, both ends of the function must be on the same side of the x-axis; therefore, if the function crosses the x-axis, it has to cross it again to get back to the same side as it started. In other words, for an even function, it is impossible for the function to cross the x-axis only once unless the function's maximum or minimum value touched the x-axis, and this scenario is eliminated in the problem. Therefore, b cannot be even, which means b must be odd. (a may be either positive or negative, and c may or may not be zero.)

49. B: Suppose you put the two hosts in two adjacent seats, as required. (It does not matter which two seats we choose since we are not worried about rotations of the whole arrangement.) Then, the other four guests can be arranged in $4! = 4 \times 3 \times 2 \times 1 = 24$ different orders. However, we have to multiply this answer by 2 because there are two possible ways in which the two hosts can be seated; in other words, if they are sitting side-by-side, the hosts can exchange seats and still be sitting together. The total number of orders is $24 \times 2 = 48$.

50. B: The equation $y = 2\sin(\pi x - \pi)$ can be rewritten as $y = 2\sin(\pi(x - 1))$. The general form of a sine function is $y = A\sin(B(x - C)) + D$, where the amplitude (the vertical distance from the peak to the center) is $|A|$, the phase shift (horizontal shift) is C, the vertical shift is D, and the period (the width of one full cycle) is $\frac{2\pi}{B}$. In this case, the amplitude is 2, the phase shift is 1, the vertical

shift is 0, and the period is $\frac{2\pi}{\pi} = 2$. All of the graphs show the same (correct) amplitude and vertical shift; they only differ in their periods and phase shifts. Consider first the period. The width of one full cycle in the graph is 2 for choices A and B, and 4 for C, D, and E. Since the given function has a period of 2, this means the correct choice must be A or B. Choice A shows what the sine graph would look like without a phase shift: it starts at $x = 0$, then rises to a peak $\frac{1}{4}$ of the way through its period at $x = \frac{2}{4} = \frac{1}{2}$, then crosses the x-axis again halfway through its period at $x = \frac{2}{2} = 1$, and so on. However, the given function has a phase shift of 1, so the entire graph should be shifted right 1 unit. Choice B correctly shows this function.

51. A: If f^{-1} is the inverse of f, then by definition $f^{-1}(f(x)) = x$; therefore, $f\left(f^{-1}(f(x))\right) = f(x) = e^{2x}$.

52. C: The given equation is the standard equation for a plane in three dimensions. More specifically, if a, b, and c are all nonzero, it is a plane not parallel to any of the coordinate axes.

53. D: To simplify this rational expression, we can first factor out the largest common power of x on both sides of the fraction: $\frac{x^7+2x^6+x^5}{x^4-x^2} = \frac{x^5(x^2+2x+1)}{x^2(x^2-1)} = \frac{x^5}{x^2} \times \frac{x^2+2x+1}{x^2-1} = x^3 \times \frac{x^2+2x+1}{x^2-1}$. Now, we can factor both the numerator and denominator of the fraction. The numerator is a quadratic equation that can be factored using the quadratic formula or by other means, but the easiest way to factor it is to recognize it as the square of a binomial: $(a + b)^2 = a^2 + 2ab + b^2$, so $x^2 + 2x + 1 = x^2 + 2(x)(1) + 1^2 = (x + 1)^2$. Similarly, the denominator is a difference of squares: $(a + b)(a - b) = a^2 - b^2$, so $x^2 - 1 = x^2 - 1^2 = (x + 1)(x - 1)$. The expression becomes $x^3 \times \frac{(x+1)^2}{(x+1)(x-1)} = x^3 \times \frac{x+1}{x-1} = \frac{x^3(x+1)}{x-1} = \frac{x^4+x^3}{x-1}$.

54. C: We can write the problem as a system of two linear equations. Let x be the number of gold coins, and y be the number of silver coins. Since there are fifty coins total, we have $x + y = 50$ as one of the equations. If each gold coin weighs 12 ounces, then the total weight in ounces of the gold coins is $12x$; similarly, the total weight in ounces of the silver coins is $8y$. Since all the coins together weigh 30 pounds, which is equal to $30 \times 16 = 480$, we have $12x + 8y = 480$. Because each term in this equation is divisible by 4, we can divide the whole equation by 4 to get $3x + 2y = 120$; this is not a required step, but does make the numbers a little smaller and more manageable.

We now have two equations: $x + y = 50$ and $3x + 2y = 120$. There are a number of ways to solve a system of equations like this. One is to the substitution method. We can solve the first equation for y to get $y = 50 - x$, and then substitute this into the second equation to get $3x + 2(50 - x) = 120$. After distributing the 2, we get $3x + 100 - 2x = 120$; combining like terms gives $x + 100 = 120$, and, finally, subtracting 100 from both sides yields $x = 20$. Therefore, the number of gold coins is 20.

55. D: The standard form of the equation of an ellipse is $\frac{x^2}{a^2} + \frac{y^2}{b^2} = 1$, where a and b are the lengths of the semimajor and semiminor axes—that is, half the lengths of the major and minor axes. The major axis is the longer axis, while the minor axis is the shorter. To put the equation $3x^2 + 4y^2 = 48$ in standard form, we have to divide both sides of the equation by 48: $\frac{3x^2}{48} + \frac{4y^2}{48} = \frac{48}{48} \Rightarrow \frac{x^2}{16} + \frac{y^2}{12} = 1 \Rightarrow \frac{x^2}{4^2} + \frac{y^2}{(2\sqrt{3})^2} = 1$. The lengths of the semimajor and semiminor axes are 4 and $2\sqrt{3}$, and the

lengths of our major and minor axes are $2(4) = 8$ and $2(2\sqrt{3}) = 4\sqrt{3}$. Since $8 > 4\sqrt{3}$, the length of the major axis is 8.

56. A: A geometric sequence is a sequence in which the ratio between any two consecutive terms is the same; this ratio is called the *common factor*. The nth term of a geometric sequence with first term a_1 and common factor r is $a_1 r^{n-1}$. In this case, the first term is 80 and the common factor is $\frac{120}{80} = \frac{3}{2}$, so the tenth term is $80 \times \left(\frac{3}{2}\right)^{10-1} = \frac{80}{1} \times \left(\frac{3}{2}\right)^9 = \frac{80 \times 3^9}{2^9} = \frac{2^4 \times 5 \times 3^9}{2^4 \times 2^5} = \frac{5 \times 3^9}{2^5}$.

57. E: If $h(x) = f(x) + g(x)$, then $h(3) = f(3) + g(3)$. $f(3) = e^{3-3} = e^0 = 1$, and

$g(3) = 2 \times 3 - 1 = 6 - 1 = 5$, so $h(3) = 1 + 5 = 6$.

58. E: The simplest way to solve this problem is to first use the trigonometric identity

$\sec^2 \theta = \tan^2 \theta + 1$, or $\tan^2 \theta = \sec^2 \theta - 1$. Replacing $\tan^2 \theta$ with $\sec^2 \theta - 1$, the given equation becomes $2 \sec \theta = \sec^2 \theta - 1$. Moving everything to one side of the equation, we get $\sec^2 \theta - 2 \sec \theta - 1 = 0$. If we let $x = \sec \theta$, this is a simple quadratic equation, $x^2 - 2x - 1 = 0$. We can solve this using the quadratic formula, $x = \frac{-b \pm \sqrt{b^2 - 4ac}}{2a}$. In this case, $x = \frac{-(-2) \pm \sqrt{(-2)^2 - 4(1)(-1)}}{2(1)} = \frac{2 \pm \sqrt{4 - (-4)}}{2} = \frac{2 \pm \sqrt{8}}{2} = \frac{2 \pm 2\sqrt{2}}{2} = 1 \pm \sqrt{2}$. So, $\sec \theta = 1 \pm \sqrt{2}$.

59. C: If the town's population triples every ten years, this is an example of *exponential growth*, which is described by the equation $P = P_0 e^{kt}$, where P is the population at time t, P_0 is the initial population, and k is growth rate. To find k, we can use the fact that ten years after 1950 the town's population will be three times what it started with: i.e., when $t = 10$, $P = 3P_0$. So, $3P_0 = P_0 e^{10k}$; we can cancel out the P_0 from both sides to get $3 = e^{10k}$. Taking the natural logarithm of both sides, we get $\ln 3 = 10k$, so $k = \frac{1}{10} \ln 3$. So our exponential growth equation is $P(t) = P_0 e^{\left(\frac{1}{10} \ln 3\right)t} = P_0 e^{\ln 3 \left(\frac{t}{10}\right)}$; using the fact that $a^{bc} = \left(a^b\right)^c$, we can rewrite this as $P(t) = P_0 \left(e^{\ln 3}\right)^{\frac{t}{10}}$. But e^x and $\ln x$ are inverse functions, so $e^{\ln 3} = 3$, and this becomes $P(t) = P_0 \times 3^{\frac{t}{10}}$.

As an alternate way of solving the problem, we can just plug in $t = 10$ to each equation and see which one then yields the proper value of $P(10) = 3P_0$. Respectively, the five choices give $P(10) = 10 P_0^{30}, P_0^3, 3P_0, P_0 \times \left(\frac{3}{10}\right)^{10}$, and $\left(\frac{3}{10} P_0\right)^{10}$; only choice C yields the correct answer.

60. B: A property of inverse functions important for this problem is that if $f(x) = y$, then $f^{-1}(y) = x$. Therefore, from the given information that $f(1) = 2$, $g(2) = 3$, $f^{-1}(3) = 4$, and $g^{-1}(4) = 1$, it also follows that $f^{-1}(2) = 1$, $g^{-1}(3) = 2$, $f(4) = 3$, and $g(1) = 4$. So $f(g(1)) = f(4) = 3$, and choice A is true. $g(f^{-1}(2)) = g(1) = 4$, and choice C is true. $g^{-1}(f^{-1}(3)) = g^{-1}(4) = 1$, and choice D is true. $g(2) = 3 = f(4)$, and choice E is true. The only choice that does *not* follow from the given information is choice B; since we do not know the value of $g(3)$, we cannot determine the value of $f(g(3))$.

How to Overcome Test Anxiety

Just the thought of taking a test is enough to make most people a little nervous. A test is an important event that can have a long-term impact on your future, so it's important to take it seriously and it's natural to feel anxious about performing well. But just because anxiety is normal, that doesn't mean that it's helpful in test taking, or that you should simply accept it as part of your life. Anxiety can have a variety of effects. These effects can be mild, like making you feel slightly nervous, or severe, like blocking your ability to focus or remember even a simple detail.

If you experience test anxiety—whether severe or mild—it's important to know how to beat it. To discover this, first you need to understand what causes test anxiety.

Causes of Test Anxiety

While we often think of anxiety as an uncontrollable emotional state, it can actually be caused by simple, practical things. One of the most common causes of test anxiety is that a person does not feel adequately prepared for their test. This feeling can be the result of many different issues such as poor study habits or lack of organization, but the most common culprit is time management. Starting to study too late, failing to organize your study time to cover all of the material, or being distracted while you study will mean that you're not well prepared for the test. This may lead to cramming the night before, which will cause you to be physically and mentally exhausted for the test. Poor time management also contributes to feelings of stress, fear, and hopelessness as you realize you are not well prepared but don't know what to do about it.

Other times, test anxiety is not related to your preparation for the test but comes from unresolved fear. This may be a past failure on a test, or poor performance on tests in general. It may come from comparing yourself to others who seem to be performing better or from the stress of living up to expectations. Anxiety may be driven by fears of the future—how failure on this test would affect your educational and career goals. These fears are often completely irrational, but they can still negatively impact your test performance.

Review Video: _3 Reasons You Have Test Anxiety_
Visit mometrix.com/academy and enter code: 428468

Elements of Test Anxiety

As mentioned earlier, test anxiety is considered to be an emotional state, but it has physical and mental components as well. Sometimes you may not even realize that you are suffering from test anxiety until you notice the physical symptoms. These can include trembling hands, rapid heartbeat, sweating, nausea, and tense muscles. Extreme anxiety may lead to fainting or vomiting. Obviously, any of these symptoms can have a negative impact on testing. It is important to recognize them as soon as they begin to occur so that you can address the problem before it damages your performance.

Review Video: 3 Ways to Tell You Have Test Anxiety
Visit mometrix.com/academy and enter code: 927847

The mental components of test anxiety include trouble focusing and inability to remember learned information. During a test, your mind is on high alert, which can help you recall information and stay focused for an extended period of time. However, anxiety interferes with your mind's natural processes, causing you to blank out, even on the questions you know well. The strain of testing during anxiety makes it difficult to stay focused, especially on a test that may take several hours. Extreme anxiety can take a huge mental toll, making it difficult not only to recall test information but even to understand the test questions or pull your thoughts together.

Review Video: How Test Anxiety Affects Memory
Visit mometrix.com/academy and enter code: 609003

Effects of Test Anxiety

Test anxiety is like a disease—if left untreated, it will get progressively worse. Anxiety leads to poor performance, and this reinforces the feelings of fear and failure, which in turn lead to poor performances on subsequent tests. It can grow from a mild nervousness to a crippling condition. If allowed to progress, test anxiety can have a big impact on your schooling, and consequently on your future.

Test anxiety can spread to other parts of your life. Anxiety on tests can become anxiety in any stressful situation, and blanking on a test can turn into panicking in a job situation. But fortunately, you don't have to let anxiety rule your testing and determine your grades. There are a number of relatively simple steps you can take to move past anxiety and function normally on a test and in the rest of life.

Review Video: How Test Anxiety Impacts Your Grades
Visit mometrix.com/academy and enter code: 939819

Physical Steps for Beating Test Anxiety

While test anxiety is a serious problem, the good news is that it can be overcome. It doesn't have to control your ability to think and remember information. While it may take time, you can begin taking steps today to beat anxiety.

Just as your first hint that you may be struggling with anxiety comes from the physical symptoms, the first step to treating it is also physical. Rest is crucial for having a clear, strong mind. If you are tired, it is much easier to give in to anxiety. But if you establish good sleep habits, your body and mind will be ready to perform optimally, without the strain of exhaustion. Additionally, sleeping well helps you to retain information better, so you're more likely to recall the answers when you see the test questions.

Getting good sleep means more than going to bed on time. It's important to allow your brain time to relax. Take study breaks from time to time so it doesn't get overworked, and don't study right before bed. Take time to rest your mind before trying to rest your body, or you may find it difficult to fall asleep.

> **Review Video: <u>The Importance of Sleep for Your Brain</u>**
> Visit mometrix.com/academy and enter code: 319338

Along with sleep, other aspects of physical health are important in preparing for a test. Good nutrition is vital for good brain function. Sugary foods and drinks may give a burst of energy but this burst is followed by a crash, both physically and emotionally. Instead, fuel your body with protein and vitamin-rich foods.

Also, drink plenty of water. Dehydration can lead to headaches and exhaustion, especially if your brain is already under stress from the rigors of the test. Particularly if your test is a long one, drink water during the breaks. And if possible, take an energy-boosting snack to eat between sections.

> **Review Video: <u>How Diet Can Affect your Mood</u>**
> Visit mometrix.com/academy and enter code: 624317

Along with sleep and diet, a third important part of physical health is exercise. Maintaining a steady workout schedule is helpful, but even taking 5-minute study breaks to walk can help get your blood pumping faster and clear your head. Exercise also releases endorphins, which contribute to a positive feeling and can help combat test anxiety.

When you nurture your physical health, you are also contributing to your mental health. If your body is healthy, your mind is much more likely to be healthy as well. So take time to rest, nourish your body with healthy food and water, and get moving as much as possible. Taking these physical steps will make you stronger and more able to take the mental steps necessary to overcome test anxiety.

> **Review Video: <u>How to Stay Healthy and Prevent Test Anxiety</u>**
> Visit mometrix.com/academy and enter code: 877894

Mental Steps for Beating Test Anxiety

Working on the mental side of test anxiety can be more challenging, but as with the physical side, there are clear steps you can take to overcome it. As mentioned earlier, test anxiety often stems from lack of preparation, so the obvious solution is to prepare for the test. Effective studying may be the most important weapon you have for beating test anxiety, but you can and should employ several other mental tools to combat fear.

First, boost your confidence by reminding yourself of past success—tests or projects that you aced. If you're putting as much effort into preparing for this test as you did for those, there's no reason you should expect to fail here. Work hard to prepare; then trust your preparation.

Second, surround yourself with encouraging people. It can be helpful to find a study group, but be sure that the people you're around will encourage a positive attitude. If you spend time with others who are anxious or cynical, this will only contribute to your own anxiety. Look for others who are motivated to study hard from a desire to succeed, not from a fear of failure.

Third, reward yourself. A test is physically and mentally tiring, even without anxiety, and it can be helpful to have something to look forward to. Plan an activity following the test, regardless of the outcome, such as going to a movie or getting ice cream.

When you are taking the test, if you find yourself beginning to feel anxious, remind yourself that you know the material. Visualize successfully completing the test. Then take a few deep, relaxing breaths and return to it. Work through the questions carefully but with confidence, knowing that you are capable of succeeding.

Developing a healthy mental approach to test taking will also aid in other areas of life. Test anxiety affects more than just the actual test—it can be damaging to your mental health and even contribute to depression. It's important to beat test anxiety before it becomes a problem for more than testing.

Review Video: Test Anxiety and Depression
Visit mometrix.com/academy and enter code: 904704

Study Strategy

Being prepared for the test is necessary to combat anxiety, but what does being prepared look like? You may study for hours on end and still not feel prepared. What you need is a strategy for test prep. The next few pages outline our recommended steps to help you plan out and conquer the challenge of preparation.

STEP 1: SCOPE OUT THE TEST

Learn everything you can about the format (multiple choice, essay, etc.) and what will be on the test. Gather any study materials, course outlines, or sample exams that may be available. Not only will this help you to prepare, but knowing what to expect can help to alleviate test anxiety.

STEP 2: MAP OUT THE MATERIAL

Look through the textbook or study guide and make note of how many chapters or sections it has. Then divide these over the time you have. For example, if a book has 15 chapters and you have five days to study, you need to cover three chapters each day. Even better, if you have the time, leave an extra day at the end for overall review after you have gone through the material in depth.

If time is limited, you may need to prioritize the material. Look through it and make note of which sections you think you already have a good grasp on, and which need review. While you are studying, skim quickly through the familiar sections and take more time on the challenging parts. Write out your plan so you don't get lost as you go. Having a written plan also helps you feel more in control of the study, so anxiety is less likely to arise from feeling overwhelmed at the amount to cover.

STEP 3: GATHER YOUR TOOLS

Decide what study method works best for you. Do you prefer to highlight in the book as you study and then go back over the highlighted portions? Or do you type out notes of the important information? Or is it helpful to make flashcards that you can carry with you? Assemble the pens, index cards, highlighters, post-it notes, and any other materials you may need so you won't be distracted by getting up to find things while you study.

If you're having a hard time retaining the information or organizing your notes, experiment with different methods. For example, try color-coding by subject with colored pens, highlighters, or post-it notes. If you learn better by hearing, try recording yourself reading your notes so you can listen while in the car, working out, or simply sitting at your desk. Ask a friend to quiz you from your flashcards, or try teaching someone the material to solidify it in your mind.

STEP 4: CREATE YOUR ENVIRONMENT

It's important to avoid distractions while you study. This includes both the obvious distractions like visitors and the subtle distractions like an uncomfortable chair (or a too-comfortable couch that makes you want to fall asleep). Set up the best study environment possible: good lighting and a comfortable work area. If background music helps you focus, you may want to turn it on, but otherwise keep the room quiet. If you are using a computer to take notes, be sure you don't have any other windows open, especially applications like social media, games, or anything else that could distract you. Silence your phone and turn off notifications. Be sure to keep water close by so you stay hydrated while you study (but avoid unhealthy drinks and snacks).

Also, take into account the best time of day to study. Are you freshest first thing in the morning? Try to set aside some time then to work through the material. Is your mind clearer in the afternoon or evening? Schedule your study session then. Another method is to study at the same time of day that

you will take the test, so that your brain gets used to working on the material at that time and will be ready to focus at test time.

STEP 5: STUDY!

Once you have done all the study preparation, it's time to settle into the actual studying. Sit down, take a few moments to settle your mind so you can focus, and begin to follow your study plan. Don't give in to distractions or let yourself procrastinate. This is your time to prepare so you'll be ready to fearlessly approach the test. Make the most of the time and stay focused.

Of course, you don't want to burn out. If you study too long you may find that you're not retaining the information very well. Take regular study breaks. For example, taking five minutes out of every hour to walk briskly, breathing deeply and swinging your arms, can help your mind stay fresh.

As you get to the end of each chapter or section, it's a good idea to do a quick review. Remind yourself of what you learned and work on any difficult parts. When you feel that you've mastered the material, move on to the next part. At the end of your study session, briefly skim through your notes again.

But while review is helpful, cramming last minute is NOT. If at all possible, work ahead so that you won't need to fit all your study into the last day. Cramming overloads your brain with more information than it can process and retain, and your tired mind may struggle to recall even previously learned information when it is overwhelmed with last-minute study. Also, the urgent nature of cramming and the stress placed on your brain contribute to anxiety. You'll be more likely to go to the test feeling unprepared and having trouble thinking clearly.

So don't cram, and don't stay up late before the test, even just to review your notes at a leisurely pace. Your brain needs rest more than it needs to go over the information again. In fact, plan to finish your studies by noon or early afternoon the day before the test. Give your brain the rest of the day to relax or focus on other things, and get a good night's sleep. Then you will be fresh for the test and better able to recall what you've studied.

STEP 6: TAKE A PRACTICE TEST

Many courses offer sample tests, either online or in the study materials. This is an excellent resource to check whether you have mastered the material, as well as to prepare for the test format and environment.

Check the test format ahead of time: the number of questions, the type (multiple choice, free response, etc.), and the time limit. Then create a plan for working through them. For example, if you have 30 minutes to take a 60-question test, your limit is 30 seconds per question. Spend less time on the questions you know well so that you can take more time on the difficult ones.

If you have time to take several practice tests, take the first one open book, with no time limit. Work through the questions at your own pace and make sure you fully understand them. Gradually work up to taking a test under test conditions: sit at a desk with all study materials put away and set a timer. Pace yourself to make sure you finish the test with time to spare and go back to check your answers if you have time.

After each test, check your answers. On the questions you missed, be sure you understand why you missed them. Did you misread the question (tests can use tricky wording)? Did you forget the information? Or was it something you hadn't learned? Go back and study any shaky areas that the practice tests reveal.

Taking these tests not only helps with your grade, but also aids in combating test anxiety. If you're already used to the test conditions, you're less likely to worry about it, and working through tests until you're scoring well gives you a confidence boost. Go through the practice tests until you feel comfortable, and then you can go into the test knowing that you're ready for it.

Test Tips

On test day, you should be confident, knowing that you've prepared well and are ready to answer the questions. But aside from preparation, there are several test day strategies you can employ to maximize your performance.

First, as stated before, get a good night's sleep the night before the test (and for several nights before that, if possible). Go into the test with a fresh, alert mind rather than staying up late to study.

Try not to change too much about your normal routine on the day of the test. It's important to eat a nutritious breakfast, but if you normally don't eat breakfast at all, consider eating just a protein bar. If you're a coffee drinker, go ahead and have your normal coffee. Just make sure you time it so that the caffeine doesn't wear off right in the middle of your test. Avoid sugary beverages, and drink enough water to stay hydrated but not so much that you need a restroom break 10 minutes into the test. If your test isn't first thing in the morning, consider going for a walk or doing a light workout before the test to get your blood flowing.

Allow yourself enough time to get ready, and leave for the test with plenty of time to spare so you won't have the anxiety of scrambling to arrive in time. Another reason to be early is to select a good seat. It's helpful to sit away from doors and windows, which can be distracting. Find a good seat, get out your supplies, and settle your mind before the test begins.

When the test begins, start by going over the instructions carefully, even if you already know what to expect. Make sure you avoid any careless mistakes by following the directions.

Then begin working through the questions, pacing yourself as you've practiced. If you're not sure on an answer, don't spend too much time on it, and don't let it shake your confidence. Either skip it and come back later, or eliminate as many wrong answers as possible and guess among the remaining ones. Don't dwell on these questions as you continue—put them out of your mind and focus on what lies ahead.

Be sure to read all of the answer choices, even if you're sure the first one is the right answer. Sometimes you'll find a better one if you keep reading. But don't second-guess yourself if you do immediately know the answer. Your gut instinct is usually right. Don't let test anxiety rob you of the information you know.

If you have time at the end of the test (and if the test format allows), go back and review your answers. Be cautious about changing any, since your first instinct tends to be correct, but make sure you didn't misread any of the questions or accidentally mark the wrong answer choice. Look over any you skipped and make an educated guess.

At the end, leave the test feeling confident. You've done your best, so don't waste time worrying about your performance or wishing you could change anything. Instead, celebrate the successful

263

completion of this test. And finally, use this test to learn how to deal with anxiety even better next time.

Important Qualification

Not all anxiety is created equal. If your test anxiety is causing major issues in your life beyond the classroom or testing center, or if you are experiencing troubling physical symptoms related to your anxiety, it may be a sign of a serious physiological or psychological condition. If this sounds like your situation, we strongly encourage you to seek professional help.

Thank You

We at Mometrix would like to extend our heartfelt thanks to you, our friend and patron, for allowing us to play a part in your journey. It is a privilege to serve people from all walks of life who are unified in their commitment to building the best future they can for themselves.

The preparation you devote to these important testing milestones may be the most valuable educational opportunity you have for making a real difference in your life. We encourage you to put your heart into it—that feeling of succeeding, overcoming, and yes, conquering will be well worth the hours you've invested.

We want to hear your story, your struggles and your successes, and if you see any opportunities for us to improve our materials so we can help others even more effectively in the future, please share that with us as well. **The team at Mometrix would be absolutely thrilled to hear from you!** So please, send us an email (support@mometrix.com) and let's stay in touch.